ב"ה

Tending the Garden

The Unique Gifts
of the Jewish Woman

Chana Weisberg

First published 2006
Third printing 2015
Copyright © 2006 by Chana Weisberg
chanaw@gmail.com
ISBN 1-56871-417-3

Dedicated to the
Courageous Women of Valor in my life
who have helped me to develop
and grow as a Jewish Woman.

To My Illustrious Grandmothers,
Rebbetzins
Sara Sosha Schochet, a"h,
and Batya Sudak, a"h,
for the solid foundation of Yiddishkeit
which you built for our family.

To My Beloved Mother,
Rebbetzin Batsheva Schochet,
for your noble example
and all that you have taught me.

To My Dear Mother-in-Law,
Rebbetzin Henchi Weisberg,
for all your kindness and concern.

And To My Very Special Daughters,
Esther,
Naomi,
Shira
and Sara Leah
May you continue to grow and to follow the paths
of the Women of Valor of our past,
and may you inspire many others
as you continuously inspire me.

Acknowledgments
Preface
Introduction

VOICES

FEMININE GREATNESS:
SKETCHES OF WOMEN OF THE PAST

❧ Chava: The Crown of Creation...7
❧ Sara: The Voice of a Leader 20
❧ Rivka: The Power of Perception 37
❧ Rachel and Leah: Two Worlds, Two Destinies 54

DEEDS

FEMININE TOUCH:
A DEEPER LOOK INTO WOMEN'S MITZVOT

Light of Eternity: The Mitzva of Shabbat Candles
❧ A Soul on Fire...77
❧ The Ultimate Harmony..79
❧ The Eternal Shabbat —Life in a Feminine Mode............ 82
❧ The Shabbat Lights—the Lights of Zion 86

Kneading G-dliness into Creation: The Mitzva of Challa
❧ Discovering G-d in the Physical.................................... 93
❧ Transforming the Physical..97
❧ Seasoning the Loaves of Mediocrity 99
❧ Torah Bread—the Feminine Link 102

Mysterious Nights: The Mitzva of Mikve
❧ Dear Child of Mine...107
❧ The Dynamics of Marriage.. 116
❧ Tuma and Tahara, Lows and Highs................................124
❧ Three Phases of Attachment 130
❧ Eternal Waters 138

TIME

FEMININE INFLUENCE:
THE ROLE OF WOMEN IN THE CELEBRATION AND
FORMATION OF THE HOLIDAYS

- Rosh Hashana—Chana's Prayer:
  A Guide to Touch the Divine 153
- Chanuka—the Paradox: Women in the Miracle and
  Celebration of Chanuka 160
- Purim—Esther: A Paradigm of Self-Sacrifice 165
- Pesach—Miriam's Tambourines: Vision and Courage 174
- Shavuot—
  Ruth, Mother of Mashiach 183
  Nitzevet, Mother of King David:
  The Bold Voice of Silence 191
- Tisha B'Av—a Feminine Journey:
  The Era of Redemption 201

IMAGERY

THE FEMININE REALM:
A MYSTICAL LOOK AT
THE FEMININE ELEMENTS IN REALITY

Two Forms of Universal Energy—Two Modes of Being

- A Cosmic Inhale and Exhale: Ratzo V'Shov 212
- Outer and Inner: The Concept of "Kav and Reshimu" 216

Malchut: The Feminine Sefira

- Sefirot in Kabbala 222
- Malchut, the Feminine Sphere and Bat, the Daughter ... 224
- Malchut and the Feminine Shabbat 227
- Malchut as the Feminine Womb 229
- Malchut as Speech and Communication 232
- Malchut as Mitzvot and the Woman of Valor 234
- Malchut, the Final Sefira 236

VISION

FEMININE MANDATE:
THE WOMAN'S ROLE

- Attuned to the Inner Self—the Role of Selflessness.........241
- Through the Eye of a Needle—the Role of Harmony......248
- Working from Within—the Role of Cultivator.................251
- Women of Royalty—the Role of Humility 255
- The Creation Story—the Role of Redeemer 265
- Acting Like a Sole—the Role of Faith and Acceptance ... 270

DIALOGUE

THE FEMININE PERSPECTIVE:
MORE THOUGHTS ON JEWISH WOMANHOOD

- Why Husbands Should Buy Their Wives Flowers:
Reflections on Women and Time-Bound Mitzvot 277
- Morning Blessings—His Version and Mine:
A Blessing of Faith 281
- Thoughts from an Unfocused Mind:
Pregnancy as a Metaphor for Exile 284
- Coffee Break:
Male and Female Differences Reflected in Their Modes of
Communication 287
- It's All in the Packaging:
A Dialogue on Equality 291
- A Different Kind of Spirituality:
The Focus on Another...296

Glossary

Endnotes

ACKNOWLEDGMENTS

The following individuals were instrumental in bringing this book to publication. To all of you, I offer my sincere gratitude and appreciation.

To an exemplary woman who wishes to remain anonymous, who loves the Jewish people and contributes generously to furthering Torah knowledge in our world. Your constant striving for growth and meaning, your continuous encouragement to me in my speaking and writing and your true friendship are a constant inspiration in my life. I am so grateful to have met you. Thank you so much for all you have done and continue to do for me. May G-d grant you health and happiness and the ability to keep on doing all that you do.

To the readers of my columns at www.chabad.org, to my students, and to the participants at my lectures—for all your feedback, encouragement, questions and challenges which undoubtedly helped me to clarify these ideas and insights.

To my beloved father, the *Moreh D'Asra* of our community, Rabbi Dovid Schochet—for your constant encouragement and support, as well as for the love of learning with which you infused our home.

To my sons, Aharon and Yisroel Pinchas, as well as my dear husband, Isser Zalman—for all that you continue to teach me and your constant encouragement through all of life's ups and downs.

To the Rebbe, whose enlightening insights about the Jewish woman have left an indelible imprint on my own life as a Jewish woman.

To the Master of the Universe, for providing me with the opportunity and privilege of teaching Your Torah. May we speedily merit the time when the knowledge of Torah will be overflowing "as the waters cover the sea bed."

PREFACE

Exactly ten years ago to this date, I completed writing my first book on Jewish women, titled *The Crown of Creation: The Lives of Great Biblical Women Based on Rabbinic and Mystical Sources.*

Four years later, *The Feminine Soul: A Mystical Journey Exploring the Essence of Feminine Spirituality* was published, followed two years later by a series of text-based workbooks titled *The Feminine Voices Series.*

Many people have asked me how I came to write these books. In truth, the books came about almost by themselves. I had been teaching a series of classes exploring the unique powers and contribution of the Jewish woman. The classes were delivered to large and small groups from all different backgrounds, shades of observance and levels of Jewish education. The common denominator of the participants was simply a will to learn and a quest to discover more about the Jewish woman.

Unfortunately, at the time, there was a dearth of material published on the Jewish woman, so I was forced to "hit the sources" and do my own exploration. Much research went into each class, but it was well worth my time after seeing how well the material was received, like living waters quenching a parched throat.

Seeing the success of the classes, I decided to commit the material to writing so that others, too, could learn and gain from the information. Once again, I was amazed by the warm reception of *The Crown of Creation*, and later, *The Feminine Soul*, which became instant best-sellers and are now completely out of print. Rather than reprinting them independently, several chapters from these works have been incorporated into *Tending the Garden*, in addition to many new subjects and new material which have been added over the years.

When *The Crown of Creation* was originally published, there were not many books on the market on Jewish womanhood. Jewish publishers simply didn't see the need or the market for a serious book on this subject. (I'll never forget how after submitting my manuscript to a large Jewish publishing company, I was graciously complimented on the depth of research, but rejected for publication because "the book was too profound for women." On second thought, the editor concluded, "But then again, maybe their husbands will read it...")

I'm happy to see that today there exist several books on the Jewish woman and the many issues facing us in modern times. As women, we have unique physiological, psychological and social needs and strengths that match our feminine bodies and feminine, emotional makeup. Similarly, we also possess spiritual needs that must be filled to satisfy and develop our unique spiritual makeup and feminine soul powers. While in the past, women may not have had the capabilities, ambition or opportunity, the time is ripe and the knowledge available for each of us to come to a fuller and deeper, more meaningful appreciation of our life and our mission as Jewish women.

Tending the Garden is a comprehensive book all about the Jewish woman from the beginning until the end of time. It explores the lives of role models from the past and translates the challenges of their lives into solutions for the myriad issues we face in our own lives. It delves into the spiritual ramifications and mystical insights behind women's special mitzvot. It examines women's cosmic role in our world and the intrinsic connection between this mission and our special spiritual makeup. It searches feminine imagery in mystical sources to broaden our awareness of the feminine perspective on life. It explores the woman's influence in the formation of our holidays to make these holidays more meaningful to us as Jewish woman. And it takes a peek at feminine dialogue and the feminine outlook on modern Jewish womanhood.

In short, *Tending the Garden* is all about being a Jewish woman in today's times.

Tending the Garden attempts to rediscover the beauty of womanhood in the Torah. It presents a glimpse of these luscious gardens to women who are searching for a better appreciation of our special feminine mission in life and our unique contribution to the ultimate purpose of creation.

I took the pains of adding extensive (although by no means complete) endnotes and sources to emphasize that, although some of the ideas in this book are expressed in an original way, they are all firmly based on Torah sources.

It is hoped that *Tending the Garden* will arouse meaningful and positive dialogue on the important issues of being a Jewish woman. As with my previous books, I can only pray that the joy, meaning and inspiration that I received from the effort expended in writing this book will be shared by each of my readers and that, together, we may all very soon experience the ultimate expression of feminine spirituality in the era of redemption, when we will have transformed our world into G-d's beautiful garden.

Chana Weisberg
6 Tishrei, 5767

INTRODUCTION

I'm often asked why it is that men have played such a major role in Jewish history. "Where are the feminine voices, the feminine role models? Why are they not leading the way?"

The short answer is that the women are there, of course, in full force, but working through their inner mode, often not noticeable to the undiscriminating eye.

But to understand why they are not at the forefront, we need a deeper understanding of the workings of our world and our purpose in being here to begin with.

"I have come into My garden, My sister, My bride" (Song of Songs 5:1).

A common perception is that the purpose of our world is for human beings to fulfill G-d's will in order to receive their reward in the world to come.

This, however, is a simplistic (and selfish) level of relating to G-d.

The Midrash explains that "G-d desired to have a dwelling place in the lower worlds" *(Tanchuma, Naso 16)*. G-d wanted a relationship with us here in this physical world. This world is G-d's "garden," where we can become connected and united with Him. We connect to G-d through the study of Torah and the practice of mitzvot, which changes our world into a more G-dly place, where G-d can feel "at home."

Ultimately, the depth of our relationship will be realized only after the redemption, in the messianic era. Our job now, however, is to prepare the world for this time.

A garden is made up of plain earth. But it is precisely within its lowly, sullied soil that the most radiant, dazzling flowers can grow. Similarly, it is specifically in our physical world that the most profound relationship between us and G-d can be forged.

Making our world into G-d's garden requires two roles.

Firstly, we must uproot the weeds and clear the debris from our garden. We must subjugate the darkness and negativity which obscures the G-dly source and essence of our world.

Secondly, and perhaps more importantly, we must tend to the garden's various plants, nurture them and ensure that they blossom fully. We must cultivate and bring out the latent inner qualities and potentials of all aspects of our world.

Both of these roles are necessary in transforming our physical world into a divine garden. On the whole, they reflect the respective roles of man and woman.

When we fight negativity—the spiritual "weeds" and "debris" around us—by drawing down new holiness to overcome it, we are employing the external, "masculine" mode.

When we reveal the inherent beauty in creation by working within the physical reality to uncover the holiness already there— cultivating the physical earth so that it brings out breathtaking flowers—we are employing the inner, "feminine" mode.

These two approaches—the "masculine" and "feminine" modes—are present in dealing with almost every facet of reality. We employ the masculine mode when we work "from above downwards"—applying external forces to reshape, bypass and overcome. We employ the feminine approach when we work "from below upwards" to cultivate, nurture and bring out the earth's inherent qualities and talents.

(This is not to say that every man will exclusively employ the masculine mode and every woman the feminine one, but generally speaking, these are the masculine or feminine energies within creation.)

In the business world, you will have those "masculine" managers who provide direction in a linear, hierarchal manner by instructing, ordering and directing from above downwards. Then you will have "feminine" managers who will brainstorm with their employees to bring out their latent talents and creative ideas.

In our school classrooms, there are those "masculine-style" teachers who lecture, dictate and "rain down" the knowledge on their students. Then there are "feminine-style" teachers who cultivate the skills within their students so that they are empowered to learn and develop on their own.

In disagreements or differences of opinion, there are those "masculine" debaters who powerfully and masterfully negate the wrongs of their opponent's argument. Then there are others who demonstrate the strengths and potency of their own approach and thereby overcome any possible challenges.

In the area of medicine, the "masculine" approach says to fight against a disease by surgically removing it or through medication aimed at eradicating it. The "feminine" healing method, on the other hand, aims to strengthen the resources of the body so it will naturally overcome the illness.

These are two roles and two directions to creating a home for G-d.

Bringing G-dliness down into our world. Or raising and elevating our reality to reveal its inherent G-dliness.

Conquering negativity and physicality. Or cultivating and uncovering the essential positivity within creation.

Man's primary role is to introduce new G-dliness to our world. He accomplishes this primarily through his Torah study.

Woman's primary role is to uncover the G-dliness that already exists within creation. Mitzvot bring out the inner spirituality within the physical realm of our world.

Man *does* by bringing in a new element of G-dliness into our world.

Woman *is* by revealing the G-dliness in what already exists.

Both roles are vital.

When evil abounds, we need to fight it headstrong. We vanquish darkness by introducing more G-dly light into creation. It is useless, even counter-productive, to sit down and negotiate with terrorists who wish to destroy you—you need to fight them head on.

But there comes a time when the evil has been largely subdued and the second approach—of finding the inherent good, and revealing the common ground of unity—is more effective.

From the beginning of time, we have fought the evil around us by defeating value systems that were antithetical to a G-dly world. The masculine energy was largely at the forefront of this battle.

But we are now at the doorstep of a new era. Mashiach will overpower all evil and then focus his energies on education and cultivation. In order to transform the very fabric of our world and reveal its implicit G-dliness, the feminine approach of nurturance and uncovering is more appropriate.

So, to get back to the original question, where are the women's voices? Why aren't they noticeable?

As mentioned, they are there, but because their role is to work from within, their approach is by necessity more hidden, more secretive. They are active behind the scenes, not always discernable to the non-discriminating eye. We need to discover and tap into their energy, their hidden, inner voices, to learn from their depth of wisdom how to deal with the challenges of our own lives.

As we stand on the threshold of this new era, the vision of the feminine role is becoming more accessible and its importance appreciated.

Geula, redemption, is the feminine era. It is an era of peace, where we no longer need to fight the negativity of our world but rather inculcate more and more goodness and G-dliness into creation. Redemption is described as the time when *nekeiva tesovev gever* ("the female shall surround the male"—Jer. 32:21), when the feminine qualities will supercede the male qualities. After resting our weapons, we will bask in and absorb the tranquility of peace. Having overcome the darkness, we will finally appreciate the splendor of the light.

Women are charged with bringing this era because they are intrinsically connected to its feminine vision. The world is ready for more of this feminine perspective. Let us not lose our feminine approach, our feminine mode or our feminine touch; let us use it to transform our world into G-d's garden.

Section One

VOICES
Feminine Greatness
Sketches of Women of the Past

- ⚘ Chava
  —The Crown of Creation
- ⚘ Sara
  —The Voice of a Leader
- ⚘ Rivka
  —The Power of Perception
- ⚘ Rachel and Leah
  —Two Worlds, Two Destinies

CHAVA
The Crown of Creation

In our search for insight into the essential physiological, emotional and spiritual makeup of women, the Torah is clearly the place to start, beginning with the creation of the first woman, Chava (Eve).

Chava is the mother of humanity, in general, and womankind in particular. Her creation encompassed all women's creation. Every woman is likened to Chava, and in some way plays her role.

By gaining an appreciation of Chava—the unique way in which she was formed, her goals and responsibilities—we appreciate better these aspects of ourselves. Understanding Chava's relationship to the rest of creation, specifically her partner, Adam, lends us understanding in our own relationships and provides insight into the uniqueness of both men and women.

The creation of woman consisted of two phases. The first was the creation of Adam, the first man, or more correctly, the first human being. Adam was created androgynous, having both male and female characteristics.[1] Only in the second phase was a separate and uniquely feminine being formed.

To properly identify women's essential nature, we must first focus on the creation of the original man, whose being included both masculine and feminine attributes.

Uniqueness of Mankind

During the six days of creation, every component of the universe was created through G-d's word. With each creation, He announced, "Let it be," as in "Let there be light" or "Let the earth give forth greenery" or "Let the waters bring forth fish," (Gen. 1:3, 11, 20).

In each case, G-d's very command caused the creation to become a physical reality. With the creation of mankind, however, there was an added step. G-d began by announcing to the angels,

"Let us make man in our form and our likeness" (Gen. 1:26) and only afterward created man.

G-d's additional "planning" can be likened to an individual planning a great event. The preparation adds to the excitement and importance of the task. Man was created with great deliberation, so to speak, on G-d's part. Such involvement of Divine providence underlines mankind's greatness over all other creations.[2]

Furthermore, Rashi (Gen. 1:27) emphasizes how all creatures were created by G-d's "words," but man, alone, was created also with the actual "hand" of G-d—a deeper, more active involvement.

Humanity's G-dly Capacity

G-d's special connection to man is apparent in the contrast between the *creation* of humanity and other species. But what in man's *intrinsic* makeup crowns him as the superior being, the pinnacle of creation?

After man's physical formation, G-d blew into his nostrils "*nishmat chaim*" (Gen. 2:7), a living soul. By receiving this G-dly breath of life, man bears a Divine spark and becomes elevated above other creatures both physically and spiritually.[3]

A breath originates in the deepest recesses of a being. When G-d "exhales," He does so from His innermost being. G-d, as it were, breathed from His essence into the essence—the Divine soul—of man. Furthermore, even after being blown into man's body, this breath is not severed from G-d. Man's soul is an extension of G-d's breath and directly connected to Him.[4] Accordingly, man assumed his Creator's image. He is the only earthly creature aware of good and evil, for only he, among all creatures, has free will.[5]

Consequently, man stands in marked contrast to plant and animal life. The plant, rooted in the soil, draws its life-giving sap from its roots, its lowest extremities. The animal has its vital center in the middle of its body, in its heart. Man's life, on the other hand, is bonded with his spirit. His spiritual aspect is only truly alive when man thinks, hopes and aspires.

The very term "*neshama*" is reserved for man's soul. All other creatures possess a far inferior "*nefesh*" or "*ruach*," a vegetative or sensitive soul.[6] Man's *neshama* is an emanation of Supreme Intelligence which causes his resemblance to the Divine. As a result, man has the capacity to appreciate G-dliness, to love and cleave to Him, and to yearn for G-dly experiences.

Love is only possible if what you love is a part of you. To illustrate, man has no capacity to love or have any relationship with an insect, as there is no connection between the two. Man, however, has in him a part of G-d that is constantly yearning to achieve a more unified state with its Source.

For this reason man is titled "*ish*," from the root "*eish*," fire. As the flame of the fire is forever aspiring to reach greater heights, the soul of man constantly strives for higher spiritual elevations.

Conquering the World

Man utilizes his *neshama*'s powerful Divine attributes by fulfilling the commandment to conquer the "*olam*," world, and fill it. This obligation extends beyond the literal translation of inhabiting the world.

Creation's purpose is fulfilled when man conquers the "hidden world" (from the Hebrew word "*helam*")—those parts of the physical world where Divinity is hidden. Man conquers this darkness by infusing it with the light of G-dliness, which constitutes his essence. Man has this power through the strength of his Divine soul.

G-d called this elevated being "Adam," mankind. He was the crown of creation due to his uniquely spiritual and intellectual capabilities. Yet this human being was not "man" as we identify him today, since he was created with two sides, male and female.

Only in the next phase of creation did the male become a separate entity from the female.

A Bond of Love

Man's two-phased creation is an enigma. Why should G-d initially create a human with both male and female attributes only to divide him later into two uniquely separate individuals? Furthermore, if man was of such supreme quality, why tamper with perfection? Conversely, if man was not meant to be an androgynous creature, why create him so in the first place?

Perhaps man's imperfection lay in his inability, as yet, to reproduce. However, the Divine blessing of "reproduce and multiply" (Gen. 1:28), received by man while still in this original form, proves that man already had the capacity for reproduction.

G-d would have enabled man, who in this stage included within him aspects of femininity, to reproduce without a mate.[7]

At this stage, though, the reproductive act was merely instinctive. The mating of man and woman was not intended to be just sexual, on par with beasts. What was lacking was that this act originate from feelings of love. G-d wanted to introduce a special, personal relationship coming from a bond of love, companionship and helpfulness.

To do so, G-d made for him his helpmate and soul mate, Chava.[8]

This does not mean that G-d changed His mind or erred in His blueprint. Rather, G-d wanted to draw humanity's attention to the precious nature of this partnership. He was emphatically demonstrating, "It is not good for man to be alone" (Gen. 2:18). Man was without woman for a brief period, so that she would be all the more dear to him after he experienced life without her.[9]

Two Half Beings

Since man and women are, in essence, parts of the same whole, each constitutes only a half without his/her partner. Looking for completion, each strives to discover and unite with that missing part.

With all other creatures, the male and female species sprang from the earth, simultaneously and independently. These creatures do not require a mate for the fulfillment of their lives' calling.

In contrast, the human female was a part of the human male. The male, therefore, is helpless and lacks wholeness without his wife.[10] Only the two together form a complete human being.[11]

By unifying these soul mates—by finding each other in our "quest for something lost"[12]—a complex and deep connection is established. Our Sages declare (*Yevamot* 62b): "A life without a wife is devoid of joy, blessing and well-being." This fuller relationship was, understandably, impossible in the initial state as one being.

Therefore, man was not only incomplete but he was "not good," as the Torah attests, "This is not good, man being alone" (Gen. 2:18). Man is merely a "half man" in his original state. G-d, therefore, announced His intention to make an "*ezer kinegdo,*" a helpmate, parallel, or on equal footing, to him.

Woman's Role

Torah depicts woman as the *"ezer kinegdo."* Our sages reveal woman's invaluable role through their explanation of this ambiguous phrase.

The woman, as a "helpmate," assumes part of man's obligations, enabling him to accomplish more perfectly the part that is left to him. This is possible only if the woman does not work at what the man is performing, but rather works "opposite him," that is, parallel to him.

Were the other being also a man, he would have to shoulder all his obligations and also be in need of this "helpmate." The female does not stand with her male, but rather at another point on the same line, so each fills a separate position, mutually complementary.

To further explain the curious description of *"ezer kinegdo,"* Rashi states (*Yevamot* 63a): "What does the text . . . mean? If he is worthy, a help; if he does not show himself worthy, against him."

This explanation contains a profound comment on the phenomenon of the male-female relationship. Constituting two parts of a whole, the male and female represent two opposites. If man is worthy, they complement one another and merge into a single whole of one Divine entity. When they are not worthy, and the bond of Divinity is not between them, then the fact that they are opposites causes her to be against him and oppose him.[13]

This is implied by their very names, *"ish"* (man) and *"isha"* (woman). The recurring letters in each word are *aleph* and *shin*, spelling *"eish,"* fire. The exclusive letters in each are *yud* and *hey*, forming the name of G-d.

When man and woman unify with sincerity and holiness, he contributes his *yud* and she contributes her *hey*, and their relationship takes on a Divine attribute. If, however, man and woman deny G-d entry into their lives, he surrenders his *yud* and she surrenders her *hey*. Remaining is *"eish,"* a relationship fraught with fiery destruction and constant strife.[14]

Taming the Fire

Fire represents the uniquely human traits of enthusiasm, lust and initiative. Simply to live and vegetate as an animal, through instinct alone, does not require G-dliness. In man's humanly fiery attributes, however, G-d must be present to prevent him from becoming a source of danger and destruction.

Taming the fire (*eish*) inside man and transforming it into a G-dly force can be accomplished through the partnership of man and woman. Fiery instincts become ennobled only by both working side by side to accomplish their separate, yet complementary, Divine goal. They transform this fire only when they form a relationship in which G-dliness (represented by the *yud* and *hey*, one of G-d's names) is an integral aspect.[15]

For these reasons, man was called "Adam" when he constituted one being. He was given the new name "*Ish*" once he received a mate. Only after he had a partner did he acquire the capacity of "*eish*," fiery instincts, and the ability to utilize this fire constructively.

Introducing Woman

After explaining the need for a female counterpart, the Torah digresses before her actual formation. The narrative shifts to forming the animal kingdom and parading them before man. After appropriately naming each species, man notices that all creatures have a partner, "but for Adam there was not found a helpmate for him" (Gen. 2:20).

G-d causes Adam to fall into a deep slumber, removes one of his ribs, and fills the vacant space with flesh. G-d proceeds to "build the rib which He had taken from Adam into a woman" (Gen. 2:22) and presents her to Adam.

Upon seeing his ultimate life partner, man declares that this creation should be called "*isha*" (woman) due to her origin in "*ish*" (man) (Gen. 2:23). The narration concludes that since man and woman are in essence one being, "a man should leave his father and his mother and cleave to his wife and they shall be one flesh" (Gen. 2:24).

Seeking a Worthy Companion

What was the urgency in forming and naming all the animal species? Why couldn't the animals wait until the sequence of man's creation was completed, with Chava's imminent arrival?

G-d manipulated the events for man's own advantage. G-d enabled man to perceive the true quality and nature of all species (implicit by his naming the animals)[16] before he, himself, received his life mate. Through this, He demonstrated to Adam his superiority over the animal kingdom. Man now realized that no species suited him as a worthy companion, since he seeks a fuller union with his partner than any other creature.[17]

G-d did not wish to remove a part of Adam before he came to his own conclusion that his very self was lacking and seeking something deeper, something external. G-d went about the creation of woman sensitively.

To illustrate this thought, a story is told about the Roman emperor, Caesar, and his precocious daughter.

Whenever the Jewish sages visited Rome, Caesar met and challenged them with questions on the Jewish religion. Days before their arrival, he would cloister himself in his library, obsessed with finding a question that the scholars could not answer.

His daughter would often listen to these debates, fascinated by the ease with which the sages invariably replied.

On one occasion, when the sages were seated, the emperor charged: "Your G-d is a thief! Isn't it written that G-d put Adam to sleep and then took one of his ribs?"

Rabban Gamliel, a leading sage, was about to reply when Caesar's daughter called out, "Summon the captain of the guards at once!"

All heads turned in her direction. "What's the matter?" asked her father in alarm.

"I just remembered what happened last night," she said. "Thieves broke into the palace. They stole a silver pitcher, replacing it with a gold one!"

"That's what you're shouting about? Replacing silver with gold?" laughed Caesar with relief. "I wish thieves like that would come every day!"

His daughter looked at him with satisfaction. "Listen to your own words," she said. "Do you think Adam complained about losing one small bone when he received a wife in exchange?"

The emperor looked in astonishment at his clever daughter. He was glad she had inherited some of his own sharpness.

"I will agree that the trade was in Adam's favor," he conceded. "But G-d still acted like a thief. Why did He put Adam to sleep? Why not carry out the exchange openly?"

Rabban Gamliel, his disciples, and all the ministers in the room waited in silence for Caesar's daughter to answer. But again she surprised them by issuing a strange command.

"Bring me a piece of raw meat!"

The servant returned with a slab of red beef lying on a silver tray in a pool of blood.

"Now bring me a knife, some coals and a grill," she commanded.

The daughter drained off the blood, hacked away large chunks of fat and cut up the meat. Then she roasted it in Caesar's presence.

"May I serve you?" she asked her father as she placed a sizzling portion of steak before him. Caesar looked away, his face taking on a greenish hue.

"I cannot eat," he mumbled. "It is so . . . unappealing."

"Isn't that just how Adam would have felt about his new bride had he been awake to witness her transformation?" asked Caesar's daughter softly.

Rabban Gamliel nodded his head in silent approval. He did not need to add a word. Wise words speak for themselves.

(Taken from *No Greater Treasure* by Shoshana Lepon (Targum/Feldheim, 1990) based on *Bereishit Rabba* 17:7, *Sanhedrin* 39a and Rashi, ad loc.)

Woman's Superior Attributes

The Torah notes that G-d built woman from Adam. The differing origins of man and woman account for some of the physical, emotional and spiritual differences between them. Man came from the soil of the earth, while woman originated from the side of a living being.

Consequently, a woman reaches maturity earlier, and certain halachic acts for her are valid from her twelfth year, while only binding for a man from his thirteenth.[18] The contrast in character and sound of voice between a man and woman is due to the difference in their original makeup, as well.

The word "built" (*vayeeven*), which is unusual in the context, is also linked to the word "*bina*," the greater understanding and intuition generally associated with women. The sages comment on this verse: "The Holy One endowed woman with greater intuition and more understanding (*bina*) than man."

Sin of the Eitz Hadaat

After appreciating the spiritual capacity of Adam and Chava, it is difficult to fathom the ensuing episode—the sin of the *Eitz Hadaat*, the Tree of Knowledge.

The Midrash expounds that Adam was so holy that when the angels saw him, they wanted to pray to him as a deity. His stature was so sublime that even after his death, his two heels—the least significant part of his body—radiated awesome holiness as bright as two suns.[19]

Furthermore, Adam extended from the earth to the heavens and from one corner of the globe to the other.[20] Nothing was hidden from him. No one comprehended better than he how his actions would determine the course of history. He fully understood the implications and repercussions of his behavior.

Adam and Chava would not have succumbed to a rash act of rebellion against G-d's command without prior reasoning or deliberation. Insight into their actions sheds light on women's unique qualities and role in the process of redemption.

Life in the Garden

After Adam's creation, G-d placed him in the Garden of Eden and presented him with every possible tree that "was pleasing to the sight and good for food" (Gen. 2:9). Man was permitted to partake of all the delicacies except for one food that was off-limits. G-d had ordered Adam, "From the Tree of Knowledge of good and bad, you must not eat, for on the day you eat of it, you will become deserving of death" (Gen. 2:17).[21]

The prohibition of eating from the *Eitz Hadaat* and the consequence of death upon its violation was intimated for Adam, Chava and their descendants.[22] Although Adam relayed this prohibition to Chava,[23] she became confused with the directive, which then set the tone for the entire sinful episode.

The cunning serpent, who was the embodiment of the evil Satan,[24] asked Chava whether G-d had forbidden her to eat from *any* trees in the garden. Although the serpent had seen Adam and Chava eating other fruits, he purposely asked this to incite Chava and engage her in conversation and open debate.[25]

Woman's Downfall

Chava played right into the serpent's scheme by answering him, "Of the fruit of any tree in the garden we may eat, just of the fruit of the tree which is in the center of the garden, G-d said, 'You should neither eat of it nor touch it, lest you die'" (Gen. 3:2-3).

Chava added the prohibition of *touching* the Tree of Knowledge. When the serpent then forcibly pushed Chava against the tree, he victoriously claimed, "See, just as death did not ensue from touching, so it will not follow from eating."[26]

Through his beguiling words, the serpent introduced doubt into Chava's mind. It now became easier to dare Chava to taste the forbidden fruit. He convinced her that G-d did not actually intend to kill her and Adam, but merely threatened them to intimidate them.[27]

The serpent enticed Chava by predicting beneficial outcomes. He lured her by promising, "Your eyes will be opened. You will become rationally aware and see whatever is around you in the proper perspective. The fruit will awaken a new desire and appreciation for the pleasures around you. It will be a source of intellectual benefit, a means of attaining wisdom and achieving understanding."

Chava was caught in the serpent's spell and longed for this new knowledge and exciting awakening. She succumbed to his alluring promises and ate the forbidden fruit. She then used her persuasive powers to convince her husband, out of her love for him,[28] to eat the forbidden fruit, so that he, too, could become wise.

The rest of the story is history.

The Power of Speech

Chava's downfall began when she expanded and distorted G-d's command, which she did not personally hear.

The Talmud (*Kiddushin* 49b) states that ten measures of speech were given to the world. Nine of them were allocated to women.

This statement is neither praiseworthy nor derogatory. In fact, behavioral psychologists notice this difference between men and women. It has been said that while women rapport, men report.

Each of us, however, has the responsibility to determine how to use our communication skills. We have the choice of gossiping, lying, plotting and talking evilly; or, conversely, we can express empathy, understanding and constructive teaching.

Woman's extra allotment of speech can have many positive or negative ramifications. In Chava's case, she employed her talent negatively.

Chava distorted G-d's command because she did not hear it directly. The command was relayed by Adam and, therefore, was slightly ambiguous to her. Elaborating on the prohibition to include something it did not, caused her to eventually be persuaded to sin.

Although the above explains the *circumstances* leading Chava to violate G-d's word, her *reasoning* is still unclear. Why were the evil serpent's promises so tempting? What did Chava perceive as so beneficial that it would warrant the flagrant disobedience of G-d's only command? What intrinsic spiritual changes did she anticipate that were so irresistible?

Outside Temptations

Prior to this sin, mankind was not a mixture of good and evil. He was essentially good, seeking to do the will of his Maker. Unlike later man, he was not born selfish. He didn't innately desire physical comfort and pleasure.[29]

Although he possessed free will, temptation came from the outside. Evil, per se, was embodied in the satanic serpent that became a vehicle for temptation.

Man's mission was to elevate himself to the level where evil would become completely senseless and unappealing. Evil would become so far removed that he wouldn't even hear its call, let alone contemplate acting on it. If man, an essentially physical being, chose to ignore temptation, he would elevate the entire physical realm.

Had humanity fulfilled this mission, our purpose would have been achieved by the time the sun had set on the sixth day of creation, at the onset of the world's first Shabbat. The future of mankind would have been a tale of perfection and sublime enjoyment of G-d's Presence. Life would have become an upward spiral of spiritual elevation and ecstasy.

Plunging into the Darkness

Chava thought she could do better. She understood that overcoming an external temptation is never as great as overcoming an internal one. Overcoming an inner unquenchable desire is incomparably more difficultᴼand rewarding than avoiding a serpent's crafty calling.

By eating the forbidden fruit of the *Eitz Hadaat*, Chava consciously caused temptation to become a part of humanity's makeup. As the serpent predicted ("your eyes will become open"), a new dimension of knowledge became integrated into man's being—the knowledge and desire for evil.

After Adam and Chava ate the fruit, "the eyes of both of them were opened"—with a new intelligence and awareness.[30] The serpent was right; they had become enlightened people. Their eyes were open to the evil of the world.[31] They now displayed a desire for base pleasure, despite its harmfulness.[32]

This is why their first realization was that they were naked. Man does not need to be ashamed of his body as long as it stands in the service of G-d. Adam and Chava had not felt their nakedness prior to this newfound knowledge. They acquired an embarrassment over their bodies only when their physicality became intermingled with temptation, lust and evil.[33]

They had thought they could please G-d by plunging into darkness while remaining spiritually unscathed. They had assumed that their service would become more meaningful by resisting this constant inner call to evil. They now realized that they had stripped themselves of the one precept entrusted to them. They felt naked of obedience,[34] and, therefore, sewed together a fig leaf to cover themselves.

Then they heard the "voice of G-d withdrawing in the garden in the direction of the day" (Gen. 3:8). This was the first tragic withdrawal of the Divine Presence.[35]

G-d began to address them. "Consider well how you have fallen from your heights. Where is your exalted status?[36] How lowly have you become! Yesterday, you were ruled by My Will, now, by the will of the serpent . . ."[37]

Though we cannot fully fathom the cosmic effect of this sin, our long exile became one consequence, to enable us to reach a new state of purification. Death, as well, became necessary.[38]

Yet man's sin was also part of Creation's design. Man had to sin to cause these effects.[39] Adam and Chava were, in a sense, correct in their assumption that the outcome of this sin would ultimately lead to a greater sanctification of G-d's Name.

In the era of Mashiach, once the world reaches its eventual state of purity, humanity will have made a greater accomplishment. Once we will have overcome temptation from within, the positive forces will be strengthened. Accordingly, man's reward will be greater, as well.

For this to happen, it was part of the Divine plan that Adam should relay G-d's command to Chava. Although Adam and Chava hoped to attain a greater spirituality by eating from the Tree, Chava would never have dared to violate a prohibition given to her *personally* by G-d.[40]

Women are stronger in this aspect of faith. Women's innate humility makes them more conducive to *"kabbalat ol,"* accepting the Divine Will, regardless of their comprehension. This quality would have prevented the entire set of circumstances leading to the sin.

Had Chava heard the direct command, in her humility, she would not have dared to make any further calculation. Humanity would not have needed the banishment from Gan Eden and exile's long purification process. Adam and Chava would have immediately attained a state of perfection.

But we also would not have achieved our ultimate objective of negating an internal evil. Thus, the greater feat would have been relinquished.

Heralding the Redemption

Since woman caused the original taint of sin to become part of man's makeup—a sin that will only be removed in the era of Mashiach—she must be the one to correct it. She is entrusted with the responsibility—and the privilege—of bringing about this ultimate rectification.

The final redemption will arrive in the merit of righteous women, who utilize their immense spiritual capabilities for positive endeavors.

As Jewish women, each of us plays a significant part in this vital role.

SARA
The Voice of a Leader

In modern times, we grapple with the roles of man and woman. The Torah has not only provided us with a clear understanding of the uniqueness of each, but has also included true-life examples of harmonious relationships between husbands and wives.

Although these stories took place over three and a half thousand years ago, as we examine the lives of the great parents of our nation, we discover timeless pearls of wisdom that can enrich any marriage.

The First Jewish Parents

There is one relationship which is unique, however, because it involves the first father and mother of the Jewish people, Avraham (Abraham) and Sara. Our first Patriarch and Matriarch were an indivisible pair who, side by side, performed the will of the Creator.

At a time when paganism was rampant, Avraham and Sara labored diligently to teach the concept of an ethical and kind, universal G-d.[41] Together, they changed the moral character of untold thousands. As Avraham taught men about G-d's existence, Sara disseminated this knowledge to women. As Avraham invited guests to his home, Sara hosted them.

A Spiritual Abode

The Midrash (cited in Rashi, Gen. 24:67) relates that throughout Sara's life three miracles took place in her home: A protective cloud hovered over the entrance of her tent, a blessing was present in her dough, and her candles burned from one Shabbat to the next.

Sara transformed her home into a spiritual sanctuary, a refuge from the prevalent ideology at the time. The Jewish home is called a microcosm of the Beit Hamikdash, the Holy Temple which stood in Jerusalem. The miracles that took place in Sara's home paralleled the miracles in the Temple.

The cloud representing G-d's presence affirmed the greatness within. Just as the Beit Hamikdash was built as a home for G-d, Sara's home, too, was a fitting abode for G-d.

Sara's dough was blessed so that her guests felt satiated for a long time. Similarly, the bread of the Temple remained warm and fresh for a whole week and was the nation's source of sustenance and prosperity.[42]

Sara's candles burnt brightly for an entire week, bringing a glow of spirituality into the darkness of the weekday. Similarly, the flame of the Temple's Menora burned brightly until the next day's lighting. The Menora's light, like Sara's, symbolized the growth from one spiritual level to a new and higher one. Sara enhanced, rather than replaced, each new Shabbat—and each new stage of spiritual growth—with the light and strength of all previous ones.[43]

The Jewish Home

The message radiating from Sara's tent was that the Jewish home has immense potential. In a sense, Sara demonstrated that a proper Jewish home is superior to the Temple, for the Temple was built to emulate *her* home, rather than the reverse.

Through the spiritual and material home that she built, Sara embodied the role of *ezer kinegdo*, a helpmate to her husband, doing her part, as he did his. Together, the two wove a beautiful tapestry of kindness and good deeds.

Sara's Superiority

Yet the relationship between Sara and Avraham extended beyond a perfect partnership. Avraham endearingly called his wife Sarai, meaning, "my princess."[44] Avraham regarded Sara, in many respects, as his superior. Although he had reached such an exalted spiritual level that he was called the "Prince of G-d" (Gen. 23:6), he realized that, in certain respects, Sara was greater.

In his eulogy for her,[45] Avraham recited the *Eishet Chayil*, the Woman of Valor song, customarily recited on Friday night before kiddush.[46]

It begins, "A woman of valor who shall find, she is more precious than pearls . . . " A righteous woman is the crowning glory of her husband, as King Solomon declared in his Proverbs (12:4), "A woman of valor is the crown of her husband."

Avraham considered Sara his crowning ornament, just as the Shabbat crowns the six days of the week.

G-d attested to Sara's superiority by commanding Avraham to follow Sara's instruction: "Everything that Sara says to you, listen to her voice" (Gen. 21:12). From this verse, the sages learn that Sara was greater than Avraham in prophetic ability.[47]

The secret of Sara's greatness was her simple faith and deep awareness of truth. She was able to see beyond the external constraints of an individual's life, right to their very core.

As we examine in greater detail the events of Sara's life, her perceptiveness, as well as her immense spiritual powers, becomes more evident.

Sara as the Sister

We are introduced to Sara at a time of severe famine in Israel. Avraham and Sara descend to Egypt to purchase foodstuffs.

As they approach the city gates, Avraham tells Sara (Gen. 12:11ff.), "I realize that you are a beautiful woman. When the Egyptians will see you, they will say, 'She is his wife.' [They will lust after you because of your beauty and] They will kill me, allowing you to live. Therefore, please say that you are my sister,[48] so that they may benefit me because of you and my life will be spared because of you."

This is exactly what occurred. "As Avraham entered Egypt, the Egyptians beheld Sara's great beauty. King Pharaoh's ministers saw her, too, and spoke highly of her to Pharaoh, and the woman was taken into Pharaoh's palace. He treated Avraham well because of her; he acquired sheep, oxen, donkeys, male and female slaves. . . Then the L-rd afflicted Pharaoh and also his household with severe plagues on account of [taking] Sara . . ."

Avraham's Strategy

The commentaries explain that when Avraham entered Egypt, he realized the potentially dangerous situation.[49] He therefore planned a two-phased strategy.

Initially, he hid Sara in a large chest. Seeing this unusually heavy box, the Egyptian customs official inquired about its contents. Avraham replied that he would pay any sum rather than open it.

The curious officer wondered if gold was inside, or perhaps an even greater treasure of precious stones. The official became suspicious, however, as it occurred to him that the foreigner, who was so possessive of his belonging, might be hiding something potentially harmful. He demanded that the box be opened and was completely mystified when he sighted the extraordinary beauty of the woman hidden inside.

Avraham's second strategy now came into effect.[50] Sara told the Egyptians that she wished to marry, but only a worthy individual who would first obtain the legal and personal consent of her brother, Avraham. This was the accepted rule for an orphaned sister. It was customary to offer silver and gold to the girl's father or brother in exchange for her hand in marriage.

Sara's Potential Dishonor

Avraham had devised this plan for his and Sara's protection. He intended to set a price so high that any man wishing to marry Sara would be unable to pay it. It didn't occur to him, however, that the king himself would desire her. When the king accepted the arranged sum, Avraham couldn't prevent Pharaoh from taking his allegedly unmarried sister.

How could Avraham allow this ruse of an unmarried Sara to save his own life, while setting the scene for Sara's potential dishonor?[51] Furthermore, if Avraham was forced to let Sara be taken, how could he hope to receive riches from Pharaoh through Sara's personal shame and violation?

Spiritual Wealth

G-d had promised Avraham that by leaving his birthplace and going to Canaan, he would (among other things), be blessed with wealth. Avraham was sure that this forced departure from Canaan to Egypt was in some way related. Seeing his journey to Egypt as a vehicle for G-d's blessing, Avraham asked Sara, "Please say that you are my sister, so that they will then be good to me."

The implication of this wealth was not merely a physical benefit. Avraham was to depart from his birthplace in order to attain spiritual elevation by making holy the physicality of the world.

Releasing Spiritual Energy

According to Kabbala, immense spiritual power is embedded and imprisoned in every aspect of creation.[52] This spiritual power can only be released and absorbed if the physical creation is used for G-dly purposes.

The task of the Jewish people is to release this spiritual energy and reunite it with its Creator. A Jew is able to do so by using the physical aspects of creation for the sake of G-d. One such example is using the energy derived from physical food to provide strength to perform mitzvot.

Due to his elevated soul, a tzaddik has more power and is capable of greater rectifications. In fact, the role designated for Mashiach is to completely release all the spiritual energy embedded within creation.[53]

When this process is completed, the spirituality of all of creation will be absorbed into the general soul of the Jewish people. The Final Redemption is but a physical reflection of the redemption of these forces. This is accomplished by our accumulation of mitzvot throughout exile.[54]

Sara's Merit

In this vein, the *Zohar* (3:52a)[55] discusses Avraham's perplexing behavior by stating that "Avraham did not rely on his own merit but rather on the merit of his wife—that he would acquire wealth in her merit, for one acquires wealth in the merit of one's wife."

Avraham realized that the physical wealth he would amass in Egypt would come as a result of fulfilling his spiritual mission. He understood that he, alone, would be unable to refine the sparks of holiness found in the spiritually bankrupt Egypt.

Towards that end, Sara's spiritual powers were crucial.

Descending into the Abyss

Avraham and Sara both had to descend into the immoral Egypt. Avraham perceived, however, that Sara alone could elevate Pharaoh's palace, the center of this corruption. This was the ultimate intent of their coming to Egypt.

Avraham allowed the Egyptians to take his beloved wife, confident that not only would G-d protect her from any dishonor, but that He would help her to accomplish their mission. Avraham correctly relied on Sara's merit: "In her merit he would not be harmed, nor would any harm befall her."[56]

The commentaries[57] explain that every time Pharaoh approached Sara, an angel beat him. He and his household were afflicted with terrible skin infections, and Pharaoh became impotent. Pharaoh could not so much as lay a finger on Sara, for G-d was protecting her to accomplish what only a *tzadeket*, a righteous woman, of her caliber could—to descend into the abyss and find and elevate the G-dliness therein.

After amassing great physical and spiritual wealth, Avraham and Sara left Egypt, confident that they had fulfilled their purpose.

It should have been a time of spiritual exultation. They were disseminating the word of G-d, expounding on His existence, and having a profound positive impact on the lives of those they encountered.

Longing for Children

Their happiness was marred, however, by their keen ache for their own child. Although they taught and helped so many others, as they progressed in years, they remained bereft of offspring whom they could educate to continue their worthy work.

This deep longing prompted Sara to perform the most selfless act. She told her husband (Gen. 16:2), "'G-d has kept me from having children. Take my slave girl, Hagar, as a wife and hopefully I will be built up through her.' And Avraham heeded the voice of Sarai."

A Sensitive Husband

Despite his own yearning for a child, Avraham was sensitive to his wife's feelings. At a time when polygamy was acceptable, Avraham acted solely with Sara's permission. Furthermore, his intention was not that *he* have a child from Hagar but that he carry out Sara's wishes so that she would find fulfillment from her maid's child.[58]

An Arrogant Maid

After ten years of marriage, Sara takes her Egyptian slave and gives her to her husband as a wife. However, after Hagar becomes pregnant, rather than appreciate Sara's selfless gesture, she views Sara with contempt.

Hagar was the daughter of King Pharaoh who had abandoned her royal lifestyle because she wisely realized the greater merit of being Sara's slave-maid. Now, Hagar loses her admiration for her mistress, boasting that Sara is not the same inwardly as she appears to be outwardly. "She cannot be as righteous as she seems, for so many years passed without her having children, whereas I conceived after just one union."[59]

Sara's Vision

Sara is devastated by Hagar's impudent talk. She is not bothered for her own honor, but rather because it was basic to her plan that Hagar remain dependent on her.

When Hagar married Avraham, she still remained Sara's servant. Sara had not freed Hagar, because she envisioned raising Hagar's child and treating him as if he were hers. In Hagar's capacity as a maid, the status of her child would be clear and the child would be trained to transmit Avraham and Sara's legacy after their death.[60]

If her plan was to succeed, Sara needed to make Hagar aware of this dependent condition. Her vision of "being built up through Hagar," would otherwise become futile. Therefore, after discussing the matter with Avraham, "Sara humbled Hagar, and Hagar ran away from her" (Gen. 17:6).

A Change of Attitude

Although Sara never really changed her behavior, Hagar's altered attitude made her present situation too difficult for her to bear.

The initial relationship between Sara and Hagar can be compared to the bond of a beloved rabbi to his disciples. Any personal service that the rabbi asks is not difficult or degrading, since they feel privileged to serve him. If any ordinary person, however, would request the same, they would be outraged.

When Hagar regarded Sara as an exalted individual, she felt privileged to be a part of her household, even in the capacity of a slave. After Hagar married Avraham, however, she grew arrogant and considered herself to be equal to, if not greater than, Sara.

Sara's routine requests became intolerable. As a result, Hagar fled what she viewed as persecution.

On her journey, Hagar met an angel who persuaded her to reaccept Sara as her mistress and spiritual superior.[61] As such, Hagar would not loathe her status or that her son was being raised by Sara. Sara would be able to accomplish what she had originally envisioned and what she so selflessly forsook her own intimacy with her husband for—a child who could continue the Abrahamitic mission.

A Better Treasure

Sara and Avraham would have contented themselves with raising Hagar's son. The Divine Plan, however, arranged that Yishmael (Ishmael) be born before their greater gem. Like silver, from which all impurities are removed before it is put to its ultimate use, all but the holiest, most spiritual forces had to be removed from Avraham before he could beget this precious jewel, Yitzchak (Isaac). Therefore, Avraham married the Egyptian, Hagar.

Into Yishmael went any spiritual impurities from Avraham's makeup. Then, purified and at an advanced age, when earthly lust was gone and birth could only be a heavenly gift, Avraham and Sara were prepared to bring Yitzchak into this world.[62]

Change of Name, Change of Destiny

When Yishmael reached the age of thirteen, and he had chosen his deviant life's path, G-d appeared to Avraham, promising him this greater offspring. He instructed Avraham to change his and Sara's names. As *Avram* and *Sarai* they were unable to have children; however, as *Avraham* and *Sara* their destiny would be changed. Not only would their personal future be altered by their name change, but their universal mission would be augmented.

Avram was to become Avraham—"Av Hamon Goyim,"[63] father of the entire world. Sarai, too, was to take on a more universal status, reflected by the new name Sara, "princess par excellence," and not just "princess of Avraham."

G-d instructs Avraham (Gen. 17:4-16): "As far as I am concerned, here is My covenant with you. You shall be the father of a horde of nations. No longer shall you be called Avram. Your name shall become Avraham . . . And as for Sarai, your wife, do not call her by the name Sarai, for Sara is her name. I will bless her and make her bear you a son. I will bless her so that she will be the mother of entire nations. Kings will be her descendants."

Implications of a Name

A basic tenet of Judaism is that nothing is coincidental. A name change by G-d Himself is a weighty act replete with meaning and symbolism.

An individual's name represents aspects of his spiritual make-up. At the time that parents name their child, they are blessed with a prophetic spirit, empowering them to choose a name connected to their child's inherent essence and spiritual life calling.

That is why, when an individual is seriously ill, it is customary to give him an additional name such as Chaim (meaning "life"), Rafael (meaning "cure") or some other name suggesting longevity. When an individual is physically ill, it reflects that something in his life-giving soul is deficient, causing the illness. By adding a name, we hope to add a spiritual life-giving power, which will bring a cure for the sickness.

Sharing Spirituality

The letter *yud* which was removed from Sarai's name has a numerical value of ten. This letter was divided into two letters; one *hey* being substituted to Sara's name, and one *hey* being added to Avraham's name.

The letter *hey* has the numerical value of five. The two additional *hey*s added to Sara's and Avraham's names have the same numerical value as the original *yud* removed from her name.[64]

Perhaps Sara was being asked to take a letter of her name—representing her spiritual powers—and divide it into two. Half of its value would remain for herself and the other half would be given to her husband and soul mate, Avraham.

The sharing of Sara's spiritual powers with Avraham was essential for the birth of Yitzchak. Only this new Avraham was capable of partaking in Yitzchak's conception.

This idea would concur with G-d's instructions regarding Avram's and Sarai's respective name changes. Avram was told, "You shall *become* Avraham," whereas of Sarai, G-d says, "Sara *is* her name." Although Avraham required a *change* in his name, for Sara, her name *is* already Sara.

Sara didn't require any new or added dimension; she already represented all the spirituality of Sara. She already was Sara. The change in her case was sharing some of her spiritual capacity with her husband.

Laughter

When Avraham hears this incredible news—that at one hundred years of age, he is to father a child—he laughs from sheer joy and amazement. Sara, too, shares a similar reaction when she is later informed.

Sara is rebuked by G-d for her laughter.

Although she believed the prophecy would occur, her laughter insinuated that she considered it abnormal and strange. An individual who recognizes G-d's infinite powers should realize that it takes no more effort to make a one-hundred-year-old, barren woman have a child than it does to perform the daily task of setting the sun.

G-d tells Avraham to relay to Sara that her reaction of momentary amazement was inappropriate.

Why was Sara so sternly criticized for her laughter, while G-d made no comment to Avraham about his similar reaction? Furthermore, why didn't G-d rebuke Sara directly, since she had attained even greater levels of prophecy than Avraham?[65]

This issue is dealt with by many classical commentaries, which differentiate between the implications of Sara's and Avraham's laughter. Avraham's laughter, they explain, was from happiness over the miraculous prophecy, whereas Sara's laughter was from disbelief. G-d did not become angry over a reaction of happiness, but sternly rebuked Sara's response and expected more from her.

Closeness with G-d

This explanation, however, still leaves unanswered G-d's roundabout rebuke. I'd like to mention one original explanation.[66]

G-d's criticism of Sara is compared to a wise woman who wishes to rebuke her daughter-in-law. Instead, she directs her rebuke to her daughter, and the daughter-in-law can infer the indirect message. Similarly, G-d rebuked Avraham indirectly for his laughter by criticizing Sara's behavior, in order to spare his feelings.

This interpretation suggests that Sara reached such great intimacy and closeness with G-d that she is comparable to His daughter, as opposed to Avraham—the more distant "daughter-in-law."

Usually when a parent rebukes his son or daughter for their misdeed, the child accepts the words, knowing that they originate from his parent's great love. The child will not become offended by criticism because she understands that any rebuke is said only out of complete devotion.

With a glimpse at the saintliness and righteousness of Avraham, we can appreciate Sara's remarkable qualities. In his life, Avraham achieved a level of utter love of and faith in G-d, to the extent that he was willing to perform the most demanding act of Akeidat Yitzchak, the Binding of Isaac, to sacrifice his only son.

Avraham's faith was unflinching throughout the many difficult tests he overcame. He steadfastly devoted his life to performing G-d's will and disseminating His teachings.

Sara, however, attained such great closeness in her relationship with G-d (comparable to a daughter) because of her ability to always perceive straight to the Divine core of the matter, unaffected by any personal biases.

Sara's spiritual capacity, in this respect, was even greater than Avraham's and is underlined by the events leading to her one recorded dispute with her husband.

The Milk of Sara

In the precise time that G-d declared, exactly one year after the prophecy was spoken, the aged and barren Sara miraculously gave birth to a son. The news that the renowned, elderly couple had a son spread like wildfire.

Amidst the joy, some cynical rabble-rousers spread the rumor that this newborn wasn't born to Sara, but was an abandoned child. G-d, however, dispelled this myth by an unusual turn of events. Miraculously, all the milk of the nursing mothers suddenly dried up. Only Sara, who had become rejuvenated when giving birth, was able to nurse her infant.

Having no other recourse, the nursing mothers pleaded with Sara to nurse their children. The miracle of Sara and Avraham's child thus became even more widespread, as people from far and near were forced to witness that Sara had indeed given birth to a son and was the only woman able to nurse him⊙as well as all the other infants.[67]

A Marred Celebration

When Yitzchak reached the age of two years and was weaned, Avraham made a great feast of thanksgiving.[68] Avraham and Sara were experiencing genuine joy and gratification at this time. Yitzchak's righteousness is apparent to them, and they thank G-d, not only for miraculously having been given a son, but also for one of Yitzchak's caliber, possessing such a lofty and pure soul.

The blissful occasion is marred, however, as Sara witnesses a troubling episode. Sara sees, with her perceptive eyes, "that the son that her Egyptian handmaid had born to Avraham was acting immorally."[69]

Sara immediately orders Avraham (Gen. 21:10): "Drive away this slave together with her son. The son of this slave will not share the inheritance with my son, Yitzchak."

Sara's Demand

The hospitable and generous Sara refuses to allow Yishmael to remain in her home, fearing he might harm Yitzchak or influence him negatively. When Yishmael became ill and feverish, unable to walk on his own, Sara did not relent. Uncharacteristically, she demanded that Avraham banish him to the heat and thirst of the desert.

Avraham was very troubled by Sara's grievous words. His conscience would not allow him to chase his son away in such a harsh and cruel manner. The kind and hospitable Avraham, whose doors were always open to all wayfarers, couldn't bring himself to such an act.

G-d's personal intervention was needed. G-d tells Avraham, "Do not be troubled because of the boy and your slave. Listen to everything that Sara tells you." Only after this proclamation did Avraham follow Sara's directive.

Incompatible Missions

In the eulogy that Avraham said for Sara in the *Eishet Chayil* song, Sara "sought out wool and linen"—she searched for this forbidden combination of *shatnez* to remove it from her home. Sara intuitively saw to the core of Yishmael and understood simply that he and Yitzchak could not remain together in the same home. Their respective missions were incompatible, and Yishmael could not be present to hinder or contaminate the holy task of Yitzchak and the Jewish people.

Sara was able to see the inherent difference between Yitzchak and Yishmael because she could sense the intrinsic G-dliness in everything. With her prophetic capabilities, Sara perceived that Yishmael was not meant to carry on the tradition of G-d, despite Avraham's attempts to teach him and raise him in an upright manner. Yitzchak and his descendants, in contrast, have this Divine inner core as the Chosen people of G-d.

Avraham, on the other hand, was constrained by his inborn kindness, blurring his vision from seeing what was at stake. Sara was also kind and hospitable, but she was able to remove her natural feelings and look objectively at what was involved.

While Avraham reasoned that he could raise Ishmael uprightly, Sara clearly and plainly perceived the truth. She, as women generally do, had a deeper insight into character than Avraham.[70] She realized that Yishmael would not change his undisciplined ways. G-d attested that Sara's judgment was correct.

Sara was speaking now, as always, not because of any personal vendetta or jealousy, but solely for the sake of G-d. Her voice was an extension of G-d's will and therefore, "All that Sara tells you, listen to her."

Consistent Objectivity

Sara merited to be obeyed in all that she said because of her consistency in looking objectively at events and perceiving the Divine Will. This consistency is affirmed by the verse relating to her death: "The life span of Sara was one hundred years, and twenty years and seven years, the years of Sara's life" (Gen. 23:1).

The Midrash[71] explains that the repetitious wording indicates that every year of Sara's life was of equal excellence. Sara was at one hundred like she was at twenty. She had attained the highest degree of integrity and consistency, so that at one hundred years she was as far from the possibility of sin as she was at twenty or at seven.

Sara attained a state of changelessness. Each of her years was exactly the same in excellence and in consistent perfection in performing the Divine Will.

Stripped of Ego

Sara achieved this consistent perfection because she removed her ego from her decisions. To Sara, there was no "me" or "you," no "Sara" or "Avraham," and no "Hagar" and "Yishmael." She saw through these external constraints to the inner core of the individual and situation.

In every predicament, Sara saw the essence of the matter, without any personal slants, and decided what G-d would want of her in that situation.

Finding the Divine purpose was her mission in life that she consistently pursued without compromises. Therefore, G-d tells Avraham to "listen to her voice," because her voice is not her own, but rather the G-dly calling in that particular mission.

Bodies and Souls

According to the *Zohar*,[72] Sara is a symbol for the body while Avraham is a symbol for the soul.

Why then did G-d instruct Avraham (representing the soul) to listen to all that Sara (representing the body) demands of him?

In man's service ultimately the body and soul should not be enemies. The mitzvot were given to the souls in bodies. Moreover, the mitzvot themselves are vested in material objects and were given specifically for the purpose of purifying and sublimating the body and the material domain.

The body should not remain an enemy to the soul, but must participate in the purification process. By helping to perform mitzvot, the body itself becomes purified.

Preoccupation with the Body

However, even if the body is not the soul's enemy, how can the lofty soul gain by listening to the demands of the body? Wouldn't it be more appropriate to tell the body to listen carefully to all the desires of the soul?

While it is not apparent to us now in exile, our ultimate preoccupation is actually with the body.

In exile, our G-dly soul vivifies the body so that when the soul departs, the body disintegrates. In the future era, however, the true essence of the Jewish body will be revealed. The essence of the body originates from a deeper level of G-dliness than even the spiritual soul.

Since the body has descended further from its exalted origin, it is currently on a lower level. In the Era of Mashiach, the essence of the body—which is actually from a higher level of G-dliness—will be revealed. Then, the soul will no longer vitalize the body, but the reverse will be true, with the soul deriving spiritual nutrition from the body.[73]

Foretaste of the Future

The Patriarchs achieved a foretaste of the future world while still in this world.[74] Therefore, G-d told Avraham to listen to all that Sara would say to him. Sara, as the body, represented a deeper aspect of G-dliness than Avraham. For this reason, she achieved her clarity of perception on all occasions.

Sara, as the "body," was the source of spiritual and material bounty in Egypt. Avraham achieved his mission of refining the spiritual elements of Egypt through her. Through Sara's greater capacity, Avraham and Sara were able to leave Egypt (and later, King Avimelech in the land of the Philistines) with great spiritual and material wealth. Avraham, the soul, became vitalized through Sara, the body.

Similarly, as the body, Sara is compared to the "daughter" of G-d, while Avraham, as the soul, represents the more removed daughter-in-law. Just as the body originates from a deeper aspect of G-dliness, so too, a child is always closer to a parent because of his very origin. Though the daughter-in-law can attain a close and warm relationship with her parents-in-law, she always remains an in-law.

Furthermore, Sara, as the body, shares spiritual strength with Avraham, the soul, by giving him a letter of her name. G-d changed Sarai's name in order to share some of her spiritual powers with Avraham. She had this capacity because she, as the body, originated in a deeper aspect of G-dliness.

Women's Spiritual Potential

As our Matriarch and as the first mother of the Jewish people, Sara represents all Jewish women.

Like the body, Sara originates from a higher level of G-dliness than the soul. Women, too, represent a higher origin of G-dliness than men. However, just as the body's true essence has not yet been revealed, this greater essence of women is also hidden. This will only be revealed in the era of redemption. Just as the body's potential powers remain obscured until that time, so do women's vast spiritual capacity and inner connection.

Beyond Subjectivity

As Jewish women, we have both the ability and the responsibility to follow Sara's example.

Perhaps Sara's greatest teaching to us was her ability to remove any tint of selfishness from her outlook. All too often, we become heated up in our views to the extent that our vision is completely obscured. We can perceive our true mandate only when we are not too wrapped up in our own biases. Removing subjectivity from a situation clarifies our perspective and prevents errors in our judgments.

The Voice of Sara

Let me conclude this chapter on Sara with a story.

Once, the chassid Reb Ber was lodging overnight at an inn. Though he was settled comfortably in his bed, strangely, he could not fall asleep. He spent the night pacing the floor and dancing for joy. The innkeeper next door was disturbed by this strange behavior and could barely contain himself until morning before demanding an explanation.

"It is very simple," responded Reb Ber, pointing his finger at the clock hanging on the wall. "That enchanted chime clock is the cause for my great joy. I recognize it as the clock of the saintly Chozeh of Lublin. I just know it must be so! You see, a clock is generally a depressing instrument because it constantly reminds you that moments of your life have passed, are gone forever. A very depressing thought.

"But not so with this clock from the Chozeh of Lublin. Each time his clock chimes, it indicates that we are so much closer to the Redemption. This is a clock heralding good tidings. It is an elating timepiece rather than a depressing one. Each time the clock chimed the hour, I felt a surge of happiness, until finally I could not restrain myself and had to get out of bed and dance for joy."

The clock in Sara's life clicked consistently and perfectly. Sara's clock, too, was an elating timepiece rather than a depressing one. Every tick of her clock of life witnessed a greater spiritual growth, built on and enhancing the previous one. Her clock attested to an uplifting life of perfection, one in which her own external self was wholly removed, while the Will of the Creator was consistently performed.

We, too, can gain proper perception by listening to the little voice nudging us. This is the voice of Sara that sees to the G-dly core and purpose, and nullifies its will in order to consistently act upon G-d's will.

Listening to the voice of Sara within means discovering your spiritual capacity as a Jewish woman.

Allow Sara's voice to ring loud in your consciousness. And, as you do, you will find the keys to heralding the era of redemption, when the Jewish woman's inherent closeness with G-d will become completely and openly manifested.

RIVKA
The Power of Perception

The Talmud[75] relates that a Roman noblewoman once challenged a Jewish sage, "If G-d created the world in six days, what is He so busy with now, after its completion?"

The sage replied, "G-d spends His time arranging *shidduchim*, marriages."

Ridiculing what she believed to be preposterous, the woman declared, "Ha! I'll show you! Arranging marriages is no difficult feat. I can accomplish in a mere hour what you presume your G-d spends all His time on."

With that, she lined up twenty male and female servants. She paired each maid to a butler, and before long all the servants were married. Content that she had proven her point and had humbled the sage, the woman departed.

A few weeks later, the sage met this woman and inquired about the well-being of the newlyweds. The woman confessed her defeat, "Rabbi, I honestly believed—until my own experience proved differently—that pairing individuals was not difficult. I assumed that by carefully choosing this male for that female, a happy couple would emerge. I never imagined all the inner workings.

"On the very day following the marriages, trouble began. Many newlyweds returned to work with broken arms or black eyes. All were fighting, bickering or angry.

"I now realize that a marriage cannot be the haphazard pairing of two individuals but involves something that goes far deeper."

It involves the intervention of the hand of G-d, Himself.

Life Mates and Soul Mates

This chapter is about the first Jewish marriage mentioned in the Torah. Like all marriages, this union was literally a match made in heaven. More so perhaps than other matches, however, the intervention of Divine Providence is clearly discernible.

When the aged Sara heard the news that she would give birth, she laughed inwardly, "*Vatitzchak Sara bekirba*" (Gen. 18:12). By closely examining these words, we learn about this unborn child and his future partner.

The Hebrew word for laughed, *vatitzchak*, contains in it the name Yitzchak, Isaac, the child for which Sara was rejoicing. The word *bekirba*, inwardly, has a permutation of the letters of the word Rivka, Rebecca, Yitzchak's future wife.[76]

This wording hints that even before Yitzchak's conception, this match was ordained. Yitzchak and Rivka were woven together cosmically on a spiritual plane as soul mates and life mates, even prior to their births. Yitzchak's conception could not take place before Rivka, too, had been "conceived" in the spiritual spheres, since she was a vital partner for the fulfillment of his Divine mission and purpose.

The Other Half

This principle holds true for all couples. Before an embryo is formed, a heavenly voice states,[77] "This individual is to marry so-and-so."

The souls of a couple are intricately woven together so that each is only one half of the other and requires his/her other half for completion. Therefore, before a soul can descend into a body, a soul mate must be identified.

When Sara rejoiced about her son's future birth, in some spiritual sense, the conception of his partner was also taking place, as is indicated by Sara's reaction. Furthermore, the allusion to Rivka's name is found specifically in the word *bekirba*, meaning the inwardness of Sara.

Rivka's inward righteous qualities and characteristics were similar to Sara's.

Spiritual Successor

The essential characteristics of Sara and Rivka were identical: virtue, kindness, humility—all the prerequisites traits for the Matriarchs of the Jewish people. Only a woman who was inwardly saintly like Sara could be a partner sharing in the accomplishments of Yitzchak's life.

In fact, when Yitzchak was mourning his righteous mother's death, Avraham realized it was time for Yitzchak to marry. Yitzchak was not comforted over his mother's loss until Rivka entered the tent and became her spiritual successor. Avraham understood that a woman of Rivka's caliber was needed to comfort his son. Avraham, therefore, sent his most trusted servant, Eliezer, on the mission of finding a suitable wife for Yitzchak.

The Divine Providence orchestrating this match began unfolding.[78]

Divine Intervention

Eliezer begins his long journey after being instructed to search for a worthy mate in Aram Naharayim, Avraham's birthplace. Miraculously, he reaches his destination on the very day that he sets out.[79] What was so pressing that his journey needed to be shortened?

To understand the urgency of Eliezer's mission, we must appreciate Rivka's qualities and the circumstances in which she was being raised.

A Rose among Thorns

In the home of her father, Bethuel, Rivka is compared to "a rose among thorns."[80] A rose grows precisely among thorns, which are important for its preservation and growth.[81] When plucking the rose from its roots, the obstacle of the thorns must be overcome. The scratches and pain inflicted by the thorns are ignored, but only if the rose is sufficiently beautiful.

The plot surrounding the rose, as well, will be irrigated to preserve and assist in its growth. All the negativity surrounding the rose will be of benefit for the rose's beauty. Once the rose has matured, however, and is no longer in need of the thorns, they are immediately discarded, no longer serving any purpose.

Irrigating the Thorns

Just as in the analogy, where the thorns are irrigated for the sake of the rose, Rivka's father, Bethuel, amassed considerable wealth on her account.[82]

When Rivka matured, she became eligible to marry Yitzchak. This change in Rivka is what constituted the motivation and reason for her to move away from the thorns. Avraham sensed this at the time and immediately sent Eliezer to search for Yitzchak's soul mate.

Avraham's instruction to Eliezer could not have been given prior to Rivka's becoming of marriageable age. Once she matured, though, there had to be a shortening of the journey to avoid her remaining in those degenerate surroundings unnecessarily.

To achieve her ultimate purpose in life, Rivka needed to be raised in the morally corrupt home of her father, Bethuel, and conniving brother, Lavan. As we will discover further in this chapter, Rivka utilized her sensitivity to evil, acquired from her childhood, later in life to evaluate her two contrasting sons, Yaakov (Jacob) and Esav (Esau).

Through this perception, she was able to benefit the Jewish people.

Descent for the Sake of Ascent

Rivka's surroundings, therefore, inadvertently served as an integral part of her maturation and developmental process.

Chassidic philosophy explains that prior to every spiritual ascent, descent is necessary. The darkness of night precedes the light of day, in part in order to amplify our appreciation for the light.

Similarly, for Rivka's righteous qualities to emerge, she had to be exposed to darkness and moral decay. Notwithstanding, once the maturation of this beautiful rose had been completed, the thorns were no longer necessary and Rivka was immediately plucked from her surroundings.

The Thorns of Exile

Rivka's spiritual emancipation from her evil home teaches an eternal lesson for her descendants, the Jewish people.

The purpose of our dark, long exile is for the Jewish people to spread the holiness of the Torah throughout the world.[83]

Once we have accomplished our mission, however, we can be plucked from the thorns of exile. Furthermore, there is no longer any purpose to sustaining the evil. Its irrigation has only been to form us into a mature and holy nation. Just as in the removal of Rivka from her negative situation, miracles could transpire to cause the Redemption to occur speedily, so that we need not remain even an extra second.[84]

Rampant Evil

Prior to Rivka's spiritual emancipation, evil was rampant. In the moments preceding the Final Redemption, evil will intensify, rising like a fever before it is broken. Evil will attempt to rear its ugly head, asserting itself in its last chance.

This explains the signs that will occur at this time. On the one hand, there will be material and technological advances and an explosion of Torah as well as secular knowledge, as never before.[85] This increased material and intellectual prosperity is a necessary prerequisite for the era which is characterized as the utopia of physical and spiritual well-being. On the other hand, social decay and disorder and personal emptiness will also be widespread.

The Talmud (Sota 49b) describes this era as the "face of a dog." Wrong will be thought of as right, and self-gratification will replace morality. The moral fabric of society will be stretched and torn, and the individual's quest for self-realization will be shattered.

This rampant evil is a prerequisite for the Redemption.[86] As with Rivka, the greatest descent can produce the greatest elevation and purity. In the midst of these thorns, Rivka remained the pure, untouched rose.

Divine Guidance

Rivka's righteousness is first recognized by Eliezer as he reaches Aram Naharayim and notices the beautiful, young girl coming to the well to draw water.[87] Eliezer had finished praying to G-d for a sign to identify which maiden would be fitting for his master's son. Eliezer understood that the hallmarks of a Jewish woman, and the characteristics which permeated Sara's tent, were kindness and hospitality. He therefore suggested to G-d that when the maiden would offer him and all his camels a drink from the well, this would be proof that she was suitable.

This scenario was highly improbable. Not only did it require that the appropriate girl come to the well at exactly the right moment, but also that she offer him and his many camels to drink. Eliezer realized the unlikelihood, and that is precisely why it would serve as a true indication of the Divine Providence guiding him in selecting the proper mate.[88]

Epitomizing Kindness

Rivka magnanimously demonstrates her absolute kindness. As Rivka approaches, Eliezer runs to meet her and asks to drink from her pitcher. She graciously lowers her vessel from her shoulder and offers it to him. When he has finished drinking, she offers his camels water, as well. She hurriedly empties her pitcher into the trough and runs back and forth to the well until all the camels are satiated. Eliezer is astounded by Rivka's gracious behavior.

Any other woman would have found many excuses in reply to Eliezer. She could have answered, "Since you are standing at the well just as I, why don't you drink directly from the waters before you?" She may also have answered, "Why do you want that I, particularly, give you to drink, when I have already placed the jar back upon my shoulder and there are many maidens who still have their jars in their hand?" Furthermore, she could have at least asked that he take the vessel and save her the considerable extra exertion of lowering the heavy container from her shoulder into her hand![89]

Rivka's offer to provide drinks for Eliezer and his camels was a mark of her wisdom and generous spirit. She concluded that this man probably had pain in his hands, preventing him from drawing water from the well or from taking the jar by himself. She reasoned that if he lacked the strength to draw water for himself, he was not strong enough to provide for his camels. She was stirred by the goodness of her heart to take pity on the suffering of these creatures and offered them water as well.

The Presents

After his detailed signs had materialized, Eliezer understood that Divine Providence was pointing to Yitzchak's future mate. Eliezer presents Rivka with "a golden ring, half a shekel in weight and two bracelets, ten gold shekels in weight" (Gen. 24:22).

All events, even minor ones that occurred to our forefathers, are meant to teach us lessons. Through the specific weight of these engagement presents, Eliezer was teaching an eternal message about the establishment of a Jewish home.[90]

Submission to G-d

The ring that weighed a half a shekel represents the mitzva of *tzedaka*, charity,[91] which is the "totality of all mitzvot."[92] The two bracelets weighing ten shekels represent the two tablets engraved with the Ten Commandments, which are the totality of the Torah.[93]

The Jewish people accepted these commandments with full submission, exclaiming, "We will keep [observe them]" even before "we will hear [understand them]."[94] They demonstrated by this that even before being aware of G-d's commandments, they were willing to accept them simply because they were G-d's will. Regardless of what would be commanded, they trusted that if this was the Divine Will, these laws must be beneficial. The Jewish people manifested *kabbalat ol*, complete submission to G-d.

The Secret of a Successful Marriage

Similarly, for a marriage to succeed it must be based on these principles. Marriage, even in the best of times, is difficult and a constant struggle. With the merging of two contrasting personalities, there is bound to be a battle of strength. Behind the petty arguments which may erupt over silly details lies a conflict of wills. At such times, the only way the marriage can be strengthened, rather than ruined, is if it has been based on the principles demonstrated by Eliezer's gifts.

The marriage can thrive only if both husband and wife submit their own will to a higher and greater one—the Divine Will.[95] Once marriage becomes a personal agenda, rather than a collective goal, feelings are bound to be hurt and harsh words uttered. Thoughts such as, "Am I really getting more than—or at least as much as—I am giving to this marriage?" are inevitably aroused. My personal gratification, as opposed to our unified spiritual mission, becomes central.

On the other hand, a marriage can thrive if it is based on submission to G-d and His commandments, as represented by the Ten Commandments and the mitzva of charity. This does not mean that, as an individual, I do not have my own rights and desires. Nor does it entail disregarding my spiritual or material needs. These thoughts, however, are secondary to the goal of establishing a thriving Jewish home.

"The greatest charity begins at home" is a well-known quote. How true that the greatest charity becomes evident when building a tranquil and harmonious spiritual abode. Each party necessarily becomes more attuned and sensitive to those issues held dear to and important by his/her partner.

An Ailing Foot

An episode is related about Reb Aryeh Levine, who once accompanied his wife to the doctor due to her ailing foot. When the elderly couple entered the doctor's room, Reb Aryeh said, "Please examine my wife's foot. It is hurting *us*."

To Reb Aryeh, the pain of his wife was the pain of the couple. There was no "I" or "you," but only "us."

The Engraved Tablets

Eliezer was teaching an indelible lesson about the foundation of the Jewish home by presenting Rivka with two bracelets to correspond to the two Tablets.

But if he was trying to demonstrate the idea of submission to G-d's will, why limit it to the Ten Commandments? Why not give something representing the vast body of the Written or Oral Torah?

The Written Torah consists of written letters, made up of both ink and parchment. The letters, or ink, are distinct from the parchment. Only by combining these two entities does the Written Torah come about.

In the Oral Torah, too, there are two distinct entities. Only in the period of the Mishna, and later the Talmud, did it become essential to commit the Oral Torah to writing. Until then, the lessons of the Oral Torah were taught by teacher to student.[96] Thus, the content matter and lessons of the Torah were distinct from the individual who studied it.

In contrast, the letters of the Ten Commandments were *engraved* on the tablets.[97] The tablets were not distinct from the Ten Commandments because the letters were *made of, and one with,* the actual tablets.

Internalizing Torah

Eliezer gave two bracelets corresponding to the engraved Ten Commandments (as opposed to the Written or Oral Torah) to demonstrate that it is not enough for the Jewish home to be based on the foundations of Torah and mitzvot. It is not even enough that the Jew observe Torah with submission. If the Jew and the Torah remain distinct from one another—even if they happen to be in agreement—the Jew has not fulfilled his ultimate purpose. The individual and the Torah must merge into one.

The individual, like the letters on the stones of the Tablets, must *become* the Torah. This can only be achieved when he strives to attain an internalization of the Torah's principles. His goal is not to master the Torah, but to allow the Torah to master him.

Furthermore, when the individual acts and thinks with the light of the Torah, he no longer sees himself as a separate self. Although he possesses his own unique attributes, talents and needs, he utilizes these characteristics for the purpose of Torah. His selfish self becomes subordinate to the higher goal of the Divine Will.

Sara's Successor

At her tender age, Rivka understood these lofty principles. Though her family was reluctant to allow her to leave with Eliezer,[98] Rivka informed them that she, indeed, would go. Though she hardly knew her distant relatives, and she had only met their servant, she was decisive, demonstrating courage and strength of conviction.

Rivka was surrounded by such evil and depravity that when she met Avraham's servant, the principles that he represented were, to her, like a breath of fresh air. With her extraordinary power of perception, she instantly sensed G-dliness and morality. Rivka was drawn to this truth and soaked it up as a rose drinks water. When asked by her family if she wanted to go with this stranger, Rivka decisively answered: yes! To her, the decision was not a question of leaving her family and homeland, but the potential of internalizing her G-dly mission in life.

In this matter, there was no question.

Rivka was not disappointed. When she arrived in Yitzchak's homeland, she noticed from afar a man praying intensely in the field and asked his identity. Eliezer answered that it was Yitzchak, and Rivka modestly covered herself with her veil. Jewish brides have learned from her to follow this custom at their weddings.

Yitzchak sees Rivka and "brings her into the tent of his mother" (Gen. 24:67). An immediate transformation occurs in the previously forlorn tent. All the miracles that had occurred in Sara's tent, which had ceased upon her death, began anew.[99] Rivka transformed the physical tent into a spiritual abode. The cloud signifying G-d's presence once again hung over the entrance, bearing witness to the righteousness within.

The strength of Sara was replaced by that of Rivka.

Love That Grows

When Yitzchak saw this, "she became his wife," and then "he loved her" (Gen. 24:64). Yitzchak only married Rivka when he was certain of her righteousness. He then loved her after their marriage.

In writing in this order, the Torah teaches a lesson about love that is particularly relevant in today's times.

The intimate closeness and deep love of a husband and wife cannot be apparent before marrying. Although infatuation can be a part of the courtship process, real love increases during marriage with the emotional, spiritual and physical sharing of the two. Real love does not decrease with familiarity. The infatuation can at times begin to dull, but the love continues to grow with their increased sharing of their inner selves. While infatuation is dependent on the external, real love involves experiencing the essence of one's partner.

This was just the beginning of Yitzchak and Rivka's growing love. It was the seed planted that would grow strong and healthy.

The Twins

Rivka's righteousness and sharp sense of perception becomes apparent when she becomes a mother. Though twenty years had passed with no voices of children's laughter heard in their tent, Rivka finally became pregnant with twins. She sensed, from the onset, that her pregnancy was out of the ordinary.[100] Through her prophetic spirits she sensed, too, a distinct and unusual contrast between the unborn fetuses.

The Cry of a Child

I am reminded of a story about Rabbi Dov Ber of Lubavitch,[101] who was so engrossed in learning Torah that he didn't hear his infant son begin to cry in his crib.

At this time, Rabbi Shneur Zalman, the grandfather of the infant was upstairs and heard the cries. He immediately came down, took the child out of his crib and tenderly caressed him. Later, Rabbi Shneur Zalman reprimanded Rabbi Dov Ber, saying, "You must never be so preoccupied with learning Torah that you don't hear the cries of a child."

At times we think of a righteous person as someone so engrossed in G-dliness and spiritual pursuits that he doesn't bother with the practicality of everyday living. Rabbi Shneur Zalman taught his son, Rabbi Dov Ber, that being involved with Torah studies does not justify neglecting what is happening around you.

If we may not neglect the physical discomforts of those around us, all the more must we heed their spiritual cries.

Rivka's Power of Perception

While Yitzchak was engrossed with the holy words of Torah, Rivka listened well to the cry of her two sons. She heard the struggle of each of them: Esav, the cry of hunting, and Yaakov, the cry of Torah and prayers. She perceived the goals and aspirations of each.

Very early in their lives, Rivka sensed that each of her sons had chosen his life's path. Esav had chosen a path of moral depravity, much like the immorality that surrounded her throughout her youth. Yaakov, in contrast, was imbued with the spiritual ideals she had found so captivating in Yitzchak. These ideals had given her the desire and fortitude to abandon her home for a life with Yitzchak.

Façade of Righteousness

Yitzchak, on the other hand, was deceived by the external trappings of righteousness that Esav flaunted. Being constantly immersed in the holy books of Torah, Yitzchak didn't discern Esav's facade. Esav would ask his father detailed questions about Torah laws in order to impress Yitzchak with his stringency in observance. Esav was a hunter in every sense of the word—he would trap his father with his crafty words. 102

Aware of the capabilities of her sons, Rivka strengthened herself to give each his deserving share. Though she greatly respected her husband, she understood that she was more discerning about her children's inherent qualities. Every time Rivka heard Yaakov's voice of Torah learning, her love for him increased. She was prepared to do everything in her power to insure that the cries of the righteous Yaakov be heeded, even if that involved deceiving her husband.

Rivka's Instructions

Rivka's plan comes into effect in the following narration (Gen. 27): "When Yitzchak had grown old and his eyesight was fading, he summoned his elder son, Esav [in order to bless him with the transmission of the Divine blessings] . . . Rivka had been listening while Yitzchak was speaking to Esav. Esav went out to the field to trap some game and bring it home [as his father had instructed him to do before the blessings could be given].

"Rivka then said to her son Yaakov, 'I heard your father speaking to your brother, Esav . . . Now, my son, listen to me. Go to the sheep and take two choice young kids. I will prepare them with a tasty recipe, just the way your father likes them. You must then bring it to your father, so that he will eat and bless you before he dies."

Rivka was instructing Yaakov to deceive his father and identify himself as Esav to receive the blessings. Yaakov objects, saying, "Suppose my father touches me. He will realize that I am an impostor! I will then receive a curse rather than a blessing."

Rivka had a back-up plan involving further deceit. She intended to put hairy goats' skins on Yaakov's arms to resemble the hairy Esav. She also reassured Yaakov in her reply, "Let any curse be on me, my son, just listen to me."

Reaffirming the Blessings

Just as Esav returns, Yitzchak has finished blessing Yaakov and discovers the truth. However, rather than cursing Yaakov for deceiving him, Yitzchak almost credits him for his behavior by reaffirming his blessing, "He should also be blessed."(The blessing should remain his.)

What was transpiring in this plot engineered by the righteous Rivka and Yaakov? Although a mother generally has astounding intuition with her children, in Rivka's scenario, more than motherly instinct appears to be guiding her. As the Torah and the commentaries attest, Esav was a murderous, blatantly evil hunter, while Yaakov was a man of the books, studying and internalizing the principles of the Torah.

How could Yitzchak so wrongly err, forcing Rivka to boldly oppose and even deceive him? Furthermore, why couldn't she discuss this openly with Yitzchak? What new insight did Yitzchak gain after Yaakov deceived him that makes him reaffirm Yaakov's blessing, originally intended for Esav?

The commentaries explain that when Yitzchak blessed Yaakov, he prophetically foresaw the destruction of the Temples and, only then, continued blessing him. Shouldn't this vision of the destruction, caused by the sins of Yaakov's descendants, convince Yitzchak to withhold the blessings?

Fighting Evil

To understand this perplexing episode, the differing positions of Yitzchak and Rivka must be clarified.

Yitzchak realized that the goal of his successor would not be to disassociate himself from the physical world, but rather to fight and overcome its negative forces. The son to assume his task would need to transform negativity into holiness.

Yitzchak believed that Yaakov was unsuitable because he was removed from this world and had little involvement with physical reality. Yaakov was "the man of the tent" (Gen. 25:28), the scholar who found refuge in the realm of Torah studies. To remain in the four cubits of study was to stay distant from the world. Being protected by this spiritual environment required much less stamina than being a part of the physical environment and overcoming it.

Warming a Cold Environment

To illustrate how to be submerged in physical reality while transforming it into holiness, we can use an analogy of a person in a cold room. There are three ways to maintain body temperature: first, he can put on a warm coat; second, he can leave the room to escape to a warmer environment; or third, he can light a fire.

Similarly, in a "cold" environment, detrimental to his standards, one's integrity can be preserved through these three methods. First, he can put on a warm coat, symbolizing strengthening himself inwardly so as not to be influenced by his surroundings. This, however, is an incomplete victory, for if he were to relax his self-control he would capitulate.

Secondly, he can leave the room, which implies separating himself from the negative influences surrounding him. Once again, this victory is only because he has removed himself from temptation. He has not met the challenge and affected his surroundings.

The third approach, lighting a fire, involves influencing the environment and raising it to a higher level. This is a complete triumph over one's surroundings, for the dangers have not only been avoided, they have been removed entirely.

Esav's Potential Spirituality

Yitzchak thought that Yaakov confronted his evil environment through the first two approaches. He strengthened himself by wearing the cloak of Torah and he escaped from its negativity by finding respite within houses of Torah study. Esav, in contrast, was a hunter, a man immersed in the physical world. Although Esav had a predisposition to evil, Yitzchak believed he had the power to overcome the negativity.

In a sense, Yitzchak was correct in his evaluation. The Midrash[103] points out that Esav had great spiritual potential, but destroyed this potential with his evil actions. Although originally Esav may have tried to ward off the evil, he eventually succumbed.

Rivka, on the other hand, perceived that Yaakov's involvement with the Torah was not to keep distant from this physical world. She understood that he was drawing strength from the Torah in order to empower him to overcome the challenges of this world.

How was Rivka able to discern Yaakov's inherent, hidden potential of transforming negativity into holiness? Why could Rivka sense this stamina in Yaakov and realize it was missing from Esav, while Yitzchak was blind to this truth?

Exposure to Evil

Yitzchak's and Rivka's differing visions resulted from their respective upbringings. Rivka's extraordinary perception was gained through her negative childhood. As mentioned, Rivka's surroundings provided a descent for the sake of an ascent. Rivka, as the rose among the thorns, was fully submerged in the evil and negativity of this world. As the rose, however, she overcame the thorns around her. She was steeped in evil, trickery and stealing, yet she remained pure. She understood, from personal experience, the inner strength needed to ward off this evil and transform it. As her two children matured, she detected this quality in Yaakov.

Yitzchak, on the other hand, was raised by the saintly Avraham and Sara. He had never experienced sin and was so pure that he was almost offered as a sacrifice to G-d. His restricted exposure to sin made it difficult for him to appreciate Yaakov's capacity for transforming evil.

Whereas Yitzchak imbued Yaakov with the power and holiness of Torah, Rivka taught him how to use this power in the involvement and transformation of the physical world. Rivka provided Yaakov with the education of challenging and overcoming sin, as is demonstrated by her plot.

When Yaakov followed Rivka's instruction and deceived Yitzchak by stealing his brother's blessings, Yitzchak realized his mistake. It was a realization that surpassed any rational convincing that Rivka could have attempted.

He saw that Yaakov had the power to overcome evil. When it became necessary, he was indeed able to use trickery and the garments of this world to achieve a spiritual elevation. Yaakov could descend into the physicality of this world and transform it.

Falling into a Pit

This point is reinforced during the blessings. Through a prophetic revelation, Yitzchak envisions the Temples' destruction but continues blessing Yaakov. The destruction of the Temples proved to Yitzchak that although the individual before him was destined to sin, he would repent. True, Yaakov's descendants would fall into the evil clutches of sin, but this only proved that he was not removed from the realm of physicality. Yitzchak foresaw that repentance would follow, thereby overcoming and transforming this very same evil.

Yaakov and his descendants had the inner stamina and spiritual strength to fall into the pit of sin—and climb out. Someone in a pit requires more energy to pull himself out than if he had never fallen in. Yaakov's descendants would undergo a long and arduous exile, but eventually the world would emerge rectified and enriched because of their service.

Disregarding Personal Risks

This was the lesson that Rivka taught Yaakov with her words, "Let any curse be on me, my son" (Gen. 27:13). Not only does this statement provide a glimpse into Rivka's greatness, it also instructs the Jewish people how to endure while in exile.

Rivka was teaching us that to receive the spiritual powers from the blessings, self-sacrifice is necessary. If our service is limited by our own calculations, we are qualifying our dedication and we cannot receive unlimited powers.

When Yaakov worried that Yitzchak would curse him because of his deceitful acts, Rivka told him not to make such calculations. She explained that at stake was the receiving of the Infinite powers for the Jewish people—blessings essential for their future survival. Rivka assures Yaakov that if Yitzchak curses him in the process, "let the curse be on me."

Through her words, Rivka was impressing upon her son that they must forge ahead regardless of personal risks, because this was vital for the future spiritual welfare of the Jewish people.

The Folly of Holiness

Rivka was willing to take personal, uncalculated risks for the benefit of the Jewish people.

We find a similar concept in what is termed the "folly of holiness."[104] This phrase describes suprarational behavior transcending reason; becoming so enthused with the mitzvot that one transcends the limitations of duty to perform them. Externally this enthusiasm for the mitzvot may appear foolish.

The Talmud (*Ketubot* 17a) relates an episode where an individual had such fervor. Rabbi Shmuel ben Rabbi Yitzchak danced at weddings, juggling three twigs to fulfill the mitzva of bringing joy to the bride and groom.

Rabbi Zeyra, a colleague of his, commented on his behavior, "The old man is putting us to shame [by behaving inappropriately and foolishly]."

When Rabbi Shmuel died, Rabbi Zeyra discovered just how wrong he had been.

Upon Rabbi Shmuel's death, a pillar of fire appeared and separated him from all the others. According to tradition, this happens only for one, or at the most two, extraordinary tzaddikim in a generation. The Talmud concludes that Rabbi Shmuel merited this privilege by virtue of his "strange" behavior.

His enthusiastic involvement in a mitzva which may appear foolish, elevated him to a superior level.

Stubborn, Uncalculated Enthusiasm

Rivka, too, demonstrated that this uncalculated enthusiasm for mitzvot and for holiness is the essential ingredient for surviving the long and difficult exile.

History has proven time and time again how an apathetic approach towards Judaism has been its prescription for obliteration. The Jewish people have been preserved through their verve and stubborn vitality in observing the mitzvot.

This stubborn persistence is needed now more than ever in believing in and demanding the Redemption. Although it may appear a "folly," this uncalculated desire for the Redemption will make it occur.

And then the beautiful rose will immediately be removed from the surrounding thorns, permanently . . .

RACHEL & LEAH
Two Worlds, Two Destinies

Rachel and Leah—two sisters, two wives of Yaakov, and two of the Matriarchs of our People. Rachel and Leah—two powerful but contrasting personalities, each representing a world of her own.

Rachel was Yaakov's first love and primary wife. But Leah was the first wife that he actually married, the first to bear his children and the one to mother the majority of his children.

At Leah's hour of need, Rachel performed the greatest act of self-sacrifice by relinquishing her own destined groom in order to spare Leah degradation. As her swindling father veils Leah, replacing Rachel as Yaakov's bride, Rachel not only remains silent, but aids her sister with the deception. She does this simply so that her sister should not feel acutely embarrassed.

Leah, too, despite experiencing the pain of being Yaakov's "unloved" wife, whose only consolation was bearing his children, demonstrates keen feelings of sisterhood and sensitivity to Rachel by praying for her to have a child. Pregnant with her seventh child, Leah prays that the fetus be female, so that Rachel, too, should have her allotted share in the tribes of Israel.

Yet, despite their enormous compassion towards one another, Rachel and Leah were very different personalities representing two entirely different planes of reality, which in later times developed into actual rivalry.

An Enduring Schism

The vast gulf dividing their respective worlds not only affected their own lives but continued as a penetrating rift in the lives of their descendants.

Beginning with the rivalry between Yosef (Joseph, Rachel's child) and his brothers (primarily Leah's children), who sought to kill him but instead were placated by selling him as a slave to a passing caravan—the schism keeps resurfacing.

It was Moshe (Moses), Leah's descendant, who redeemed our people from their slavery in Egypt, but only Yehoshua (Joshua)—Moshe's disciple and Rachel's descendant—who was able to lead the nation into the Holy Land.

The rulership of our first national king, King Shaul (Saul, descendant of Rachel), was cut short by King David (Leah's descendant), through whom the dynasty would be established. But the schism again resurfaced with the constant strife and divisiveness between Malchut Yisrael (the kingship of Israel) and Malchut Beit David (the Davidic dynasty).

And this schism is set to remain until the end of time. Mashiach ben Yosef (from Rachel) has the task of preparing the world for redemption, but it is Mashiach ben David (from Leah) who actually accomplishes the final redemption for eternity.

What is the mystery of the spiritual qualities represented by these two sisters? What was the secret cosmic schism that would span centuries of history?

The Life of the Tzaddik

Our first introduction to Rachel presents a young woman who is "beautiful and shapely," of sterling character and overflowing kindness, shepherding her father's animals. Yaakov's keen spiritual sensitivity immediately senses that he has found his soul mate.

Like her father's sheep that she tended, Rachel's name means "ewe"—an animal characterized by its bright white color and serene, loveable nature.[105] The beautiful Rachel, loved immediately by Yaakov for the shining qualities of her soul, is associated with the revealed, beautiful world of the present.

Rachel represents the tzaddik (literally, saintly individual) personality,[106] a pure and righteous individual whose very being reflects the harmony and goodness of her Creator. Her task is to elevate our people to reach a higher reality. Her beauty is openly apparent.

A World of Perfection

In the original design for our world, it was intended that we taste the sweetness of the fruit, even as it was developing within the wood of the tree.[107]

In a perfectly functioning world, the present is meant to be revealed in all its radiance as a prelude to a more sublime future.

Rachel represents this state of simple and natural, revealed beauty. She epitomizes the world of perfection in the here and now of the tzaddik personality. She personifies the world of personal success, self-realization and spiritual perfection.

Her oldest son, Yosef, the handsome, enterprising and charismatic viceroy over the Egyptian empire, also strongly embodied Rachel's qualities. His handsomeness, too, mirrored an inner drive for spiritual perfection, retaining his righteousness even in the most corrupting of environments in Egypt, while working to achieve his spiritual goals for himself and the world at large. [108]

The Life of the Baal Teshuva

On the other hand, Leah's name means "one who is weary."[109] She is described as the weak-eyed sister, weakened from her incessant tears and anxiety.

Leah personifies a more complicated individual who struggles with the darker forces of our world and faces an exhausting, perpetual struggle. Leah is associated with the *baal teshuva* (literally, master of return) figure, the repentant, an individual continuously plagued with battling, and overcoming, the negative urges rooted in her psyche.

The *baal teshuva* personality does not only mean one who simply sins and repents. The righteous Leah did not commit any act of sin. The path of the *baal teshuva*, however, refers to a specific Divine service where one is charged with dealing with the negativity of this world and exploiting its goodness. The *baal teshuva* has the power of transforming the negativity by dealing with it, and thereby elevating it and causing it to become holy.

Teshuva (literally, repentance or return), in its ultimate sense, redefines and transforms negativity and reaches a new level of attachment to G-d. One who strays and then rebounds is fueled by his deficient state with a stronger yearning for Divine life.

But the interaction with the negativity is strenuous and often painful. The *baal teshuva* must be vigilant, on constant guard in each of his interactions with the world, for fear of succumbing to its embrace.

A World of Struggle

Though our world was initially created in perfection, it didn't take long for the universe to experience decline. The earth failed to produce trees tasting like its fruit. The sin of the Tree of Knowledge forced humanity to be expelled from the perfect world of Eden.

The beautiful future in store for our world and the Jewish people, in Messianic times, is profoundly hidden. Though the end result of our service of *teshuva*—ultimately manifested in the future redemption—is an even greater attachment with the Divine, the path leading to it throughout exile is obscure, full of wearisome battles.

"In the place that a *baal teshuva* stands, a tzaddik cannot reach."[110]

Ultimately the path of the *baal teshuva*, precisely due to his digression from the road of righteousness, evokes in him a striving and yearning for home that he would never have mustered otherwise.

Leah, typifying the *baal teshuva* personality, represents this future state of our people. Like Leah, we can raise our sights, overcome the present difficulties and actualize a lofty future. Leah, who symbolizes the destiny of our people, is the twisted path towards that ultimately higher future reality.

Yehuda and King David: Paradigms of Teshuva

Leah's son, Yehuda, who is destined for kingship, is held as a prime example of someone who perfectly accomplishes *teshuva*, by publicly admitting to his sin with Tamar and repenting over it.

Early in his life, King David, Yehuda's descendant and from whose dynasty Mashiach descends, also represents the life of a *baal teshuva*, breaking any trace of evil within him through his constant fasts and prayers.[111]

Yehuda and King David are both characterized not by their magnetism, ambition and self-actualization, but by their humility, commitment and self-effacement. They faced the trials of their lives, not as Yosef, with a determined self-confidence mirroring an inner spiritual perfection, but rather with a sense of weary self-abnegation and commitment.

Leah's life, like that of her descendants and the Jewish people as a whole, bears witness to one who has been riding the ups and downs of the roller-coaster ride we call life. Only in retrospect can one fathom a beauty in the downs as well as the ups, in seeing how the descents ultimately lead us to higher ascents.

Leah's Marriage Partner

For this reason, initially, Leah was destined to marry Esav (Esau), while Rachel was destined for Yaakov.

People would say: "This is the arrangement. The elder daughter (Leah) is for the elder son (Esav), while the younger daughter (Rachel) is for the younger son (Yaakov)".[112]

Leah sat at the crossroads asking about Esav. She was informed, "Oh, he's a wicked man!"

Hearing this, Leah cried bitter tears, "My sister and I were born of the same womb, yet Rachel is to marry the righteous man and I, the wicked Esav!"

Leah wept and fasted until her eyes became weak.[113]

She would cry until her lashes fell out saying, "May it be Your will that I do not fall to the lot of that wicked man!"

Rabbi Huna said, "Great is prayer that it annulled the decree and Leah even took precedence over her sister."[114]

A Hidden Marriage

Leah's weak eyes bespeak a weariness borne from her struggles. She battled with all her strength to avoid interaction with the evil of the world, for fear of succumbing to its gravity. Leah feared any connection to Esav and was able to change her destiny with her steadfast prayers.

The Kabbalists explain that Yaakov's marriage to Leah was also part of the Divine plan, but part of a secretive plan, primarily for the future.

R' Elazar remarked: "Since Yaakov had to find his wife by the well, why did he not meet Leah there, who was to mother the majority of the tribes? The answer is that it was not the will of G-d that Leah be espoused to Yaakov openly. Yaakov, in fact, married her without his knowledge."[115]

The Prearranged Signs

When Yaakov meets Rachel, he proposes.

Rachel answered, "Yes, I agree to marry you. But you should be aware that my father is a trickster and you will not prevail against him."

"What is his trickery?" Yaakov inquired.

"I have a sister who is older than I," Rachel replied. "My father will try to marry her off first."

Yaakov said, "I am his brother in trickery."

Rachel asked, "May the righteous indulge in trickery?"

"Yes," he replied. "With the pure, you act in purity and with the crooked you are wily" (2 Sam. 22:27).

Yaakov then gave Rachel secret signs to prevent Lavan's trickery. On the night of the wedding, Rachel saw Leah being led to the wedding. She thought to herself, "My sister will now be disgraced!"

With her enormous compassion, Rachel told Leah the pre-arranged signs.

This explains why it is written, "When the morning came, there was Leah!" This implies that until then she was not Leah. Because of the signs that Yaakov gave to Rachel who gave them to Leah, he didn't know who she was until then.[116]

The pure, righteous Rachel couldn't remain quiet while her sister would be utterly humiliated. Shattering her own dreams for a beautiful future and forsaking her personal happiness, the compassionate Rachel shares the prearranged signs with her sister.

Learning by Example

The morning after consummating his marriage with Leah, Yaakov awoke and realized the treachery.

He was furious with his new bride. "You are a deceiver and the daughter of a deceiver! All night long I called you Rachel and you responded as if you were she."

Leah responded, "Is there a teacher without pupils? Your example taught me that it is permissible to lie for a good cause. Twenty-one years ago, your father sent Esav to bring him food and you rushed to set it before him. Did not your own father call you Esav and you answered him! [Gen. 27:29] You called me, too, and I answered you."[117]

Two Names: Yaakov and Yisrael

Through this obscure interchange, Leah is explaining to Yaakov the workings of the Divine plan.

Yaakov had two names: Yaakov, which was given to him at birth, and Yisrael, which was bestowed upon him after defeating Esav's guardian angel, Samael, and receiving his blessing.

The name Yaakov symbolized Yaakov as the scholarly man, who remained immersed in study in the tent, issuing forth the voice of Torah and prayer (Gen. 25:27).

The individual named Yaakov fell in love with Rachel. Their union is referred to in Kabbala as the union of "voice" and "speech."[118]

Yisrael's Marriage Partner

But when Yaakov takes the blessings intended for Esav from his father, he dresses up in the clothes of Esav. In order to wrest his father's blessing from his brother, in a sense, Yaakov needed to "become" Esav. There needed to transpire a merger between the hands of Esav and the voice of Yaakov. The implication of this merger would continue to live on in the personality of Yisrael.

Through her words, Leah was explaining to Yaakov that by deceiving his father, on some cosmic level, he became Esav and must fulfill Esav's spiritual role. Part of that role was in his union with Leah.[119]

His marriage to Leah was a result of his own actions and his new identity as Yisrael. Rachel married Yaakov as his first match, a match preordained in heaven, while Leah was married to Yisrael, a second and additional marriage which was earned through his actions.

Exchanging the Mandrakes

An interesting episode is described several years after Rachel's and Leah's marriages to Yaakov. Leah has already given birth to a number of children when her oldest son, Reuven, brings her a present of mandrakes, a flower known to aid fertility.

The barren Rachel requests these mandrakes. After some negotiation, Leah agrees to give Rachel the mandrakes, in exchange for spending the night with Yaakov.

When Yaakov comes home from the field, Leah goes out to greet him, explaining that it is his turn to spend the night in her tent.

The verse then records that *"He* lay with her that night."

"He" is not called Yaakov, but rather a mysterious, nameless "he." The Kabbalists explain that while Yaakov was Rachel's marriage partner, this nameless "he" who is identified as Yisrael was married to Leah.[120]

Yisrael's Destiny

Yaakov only assumes the name Yisrael after "struggling with strong forces and emerging victorious."[121]

Yisrael represents the encounter and personal struggle with the negativity in our world. Yaakov is unable to comprehend this inner struggle; he is entirely removed from it. But Yisrael understands it very well.[122]

Yisrael appreciates the spiritual level of Leah, her hidden and inner beauty which is very different from the revealed, open magnetism of Rachel. Leah's beauty is a veiled, austere beauty, bereft of adornments. It is a majesty reflected in all of our people, in the wonder of exposing our potential—within our hardships, our struggles and our uncertainties.

Dina's Outgoingness—Leah's Spiritual Heir

Leah's hidden, wearisome journey, traversing the twisted paths of this world, is echoed in the life of her daughter, Dina.

Dina was originally a male fetus, transformed into a female due to Leah's prayers.

"'Afterwards she bore him a daughter and she called her name Dina' (Gen. 30:21).

"What is meant by afterwards? Rab said: After Leah had passed judgment on herself, saying, 'Twelve tribes are destined to issue from Yaakov. Six have issued from me and four from the handmaids, making ten. If this child will be a male, then my sister, Rachel, would not even be equal to one of the handmaids.'

"Immediately the child was turned into a girl, as it says, 'And she called her name Dina.'"[123]

Like Mother, Like Daughter

Dina is considered Leah's daughter. When the Torah speaks of her abduction by Shechem, the prince of the land, she is introduced to us as "Dina, *the daughter of Leah*, whom she bore to Yaakov who went out to see the daughters of the land."

The Torah does not refer to her as the daughter of Yaakov or even Leah and Yaakov, but only the daughter of Leah, since Dina is Leah's spiritual daughter, inheriting her strengths and her destiny.

Rashi explains, "Because of her going out she is called the 'daughter of Leah.' For Leah, too, was outgoing, as it is written, 'and Leah went out to greet him' (Gen. 30:16). Regarding her it has been said, 'Like mother, like daughter.'"

Leah Greets Yaakov

At first glance it may seem that this "outgoingness" was a negative characteristic, the opposite of the trademark of modesty expected from a Jewish daughter.

The occasion of Leah's outgoingness that Rashi cites, however, is when Leah gave her mandrakes to Rachel in exchange for spending the night with Yaakov. Leah goes out to the field to greet Yaakov and to inform him that he will be spending the night with her.

The Midrash[124] explains that G-d rejoiced in this act of Leah's and participated in her conception. G-d considered the episode with the mandrakes very precious, resulting in the birth of two important tribes: Yissachar and Zevulun.

From this, it is learned that a woman who makes herself attractive and desirable for her husband will be rewarded with pious, scholarly children, just as Leah was.[125]

Keeping Dina Hidden

Attributing Leah's praiseworthy outgoingness to Dina at the time when she was abducted cannot be inferring a negative trait in Dina that would cause her terrible ordeal. Her outgoingness—in the sense of a lack of modesty—was not the cause for the tragedy.

Rashi explains an entirely different underlying basis for Dina's abduction.

Earlier on, when Yaakov was preparing for his encounter with his wicked brother, Esav, "Yaakov took his two wives, his handmaidens and his eleven sons and crossed the river of Yabbok" (Gen. 32: 23).

Rashi comments: "Where was Dina? Yaakov placed her in a chest and locked her in, lest Esav set his eyes on her.

"For this Yaakov was punished, for had he not withheld her from his brother, perhaps she would have brought Esav back to the proper path. The punishment was that she fell instead into the hands of Shechem."

Dina's abduction by Shechem occurred as a punishment to Yaakov for hiding Dina from Esav, out of fear that Esav would take her as his wife.

Dina's Spiritual Powers

Leah was initially destined to become the partner of Esav. Feeling unequal to the challenge, Leah avoided this outcome through her incessant prayers. Dina, however, as Leah's spiritual heir, with her spiritual qualities (as reflected in her "outgoingness") could have been the instrument for Esav's redemption.

It was not Dina's outgoingness that caused the tragedy in Shechem, but rather Yaakov's preventing Dina from using this trait to potentially improve the wicked Esav.

While Yaakov feared that Esav would corrupt his daughter, in truth, Dina had the strength and moral grounding to influence him. Dina, like her mother, and like the *baal teshuva* figure, was destined to encounter the negative forces of the world. She had the power to elevate these forces and bring them to redemption.

Her outgoingness was not the reason for her downfall, but quite to the contrary, a quality from which she could derive strength. In her exposure to the alien environments of our world, this strength would enable her to be uncompromising regarding her integrity and morality.

Yaakov hesitated to allow Dina to use these potent powers to have a positive effect on his brother. As a result, Dina experienced an even more degrading abduction.

These powers of Dina eventually were actualized. She later met Iyov (Job). Although he was a non-Jew, she influenced him to convert and he eventually became a great individual.[126]

If Dina was able to accomplish such enormous change with Iyov, she certainly could have improved Esav, who was already circumcised and who was a son of Yitzchak and Avraham.[127]

Yosef: Esav's Adversary

When Leah prayed that the fetus she was carrying become female, it became Dina. Interestingly, the Targum comments that "The fetus inside them switched. Yosef came into Rachel's womb and Dina into Leah's womb."[128]

Dina had the ability to transform and redeem Esav. On some level, as seen by the switch of the fetus, Yosef was her spiritual counterpart.[129] He was charged with *destroying* the negativity of Esav, however, rather than Dina's role of *elevating* him.

When Yosef was born, Yaakov learned prophetically that his sons would have the power to defeat Esav, as it is written, "The house of Yaakov shall be fire, and the house of Yosef shall be a jet of flame, while the house of Esav shall be straw" (Obad. 1:18). Yaakov was likened to an ordinary fire that cannot burn something at a distance. Yosef, on the other hand, was like a jet of flame which could burn something far away. For this reason, Yaakov said, "I am no longer afraid of Esav. Yosef, his adversary, has been born. Now I can return home" (*Bereishit Rabba* 73, 5).[130]

Transforming or Destroying

Yosef's power as Rachel's descendant to destroy anything opposing holiness was openly revealed. His strength to demolish the forces of evil was readily manifested.

As Leah's descendant, Dina's abilities, however, were more hidden. Had she joined Esav on his twisted journey through the mire that the *baal teshuva* must traverse, at the same time steadfastly maintaining integrity and morality, Esav would not have needed to be destroyed or consumed. Instead, he would have been transformed positively, through the powers of Dina.

Dina could have actualized her potential by living through what her mother prayed with incessant tears to avoid. With her spiritual qualities of outgoingness as *Leah's daughter*, coupled with being her father Yaakov's daughter ("whom she bore to Yaakov"), with his moral traditions, Dina would have had the ability to redeem the negative forces within her uncle, Esav.

Advantage of the Baal Teshuva

Though Rachel was the beautiful individual, favored by Yaakov and leading the life of the tzaddik, Leah's path ultimately led to greater heights.

It was Leah who mothered the majority of the tribes of Israel. It was she who lived with Yaakov for a greater part of their lives, while Rachel's life was cut prematurely short. It was Leah, too, who was buried at Yaakov's side as his eternal partner in the Cave of Machpela.

Because ultimately, though the path of the *baal teshuva* is a difficult and tortuous one, its impact on the world is weighty. It is when we victoriously face the wearying struggles and tempting choices in our lives that we emerge, finally, as a greater people.

The dramatic splendor of the *baal teshuva* is hidden[131] and can only be fathomed in the future, in retrospect. After the passage of time, after experiencing the darkness of life's nights and desolate winters, an even more intense and meaningful bond with G-d has been reached.

Leah's journey to her destiny starts off shakily, moving towards a hidden, unknown outcome, but ultimately it will lead us to reap rewards in the future, as a redeemed people in a redeemed world.

The Mothers of Israel

Rachel and Leah were two special personalities who, together with Sara and Rivka, became the mothers of Israel. Whether it be through the revealed path of righteousness of Rachel, or the more hidden but ultimately higher path of Leah, the qualities and mannerisms modeled by our Matriarchs in dealing with the challenges of their lives are vital lessons for their children, for all times.

Even through her burial place, however, Rachel continues to teach a valuable lesson. Her choice of that location reminds us of the enormous compassion and self-sacrifice that she personified in her lifetime.

Rachel's Place of Burial

On his deathbed, addressing his much-loved son Yosef (Joseph), Yaakov expresses his desire that his remains be transported to the Holy Land, to be interred alongside his ancestors in Hebron.

"Do true kindness with me," says Yaakov to his son, "and do not bury me in Egypt. Let me be with my fathers. Carry me out of Egypt and bury me in their burial place" (Gen. 47: 29-31). He even asks Yosef to take a solemn oath to fulfill this request.

A few passages later, Yaakov clarifies what happened decades earlier when Yosef was still a youth and Yaakov experienced the traumatic and sudden passing of Yosef's mother, Rachel.

Yaakov recalls that painful moment. "And I, when I came from Padan, Rachel died on me in the land of Canaan, on the road, a short distance away as we came towards Efrat. I buried her there, alongside the road to Efrat near Beit Lechem [Bethlehem]" (Gen. 48:7).

Yaakov was only a short distance, about two-thirds of a mile, from Efrat. Yet he did not bring his beloved Rachel there, nor did he carry her to the more distant Hebron, but laid her to rest "alongside the road."

Yaakov now explains his actions. "This was not during the rainy season, that I could claim it was because of the mud that I did not bring her to Hebron. The roads were dry and good. Still, I buried her alongside the road to Efrat.

"Not only did I not bury your mother in our family plot in the Machpela Cave in Hebron, as I should have, I did not even bring her as far as Beit Lechem, a nearby village.

"Let me explain the reason," Yaakov says to Rachel's eldest son. "I did it because G-d commanded it.

"I will reveal to you a mystery regarding the future," Yaakov discloses. "There will come a time when your children will go into exile, driven from their homes by Nebuzaradan, marched in chains to the distant land of Babylonia.

"On the way, they will pass your mother's grave. Rachel will come out and cry and beg G-d for mercy. G-d, in turn, will respond to her, 'There is reward for your actions. Your children will return to their borders'" (Rashi, Gen. 48:8).

Thus the prophet Jeremiah declares, "A voice is heard in Ramah, lamentations and bitter crying; Rachel is weeping for her children..." (Jer. 31:15).

Voices of Defenders

Of all the great leaders of Israel, it was Rachel who waged war against the heavenly accusers, demanding from G-d that He have mercy on her children. Only she was capable of eliciting G-d's compassion.

The Midrash relates: As the Temple lay in ruins and the Jews were being led into exile as slaves, Avraham came before G-d and said, "Master of the universe, when I was one hundred years old, You gave me a son, and when he was thirty-seven years old, You told me, 'Raise him as a sacrifice before Me.'

"I overcame my natural mercy and bound him myself. Will You not remember my devotion and have mercy on my children?"

Next, Yitzchak approached: "When my father said, 'G-d will show us the sheep for a sacrifice, my son,' I did not hesitate but accepted my fate and extended my neck to be slaughtered. Will You not remember my strength and have mercy on my children?"

Then Yaakov beseeched, "I worked for twenty years in the house of Lavan and when I left, Esav came to harm me. I suffered all my life raising my children. Now they are being led like sheep to the slaughter in the hands of their enemies. Won't You remember all the pain and suffering and redeem my children?"

Moshe rose up and said: "Was I not a loyal shepherd for Israel for forty years? I ran before them in the desert like a horse. When the time came to enter Israel, You decreed that I would die in the desert. Now they go into exile. Won't You listen to my crying over them?"

Before all these virtuous defenders, G-d remained silent.

Then Rachel lifted her voice. "Master of the Universe, You know that Yaakov loved me intensely and worked for seven years in order to marry me. When the time of my marriage came, my father substituted my sister for me. I did not begrudge my sister and I didn't let her be shamed; I even revealed to her the secret signs that Yaakov and I had arranged.

"If I, a mere mortal, was not prepared to humiliate my sister and was willing to take a rival into my home, how could You, the eternal, compassionate G-d, be jealous of idols, which have no true existence, that were brought into Your home? Will You cause my children to be exiled on this account?!"

Immediately, G-d's mercy was aroused and He responded, "For you, Rachel, I will bring Israel back to their place."[132]

Rachel's Self-Sacrifice

Yaakov revealed the essence of Rachel's character and self-sacrifice.

More than anyone, Rachel understood the spiritual merit and pleasure of being buried in a place as blessed as the Machpela Cave, side by side with the holy Yaakov—a place so sacred that on his deathbed, Yaakov instructs Yosef to vow to bring his remains up from Egypt to there. Yet Rachel was willing to forego the immense benefit of being buried there together with Yaakov, for all eternity.

Instead, she readily accepted a burial in solitude and loneliness, on the side of a deserted road.

During her lifetime, Rachel forfeited her own happiness in order to spare her sister, Leah, embarrassment. She didn't hesitate or pause to consider the effect of her actions on her own future plight.

After such immeasurable sacrifice in her lifetime, surely, in her death, Rachel was entitled, as the *akeret habayit*—Yaakov's primary wife and first love—to be buried next to her rightful husband for all perpetuity.

Surprisingly though, Rachel relinquishes this privilege in order to be buried alongside a neglected, forlorn road.

She does this for the sake of her children—descendants of Yaakov—who would live tens of centuries later.

Were these children special? Did they possess endearing qualities or exceptional merits?

These children were *sinners*. *Sinners*, who were exiled from the Holy Land due to their reprehensible behavior. *Sinners*, whose wicked deeds caused the Holy Temple—G-d's home and the source of the most intense Divine lights shining forth for the world—to be destroyed.

They engaged in the worse possible sins, committing acts of idolatry, sexual immorality and murder.

Was Rachel not aware of the deeds of these far-off descendants? Did she not know to what spiritual lows they would descend?

A woman of Rachel's stature knew far better than we to what depths of lowliness these descendants would reach. But when she looked far ahead into the future, Rachel was determined to sacrifice her eternal pleasures so that these sinners could pass by her gravesite and she would pray on their behalf.

On no other occasion had Rachel pleaded to G-d in the merit of having enabled Leah to marry her own intended husband. At the lowest point in her life, after years of aching barrenness and keenly feeling that her life was worthless without offspring, we do not find Rachel citing this meritorious act.

But now, as she pleads on behalf of these children—who were dragged out of their homeland due to their iniquity—Rachel begs G-d to consider her deed.

For centuries, Rachel waited patiently, in utter solitude, buried alongside the road, simply so that these pitiful sinners would find encouragement as they passed by her gravesite, and she beseeched G-d on their behalf.

The Quintessential Jewish Mother

Why? What compelled Rachel to such sacrifice?

Because to Rachel, these were not simply evil sinners. They were *her children*.

Children who may have strayed. Children who may have fallen. But, nevertheless, *her* children, who were worthy of love and compassion.

Rachel, as the tzaddik personality, sees the Jewish nation as her children, deserving her defense regardless of how low they have fallen.

But Avraham, Yitzchak, Yaakov and Moshe also embodied the tzaddik personality, rising in defense of their nation. They also raised their voices in protest against their children's exiles.

But to their voices, G-d remains silent.

It is only Rachel's voice of dissent that is answered with words of comfort. And it is only our matriarch Rachel who willfully chooses to be buried alone, on the side of the road, for the sake of these children.

Because Rachel is the quintessential Jewish *mother*, sacrificing for the sake of her children. With her boundless wellspring of mercy and compassion, Rachel saw beyond their iniquities to the innocence of their essence, to the inherent goodness and beauty of their soul.

No matter how low they would fall, they were unconditionally *her children* and the children of G-d.[133]

Discovering Rachel's Compassion

Unlike the destruction of the First Temple, the Second Temple's destruction was not due to sins of immorality or idolatry, but rather sins of senseless hatred.

Can we, Jewish mothers, spiritual descendants of Rachel, learn from our matriarch's sacrifice?

Can we look beyond the sins, faults or inadequacies of our fellow Jews, and envision what our matriarch saw, children of G-d, deserving of His mercy and compassion?

As we search deep within ourselves for that vision, modeled by our quintessential mother, Rachel, we have G-d's promise, "and your children will return to their borders."

For Further Reflection

- ❧ What are the defining qualities of each of the matriarchs?
- ❧ What have you discovered about the unique spiritual powers of each of the women mentioned in this section? How do they differ? How are they similar?
- ❧ How can you apply this insight to areas in your own life?
- ❧ Did the women in this chapter complement their soul mates? How did they differ? How were they similar?
- ❧ Is there such a thing as "a woman's intuition"?
- ❧ In what ways are humans created in the image of G-d?
- ❧ "The end is wedged in the beginning" (*Zohar*), i.e., the end goal is the ultimate intent of the initial purpose. Share some insights on how you see this principle in action.

Section Two

DEEDS
The Feminine Touch
A Deeper Look into Women's Mitzvot

❧ Light of Eternity: The Mitzva of Shabbat Candles
  - A Soul on Fire
  - The Ultimate Harmony
  - The Eternal Shabbat—Life in a Feminine Mode
  - The Shabbat Lights—the Lights of Zion

❧ Kneading G-dliness into Creation: The Mitzva of Challa
  - Discovering G-d in the Physical
  - Transforming the Physical
  - Seasoning the Loaves of Mediocrity
  - Torah Bread—the Feminine Link

❧ Mysterious Nights: The Mitzva of Mikve
  - Dear Child of Mine
  - The Dynamics of Marriage
  - Tuma & Tahara, Lows & Highs
  - Three Phases of Attachment
  - Eternal Waters

LIGHT
OF
ETERNITY
The Mitzva of Shabbat Candles

The Lamp

A light burning bright
In the blackness of night
Dispelling the darkness around it
A lamp
Three distinctive components
The flame
The wick
And the oil.

The Flame

Fiery, intense
Ethereal
Ablaze with passion and luminosity
Dancing towards the heavens
Surging back earthwards
Only to begin its rhythm of motion
Once again.

The Wick

A piece of matter
Grounded, lifeless
Steady, immobile
Housing the flame on its tip
Saturated with the fuel beneath
Imprisoning the flame
While granting it
Its very existence.

The Oil

Pure, clear, serene
Enlightening, iridescent
Potent fuel
Empowering the flame
Igniting its wick
The source inspiring
The bright light.

A SOUL ON FIRE

The soul of man is a lamp of G-d" (Prov. 20:7).
Man is a complex conglomeration of heaven and earth, spirit and matter, fire and wick. Like the lamp, man, too, is comprised of three elements which determine the direction of his actions. The candle's wick, flame and oil resemble man's body, soul and source in the Torah and its mitzvot.

His soul, like the flame, is aflame with yearning and inspiration. It burns brightly within him, inspiring him to connect to his Creator. It desires fiercely to break the bonds of this physical world, to transcend the barriers of a material existence and unite with its Maker.

When allowed full expression, the soul encourages man to seek spiritual pursuits, to almost tear itself free from the gravity of physical reality that grounds it. Yet, like the flame of the candle, after the soul performs its celestial dance it also falls back, returning to illuminate this world and leave its mark on physical reality. By cleaving to the ultimate Source, the soul would be encompassed within it. Only as it exists within a seemingly distinct being can the soul accomplish the very purpose of its descent.

The body of man, like the wick of the candle, is both grounded and physical. With its many limitations, many real needs and desires, the body entraps and enslaves the soul within it. Yet, while imposing its restrictions, the body also houses the soul and provides an outlet for its unique expression. The soul can only feel, perceive and savor reality through the body's senses; it can only move about freely with the body's limbs; and it can only think and analyze with the body's mind. The body's very groundedness, then, provides a means and opportunity for the soul's relationship with creation.

Torah, like the oil of the lamp, is the source for man's ideals, providing the direction for a meaningful life that connects him with his Creator. Mitzvot ignite man's potential, showing him in a concrete way how to utilize his abilities and talents for a G-dly end.

Enlightening, pure and clear, like the oil,[134] the Torah and its mitzvot direct the potential in man to its ultimate purpose.

"The spirit of man gravitates upward" (Eccles. 3:21).

When man is true to the yearnings of his soul, directs them with the wisdom and enlightenment of Torah, puts them into practice by fulfilling the mitzvot with the faculties and limbs of his body, he generates light and becomes "a lamp of G-d."

This is not an elusive light, removed from worldly concerns and dynamics, but an inspiration that imbues the deepest darkness of this physical reality. It elevates its earthiness and saturates humanity and creation as a whole with a brighter goodness and truer perspective, in harmony with the will of its Creator.[135]

Every Friday eve, as a woman strikes her match, charring the wick while igniting the flame that drinks in the oil of her Shabbat lights, she is drawing down, in a very real and physical way, this light.

Just as the physical lights represent man's soul and being, every mitzva brings a real spiritual light into this world. The Shabbat candles, however, physically dispel any spiritual darkness or gloom surrounding us. Since they involve physical light, the Shabbat candles, more than any other mitzva,[136] harmonize this vacillating dichotomy between body and soul in the essence of man's being, bringing light and inspiration to the temporality of life.

"A perpetual fire shall remain aflame on the altar; it shall not be extinguished" (Lev. 6:6).

"Our heart is the altar. In all you do, let a spark of holy fire burn within, so that you may fan it into a flame" (Baal Shem Tov).

As her match kisses the candle, creating a holy light, the woman reveals and elicits unseen and intangible, yet vast and potent, G-dly energy which surrounds, while at the same time imbues, all of creation. By kindling the Shabbat candles, the woman has the special power to usher in the holiness of Shabbat. Her act of lighting the candle and reciting its blessing draws down the special aura of the holy Shabbat for us all.

THE ULTIMATE HARMONY

A nd there was evening and there was morning, the sixth day.

"Thus the heavens and the earth and all their array were completed.

"On the seventh day, G-d completed His work which He had done and He rested on the seventh day from all the work He had done.

"G-d blessed the seventh day and sanctified it, for He rested on it from all the work which He created to do."

(Gen. 1:31–2:3)

"What was the world lacking at the end of the sixth day? Rest. Shabbat came, rest came. The work was completed and finished."

(Rashi, Gen. 2:2)

On the seventh day, G-d added His final strokes to His masterpiece. He introduced the last remaining touch to complete creation—G-d added the concept of rest, tranquility and harmony to the world.

Unlike the other six days of creation, on the seventh the world was no longer changing. It was no longer in a state of flux, but in a state of being and absorption. During the previous six days it was undergoing development and creativity; on the seventh day, creation was able to partake of G-d's serenity. The day and the creation then became holy and blessed.[137]

The builder had worked long and hard for many months, days and hours. From the initial conception to the final implementation, no detail had been neglected. No area had escaped his scrutiny. The foundation was laid, the bricks were cemented, the floorboards and walls aligned. Rooms began to take shape.

The building had a form.

Next, the inner, finer craftsmanship began. The doors and windows were installed, the circular staircase was put in its place, the elaborate moldings were crafted, and the plush carpets and gleaming flooring were cut to size and carefully installed.

The building became a house.

Next, the furniture was moved in: the mahogany beds and dressers, the marble tables, delicate chairs and plush couches. The expensive clothing was placed on its closet racks, the ornate mirrors and costly artwork hung on the freshly painted walls, and the crystal and antique knickknacks carefully set on their decorative side tables.

The house became a home.

Finally, the owner moved in. All was prepared, all the work complete, the vision implemented. Now he could enjoy the fruits of his labor, exult in the completion of his toil. At peace with his home and at rest with his environment, he would now absorb its blessing.

The home became lived in and blessed.

During the six days of creation, G-d asserted His mastery over the universe by changing it. G-d did not rest on the seventh day because He was tired from the exertion of the previous days, for "The everlasting G-d, Creator of the wide world, grows neither weary nor faint."[138] Indeed, the creation of the universe involved less effort for Him than pronouncing a single letter. [139]

On Shabbat, G-d transformed this world into His dwelling place by refraining from changing it. Therefore, the word Shabbat is related to *"shevet,"* to dwell. For the Shabbat brought an integral harmony between G-d and His world. The creation became G-d's dwelling place, His home.

The mystery of Shabbat is Unity. On the Shabbat, G-d created harmony between Himself and the universe.[140]

Similarly, we emulate G-d by relinquishing our mastery over the world by not performing any "work" on Shabbat.

Work, as a Shabbat definition, is an act that demonstrates man's mastery over the world by means of his intelligence or skill.[141] *Rest*, as a Shabbat definition, means not interfering with nature or exhibiting any mastery over it. It is a state of peace between man and his world.

Therefore, even the most trivial act of interference with creation can be considered work and a violation of the Shabbat. At the same time, strenuous exertion that does not interfere with creation, in a literal Shabbat sense, is permitted on Shabbat.

All week long, man struggles to attain mastery over creation. He asserts his dominance over nature by utilizing it, by plowing the earth, extracting the wheat, kneading and baking the flour into bread. But by his very involvement with nature, man is also bound to the material world. He becomes a slave to it, ruled by his need to dominate it for his personal needs and desires.

On Shabbat, on the other hand, man is liberated and exists in harmony with the world without the need to battle it. He can now appreciate the fruits of his labor. He can restfully absorb the blessing of his weeklong efforts.

The mother of Rabbi Menachem Mendel of Rymanov once asked him, "What is the real meaning of the expression 'holy Shabbat'?"

Rabbi Menachem Mendel answered: "The Shabbat makes you holy."

"True," commented his mother. "But the Shabbat does not only make you holy, it also makes you whole."

The concept of peace is so integral to Shabbat that we even greet one another with *"Shabbat shalom,"* a peaceful Shabbat.[142] This day, like no other, brings peace between man and all of nature, and harmony between G-d and His creation.

Man has completed his weekday task of "filling the earth and conquering it." He now begins anew his seventh day, his *"shevet,"* occupying and dwelling with *"shalom,"* in a peaceful and harmonious manner.

THE ETERNAL SHABBAT
Life in a Feminine Mode

The word *Shabbat* is composed of two parts: the letter *"shin,"* which stands for *"shoresh,"* root; and *"bat,"* daughter, which stands for *"Bat Yisrael,"* daughter of Israel or Jewish woman. *Shabbat,* then, is the root and source from which the Jewish woman draws her strength.[143]

Throughout the six days of the week we are embattled in a struggle to dominate and exert influence over our surroundings. We are in a constant state of conflict, choosing between those elements of our world that we are to embrace and develop, and those that must be rejected and overpowered.

The Torah helps us distinguish between that which can be positively harnessed and that which must be rejected. It guides us as to which foods, materials, items and relationships energize our being and sanctify our lives, and those which deaden our spiritual sensitivities and coarsen or debase our hearts and minds. Our job, in turn, it to extract the kernels of holiness from within their material husks in each and every one of our endeavors and activities.

During the six weekdays we operate in a masculine mode of conquest and assault, in a constant state of restlessness.

Every Shabbat, on the other hand, we enter afresh into a spiraling new cycle of harmony, serenity and peace. After having asserted ourselves and having accomplished our goals during the weekdays, we take a respite from our battle against evil.

On the Shabbat, we refrain from the selection and suppression process altogether. As we reach a new awareness and unity, we can begin to appreciate and nurture the good inherent

---

within all elements of creation. Tapping into the spiritual, Divine origin, we can absorb its blessing into our psyche.

On the Shabbat, we enter into a feminine mode of harmony and peacefulness within ourselves and within creation, a state of restfulness and receptivity. For this reason, Shabbat is always referred to in the feminine, as in Shabbat Hamalka,[144] the Shabbat Queen, or Kalla, bride.

The physical rest experienced on the Shabbat is reflective of the day's qualities of spiritual rejuvenation, a day in which we can become attuned to our essence and the quintessential core of all of creation. Having achieved the goals of our weekday, the Shabbat bestows new meaning and purpose to our lives.

Shabbat is the source of blessing[145] both for the week that preceded it as well as the one that follows.

Similar to the feminine Shabbat, a woman is the source of blessing for her husband and home. As our Sages declared, "A man receives sustenance only through the merit of his wife,"[146] and "Happiness, blessing, goodness, Torah and protection come from the wife."[147]

On Shabbat, we can finally absorb the blessing of our previous week's toil, as well as invigorate ourselves to continue on in the new journey awaiting us in the upcoming weekly cycle. We give meaning to the past while we renew our energies to take on the new onslaught, albeit on a spiraling higher level, once again, come the weekday.

Thus the cosmic, universal "Shabbat" will be experienced in the era of Mashiach, a time that is termed "a day of eternal Shabbat and repose for everlasting life" (*Tamid* 7:4).

Once the ravages of exile have been fought and all the weekday evils of the world have been slayed, we will enter this new state of "a day of eternal Shabbat."

G-d promises that this will be a time when "I shall remove the spirit of impurity from the earth" (Zech. 13:2), when all evil shall cease and the positive essence of every creature and phenomenon will come to light. This will be the timeless Shabbat era, when we will be saturated with "the knowledge of G-dliness just as the waters cover the seabed" (Isa. 11:9).

No longer will we face the daily "weekday" challenges of winnowing the holy from the profane. Our world will enter a new state of unity and harmony, a foretaste of which we experience in microcosm for a twenty-five-hour period starting every Friday eve.

After the six mundane weekdays, or on a universal level, the six long and hard millennia of persecution and exile, we will have collectively arrived at Shabbat, a time when G-dliness can fully dwell within us. In this era, the weekday will no longer follow the Shabbat, in the sense of returning to the weekday jungle of dominion and assertion, selection and suppression.

Our masculine, almost six-thousand-year, journey will then have been completed. Unity will prevail throughout creation as the forces of evil will all have been vanquished.

Our feminine journey will now be accentuated as we begin its spiraling cycle of reaching ever-higher levels in absorbing the spiritual, developing and nurturing its inherent good, and cultivating and refining the positive throughout creation.

For this reason, when we begin the Shabbat service on Friday night, we begin with *"Kabbalat Shabbat,"* the welcoming, or reception, of Shabbat. The first act once the Shabbat is upon us is termed *Kabbalat Shabbat*, epitomizing receptiveness, which is the essence of the day.

A Chassidic sage once commented: "The succa is one mitzva into which you can enter even with your boots."

Added Rabbi Yaakov Yitzchak of Peshischa, known as the Yid Hakodosh, the Holy Jew: "You can walk out of the succa, but you spend every instant immersed in the Shabbat."

This is also why the word haShabbat, "the Sabbath," also contains the same letters as the word *teshuva*, "return." *Teshuva*, often defined as repentance, really means our ability to rectify and sublimate past wrongdoings by returning to the timeless, inviolable core of self that was never tainted by sin in the first place. *Teshuva* is the most potent of human deeds, enabling us to redefine the past as we mold our new future.

A true Shabbat experience is when one returns to one's source, to one's quintessential core of unity and G-dliness permeating all of creation. Every Shabbat in our exile accomplishes this, and is a precursor to the ultimate Shabbat when the world as a whole returns to its collective source,[148] when "No longer will your Master be cloaked, your eyes shall see your Master" (Isa. 30:20).

The Divine essence of creation will no longer be shrouded in a guise of corporeality, and the positive use of all created matter will be accessible.

Our weekly Shabbat on a small scale, and the day of eternal Shabbat on a cosmic scale, is a time of spirit and tranquility when we get in touch with our deepest, most essential self. We have completed our refinement of evil; now we can devote ourselves, body and soul, to exulting in the feminine experience of redemption.

THE SHABBAT LIGHTS
The Lights of Zion

A dark room,
Shrouded in blackness.
Heavy. Morose. Deadened.
Lacking energy and vitality,
Cloaked in gloom.
A tiny spark
Begins to flicker,
Dispelling so much darkness.
Alighting its surroundings,
Energizing and vitalizing.
The tiny flicker
Soon joins another tiny flame
And another.
Before long a powerful fire
Dances alive.
The darkness is gone,
Replaced with a shining brightness,
Imbuing its warmth and splendor,
Its life and energy.

"If you cherish the lights of Shabbat, I will show you the lights of Zion."

(Yalkut Shimoni, parshat Behalotcha, sec. 719)

On an individual level, by lighting the Shabbat candles, we usher in the holiness of the Shabbat. On a more universal level, we draw down a spiritual light that reveals and uncovers the G-dly unity and harmony within creation.

As individuals, after implementing our weekday role of differentiating between the mundane and holy, we have prepared ourselves to receive the sanctity of the Shabbat. On a cosmic plane, we are preparing the world for the G-dly revelation of the era of eternal Shabbat by eliciting samples of these rays as we kindle the lights of the holy Shabbat.

After nearly six millennia of infusing spiritual light into our corporeal world, symbolized in a very real way by the millions of candles kindled every Friday eve by Jewish women, we have a virtual explosion of G-dly light in our midst. Our collective efforts must therefore culminate in completion of their ultimate mission, as G-d promised, to bathe all of creation in this visible G-dly energy.

Every Friday eve, as we kindle our Shabbat candles, we add our sparks to this global bonfire of G-dliness, brightening the darkness of the exile and igniting the "lights of Zion."

"It is mandatory for both men and women that a candle be lit in their home on Shabbat. Women are especially enjoined concerning this" (Shulchan Aruch, Orach Chaim 263:2, 3).

"Even if the husband wants to kindle the candles himself, his wife takes precedence" (Mishneh Brura, ad. loc. 11, 12).

Woman has been charged with lighting the Shabbat candles. It is her act that ushers in the unity and holiness of the Shabbat day.

The Shabbat day epitomizes the feminine mode and the woman's role of working from within creation to uncover, cultivate and nurture its G-dly potential. Therefore, precisely because the Shabbat day exemplifies the feminine experience of peace, harmony and receptivity, as mentioned previously, it is appropriate that woman has been enjoined with the climactic act that brings this atmosphere upon us.

Therefore, even "if the husband wants to kindle the candles himself, his wife takes precedence." Only in a situation where the wife cannot light the candles herself, should her husband do so. For the essence of the woman's being is in harmony with the essential message of Shabbat, and accordingly, she especially has been entrusted with drawing this sanctified atmosphere into her home.

Parenthetically, for the same reason, it is preferable for a man to recite the Havdala prayer at the conclusion of the Shabbat, ushering in the weekday work. Appropriately, the man, who epitomizes the struggle and the battle against negativity, as experienced during the weekday cycle, ends the Shabbat experience as he separates it, by Havdala (meaning separation), from the weekday's work. As the woman ushers in the Shabbat, by kindling and blessing its candles, the man bids good-bye to the Shabbat as he brings in the weekday, through his recital of the Havdala service.

Similarly, women have been enjoined with ushering in the era of eternal Shabbat.

Our sages said, "In the merit of righteous women we will be redeemed."[149] In the merit of women, we will collectively experience the era of the redemption. Just as a woman ushers in the feminine Shabbat precisely because it is in accord with her spiritual makeup and essence, it is her culminating acts and merits that will bring about the feminine era of the eternal Shabbat.

KNEADING
G-DLINESS
INTO CREATION
The Mitzva of Challa

THE REBBE, RABBI ZUSYA,

remarked: "I would like to abstain from eating, but what can I do, since my Creator created me with a mouth?

Surely, G-d did not create anything in His world unless it can be used exclusively to serve Him. If so, why did He create us with a mouth to eat?

In order that we serve Him with our mouths!

Everything in this world has a spiritual essence that needs to be elevated to G-d."

DISCOVERING G-D
IN THE PHYSICAL

The kitchen. The center of the home. Frequented by all members of the family. From the youngest to the oldest, in all sizes and shapes, guests and home dwellers, it becomes the focal point of the house. It hosts lavish meals; produces delectable treats for those special occasions; stands ready with modest foods at all times and quenches all sorts of thirsts.

Here the secrets of the day unfold. Seated around the kitchen table or standing near the sink full of dishes, hearts and mouths open and share with one another the day's events. Gathered around, each pitches in to do his share, the individual members of the household mold together to become a united family.

In the center of the kitchen, whether large or small, with granite countertops and marble floors or plain linoleum tiles, the oven is always to be found. Gas, wood or electric, with all kinds of gadgets, mirror tops or plain functioning, the oven warms the room. Tantalizing aromas waft from the door of this room, which defines the mood and sets the tone for the whole house.

"From the first of your kneading bowl, you shall lift up a dough-offering (challa) to G-d" (Num. 15:20).

Bread—the most basic of foods. Food—the most pedestrian, rudimentary need of man, necessary for his very survival.

The swollen, raw dough in the kneading bowl encompasses and unites all the physical needs of the family. It represents mankind's most fundamental need and desire, in its barest and most basic sense, stripped of any coverings or trappings.

From this physical, raw material we are commanded, "lift up a dough-offering to G-d."

The mitzva of *challa* is the commandment to separate a portion of dough each time we mix a certain amount of flour with water to make bread. In the time of the Temple, this dough would be given to one of the priests. In today's time, this small portion is burnt in the oven, and may not be eaten by anyone.

If there is a certain minimum amount of dough, a blessing over this mitzva is recited.[150] Although both men and women may perform this mitzva, women have traditionally been responsible for carrying out it out, and it is thus counted as one of their special mitzvot.

By "lifting up a dough-offering to G-d," we direct our physical foods, needs and urges to a spiritual purpose. The very dough takes on a new "life," one that becomes consecrated for holiness, directed and hallowed for a greater purpose. The physical thereby merges with the spiritual, infused with a new life and vitality enabled to fulfill the Divine Will.

The hand that separates the dough, too, is attached to a mind that has gained a newfound awareness. It has become permeated with the realization that the dough it holds is a gift to G-d. Man's efforts are not for the sake of mere self-preservation or for the sake of quenching a gnawing hunger. Rather, his efforts are the means of connecting to G-d's benevolence and appreciating His goodness.

Why is the law of challa recorded in the Torah adjacent to the law of idolatry? To teach you that whoever upholds the mitzva of challa is as if he has negated idolatry; and whoever neglects the mitzva of challa is as if he has affirmed idolatry.[151]

Idolatry is the perverted image of an independent self outside of G-d. It is the worship of self-actualization, without the acknowledgment of a greater Being. Idolatry separates the body from the soul, the physical matter from the spiritual, robbing the corporeality of its inner, deeper connection with its purpose and focus. Consequently, physical reality assumes a life of its own, devoid of its spiritual component, lacking true direction and meaning.

"In all your ways you shall know Him" (Prov. 3:6).

"A person should direct his heart and all his deeds. . . resting, walking, talking . . .doing business, working . . .eating, drinking and procreating . . .as a means of knowing G-d . . ."[152]

Judaism does not confine G-d to the synagogue. Mitzvot involving physical activities make G-dliness the focal point of our lives. Whether it be an "up in the clouds" spiritual endeavor or an earthly grounded need, whether in the bedroom or in the kitchen, whether in the realm of the abstract or in the world of action, G-d's presence must be felt hallowing all aspects of creation.

Therefore, compartmentalizing our lives and schedules so that some areas involve G-d while others do not is a form of idolatry. Excising G-d and relegating Him only to specialized components of our lives while we remain preoccupied with our own needs and wishes, is also admitting to a force outside of G-d's domain, bereft of His providence.

"If only...you could comfort me like a brother nurtured at my mother's bosom! If I would find you in the streets, I would kiss you and embrace you" (Song of Songs 8:1).

The Baal Shem Tov: Our love of G-d should be like the love between brother and sister or between mother and child, rather than the love between husband and wife. Siblings may display their love in private and in public, whereas husband and wife may do so in private only. Our love of G-d must not be demonstrated only in the synagogue . . .

The small rounded piece of dough that we separate for G-d shatters this idol. It represents the soft, elastic piece of faith within each of us that can be applied in all situations. It is the gift to G-d that we take along with us in every circumstance, in spite of its mundanity.

The blessing we recite before separating the *challa* ignites that faith in each of us, reminding us to bring G-d into every aspect of our lives and aspirations. It reminds us that G-d and His goodness need to occupy an integral part in our every action and deed. Even within the world of the physical, even while kneading together the most base, pedestrian components of corporeality, we must suffuse creation with its G-dly mission.

The offering of this G-dly gift is not to be regarded as "only" a mitzva, albeit an important one. It is rather a reaffirmation of our belief, a restatement of our purpose and mission within creation. It negates idolatry and sustains our faith. By separating the small piece of raw dough, we attest that there is no corner of the earth devoid of G-d's presence.[153]

TRANSFORMING THE PHYSICAL

R abbi Yaakov Yitzchak of Lublin used to invite poor wayfarers into his home and would serve them himself. After providing his guest with a hearty meal, he would stand beside his chair ready to bring him whatever else he needed. After the meal, Rabbi Yaakov Yitzchak would carry away the empty plates and platters into the kitchen.

Once, his guest questioned his behavior. "Master, please explain something to me. I know that in serving me, you fulfill the command of G-d who wishes that the beggar be honored and treated respectably. But why do you trouble yourself with carrying out the empty dishes?"

The Rabbi replied, "The removal of the spoon and the coal-pan from the Holy of Holies was also part of the service of the High Priest on the Day of Atonement!"

Thus the Sages comment, "The mitzva of receiving guests takes precedence over receiving the Divine Presence" (Shabbat 127a).

Everything in this world contains sparks of G-dliness, which are concealed by the veil of nature. Mankind has been given the task of refining the material and revealing its innate G-dliness. Every individual is destined to elevate certain "sparks." This Divine service is necessary not only for the refinement of the created matter, but also for man's own personal growth. If these G-dly energies are not elevated, that individual's soul remains incomplete.[154]

"Hungry and thirsty, their soul longs within" (Ps. 107:5).

The Baal Shem Tov asks, "Why are they hungry and thirsty? Because 'their soul longs within.' Their soul seeks a bond with the G-dly energy contained in the food and drink."[155]

We may be unaware of the spiritual motive underlying our physical desires—the deeper driving force that directs our will. The Baal Shem Tov's innovative interpretation demonstrates why we want children, possessions or material success. It is to fulfill our soul's unspoken desire to accomplish the G-dly purpose associated with these seemly material blessings.

As the woman holds the fistful of dough to be consecrated to G-d, she achieves the very purpose of creation through her specially attuned feminine qualities. She works from within, within nature and physicality, elevating the very G-dliness embedded within it.

Woman, whose many moments and hours tend with such tenderness to the physical needs of her family, utilizes these very needs for a greater purpose and meaning. As she recites the blessing and throws the dough over the burning coals, the very bread becomes consecrated. Indeed, all the many morsels of delectable treats, the warm oven, the marble-tiled kitchen floor and the very home itself, together with its inhabitants, become elevated and differentiated, redirected to a higher purpose.

As she lifts her arm, the woman has listened to the innermost, still voice of her soul which seeks a bond with the G-dly energy contained in every material blessing of created life.

Her seemingly simple act reflects the accomplishment of perhaps one of the deepest mysteries of creation, allowing her to become a partner with G-d Himself in carving out for Him an abode down here in the earthly, grounded world among the most basic, physical needs of mankind.

She has transformed her house into a G-dly home where spirituality saturates the very flooring. She has set the tone for the members of her household, too, so that each in their respective unique ways will leave a united mark on creation, uplifting it and thereby revealing the very essence of their soul.

SEASONING THE LOAVES OF MEDIOCRITY

R abbi Shimon Ben Elazar ruled: "A woman may fill her entire oven with bread [when baking on a festival day] since bread bakes better when the oven is full."[156]

Unlike the laws of Shabbat, on the *Yomim Tovim* (Jewish festivals) Torah law allows us to transfer (but not create) fire, thereby permitting us, within a very specifically defined halachic framework, to cook on these days. The limitation imposed, however, is that the food cooked be needed for, and consumed on, that festive day. In other words, preparing a large feast which will be eaten (even mostly) as a festival meal is permitted, while preparing foods to be eaten at a later date is forbidden.

An exception is made when cooking additional food will actually enhance the flavor or texture of the food to be consumed on the holiday. Then the law stipulates that if a woman is baking a small quantity of bread to be consumed on the festival, she may fill her entire oven with loaves. This applies even if these loaves are to be eaten after the festival, since these extra loaves will enhance the flavor of the loaf eaten on the festival.

With this seemingly simple Torah law, we are taught a deep and penetrating principle applicable to our own self-styled ovens of life.

As we stoke the flames of our own individualistic lifestyles, we will experience many "loaves" of mundanity. Many of these breads are pursuits that will not be eaten directly, or utilized, for the festivals—for holy spiritual activities. In fact, many of these activities may even seem to distract us from the true purpose of our being.

In the deep recesses of our soul, we may long to avoid these undertakings, absolve ourselves from these "unnecessary" obligations and focus exclusively on the sole bread of the festivities. In fact, we may become saddened at a realistic evaluation of our lives, when we note just how many hours of our day are filled with these "loaves of mundanity," and how, in truth perhaps only a small measure is utilized for "the festivals."

Yet the Torah both cautions and comforts us, teaching us that we are permitted to bake these extra loaves in our oven of life. Nay, the Torah convinces us that these mundane, physical breads actually augment and improve the flavor of the singular festive bread. These seemingly extraneous loaves can serve a very important role in life, enhancing our being and flavoring our very purpose of existence.

G-d did not choose to reign only over the spiritual spheres, but rather to infuse the lowest of the physical domains as well. Similarly, a person must not avoid these mundane realms, but should question rather, in each situation, what is his intent and how will he utilize this opportunity.

The loaves over the flaming coals of life beckon to man and question him. How many loaves and hours of each day will be devoted just to eating, drinking, sleeping and other bodily needs or pleasures? How much of the energy of life will be squandered on simply earning a living, fulfilling social obligations and merely flowing with the natural ebb of life?

Or, will these loaves baking over the fiery coals be a means to an end—a way to enhance the fulfillment of one's truest and innermost needs and desires? Will these activities be utilized to enhance the flavor of the festivities and of one's spiritual needs, thereby elevating and suffusing these very loaves and moments with a higher purpose and meaning?

G-d declares: "I created the evil inclination, and I created the Torah as spices for it" (Kiddushin 30b).

At first glance this statement is perplexing. Shouldn't the evil inclination be eliminated? Our sages teach us, "If this disgraceful one [the evil inclination] meets you, drag him into the hall of study. If he is like a rock he will dissolve. If he is like iron, he will be shattered" (ibid.).

Spices, however, do not destroy food. On the contrary, they flavor and season it. What is G-d's intent in considering the Torah as spices for the evil inclination?

Indeed, our sages explain that it is necessary to destroy the evil inclination "when he meets you"—when he comes upon you and incites you. But the essence of the evil inclination is simply the power of craving per se. This force must not be eliminated, but rather seasoned, flavored and transformed into a positive force.[157]

G-d desires that the Torah be used as seasoning to sublimate desire and craving. Desire is not an evil or negative emotion, in and of itself, but it depends on how we harness and direct it.

Women have been entrusted with the task of seasoning, according to the specific tastes of their family members. The woman's intuition helps her spice life's lessons so that they are neither too sharp nor too bitter, neither too salty nor too sour. Yet she realizes that excessive sweetness is not always positive. She is the one who is charged with flavoring life's lessons to suit the taste buds of her family members.

She is the one who is charged with consecrating the dough—and in her own intuitive way, directing her family's pursuits to worthwhile endeavors.

Indeed, the Torah advises us: Bake as many loaves as will fit over the coals of the fire! Just remember the main loaf of the festival, and keep in mind that the purpose of the other loaves is to enhance and flavor the loaf of spirituality, which must dominate.

TORAH BREAD
The Feminine Link

The Torah is referred to as bread,[158] as it is written, "Come partake of My bread" (Prov. 9:5) and "Bread satisfies the heart of man" (Ps. 105:15)—strengthening him and giving him the power to conquer his animalistic inclinations. Torah endows the G-dly soul with strength and power, enabling it to overcome the material nature and coarseness of the body and the animal soul.

Therefore, the Torah is called "bread." For bread connects and binds the vitality of the soul to the limbs of the body, eliciting additional life energy from the soul. When a person does not eat, the vitality enclothed in the limbs of his body is weakened; it is reduced and withdraws. And by eating, he obtains energy from his soul and vitality that is enclothed in his body.

Similar concepts apply with regard to the "bread of the Torah." It draws down added vitality to the G-dly soul that is enclothed in the animal soul and empowers it, enabling it to overcome the material nature of the body and animal soul. *(Kuntres Eitz Chaim,* chap. 4)

Although both men and women may fulfill the obligation of "taking *challa,*" it is the woman who has specifically been entrusted with this mitzva.

It is appropriate that one of woman's special mitzvot involves bread, which "connects and binds the vitality of the soul to the limbs of the body eliciting additional life energy from the soul." [159]

Bread is analogous to Torah, which likewise connects the spiritual soul of man and his physical life force with the world in which he lives and interacts. Bread enables man to draw the necessary strength from his soul's life force to fortify his body, making him capable of breathing, thriving and accomplishing. Bread, like Torah, serves as the link, then, between the world of spirit and the world of matter.

Therefore the word *lechem*, bread, comes from the linguistic root meaning to join or connect,[160] since it connects and holds together the two basic elements comprising man: his body and his soul.

Similarly, a wife is sometimes referred to as *lechem*.[161] Bread, and on a larger scale all the household's material prosperity, come through the wife's merit, as it says, "Blessing only comes to a man's household for the sake of his wife" (*Bava Metzia* 59a). Furthermore, "a man who does not have a wife, lives without joy, without blessing and without goodness" (*Yevamot* 62b).

A woman represents the link between the physical and the spiritual realms. By nurturing the physical, developing and revealing its spiritual capacity, she connects and joins the spiritual life to its material life.

This ability and innate characteristic of women is demonstrated on several planes.

Biologically, man implants the seed of potential into woman. Woman develops this potential into a viable life form. She nurtures it within her, bringing out all its latent abilities to develop it into a living being.

Man gives, while woman receives. But part of her receiving is completing and nurturing what she receives into a completed being. While man initiates, it is woman who patiently develops the potential within her into a thriving, healthy, physical and spiritual being. She gives of herself wholly, with all her physical, emotional and spiritual capacities to develop this nascent life into a functional individual, capable of discerning right from wrong.

Rabbi Dov Ber, the Great Maggid of Mezeritch, disciple and successor of the Baal Shem Tov, merited fathering a very righteous and saintly son. This son, Reb Avraham, was so holy, in fact, that he was commonly referred to as "the Malach," the Angel.

Unfortunately, the Maggid's wife and mother of "the Malach" died at a young age and the Maggid remarried soon after. His second wife once asked the Maggid that he should bless them so that she too would have a child. "After all, would it be so bad to have two holy Malachim in this world?" she beseeched him.

Replied the Maggid: "The Malach was not born to me due to my own merits or righteousness. It was solely due to the greatness of my first wife that a life as pure as the Malach came to be."

On a spiritual plane, woman also represents the link between the world of the spiritual and the world of the physical. [162]

In her spiritual role, woman acts as the unifying force, harmonizing and directing the various physical forces around her for a higher goal. While the man is the paradigm of diversity, woman represents the axis or focal point, unifying and focusing physical reality towards its spiritual epicenter.

Just as her physical womb receives the seed, completes and develops its potential and then channels a real life into this world, similarly, on a spiritual plane, woman completes and channels each morsel of physical reality towards its singular Divine purpose. In doing so, she peels away the many layers of its physical externality to reveal its singular, inner essence.

The hand that separates challa dough consecrates the physical and unites it with its spiritual purpose. It focuses not on its own capabilities. Its aim is to unify all of creation, and to unite the physical with its ultimate Divine fulfillment.

It is appropriate, then, that "From the first of your kneading bowl, you shall lift up a dough-offering [*challa*] to G-d," should be one of woman's special mitzvot, since her life's mission, and biological and spiritual roots, are endowed with just this capacity.

MYSTERIOUS
NIGHTS
The Mitzva of Mikve

THE GREAT
CHASSIDIC MASTER,

Rabbi Yisroel Baal Shem Tov, explains: "When a father teaches his young son how to walk, he stands the child on his feet and holds out his own arms to safeguard the child from falling. As the child waddles to the father's outstretched arms, the father slinks back further, bit by bit, and the child follows. The more the father retreats, the more tenaciously the child tries to reach him. That's how a child learns to walk."

Continues the Baal Shem Tov: "G-d relates to man in a similar manner. When an individual passionately seeks a connection with G-d, G-d in turn distances Himself. This only intensifies the person's yearning. The more detached from G-d the individual feels, the stronger is his longing to be near Him."

The closer we attempt to come, the more we realize His infinite greatness. As we approach Him, He seemingly withdraws. Just like the toddler, we continually advance, and in the process, we are elevated.

Dear Child of Mine

Dear Baby,

I cuddle you tightly in my arms, as if my arms can safeguard you from the woes of the world.

As I embrace you, I wish to keep you secure, warm and protected.

But as I do, I realize that I must let you go.

I stand you in the middle of the room, now looking ever so large compared to your tiny figure.

I move away.

Come, baby, walk towards me. My hands are held out, yet beyond your grasp.

You tumble over and fall. You've scraped your delicate knee. You cry.

I kiss your hurt, wipe away your tears. Then I put you down once again.

You look at me with a wounded look.

Why have I abandoned you? Why do I make you stand alone? Why do I keep retreating just beyond your reach, making you take one step and yet another?

But look, dear baby, you are starting to walk. Unsure. Unstable. Yet you are using your own two feet to move yourself forward.

I smile at you reassuringly. Enthusiastically, I applaud your efforts.

You begin to feel proud of your accomplishments. You begin to realize how to advance.

You fall down many more times, but each time you get up, increasingly more willing to keep trying, again and again, until you accomplish this feat.

You realize that I am here, smiling at your achievements, shedding tears when you stumble, waiting for you, just a little further away.

THE MAGGID OF MEZERITCH

taught the following parable:

A father was playing hide-and-seek with his little son. The father hid behind a large tree, and the boy, after searching, finally found him.

Similarly, G-d sometimes hides Himself from us. After searching for Him, and eventually finding Him, we become all the more beloved.

Dear Child,

Come, little one, today is your first day of school.

Let me brush your golden locks and adjust your freshly pressed collar. What excitement! Today you begin a whole new phase in your journey of learning.

Here, take my hand. Let's walk together to your classroom. A new horizon is opening before you; a new circle of friends in whom to place your trust; a new teacher to answer your queries.

A new world, somewhat separate from me.

I blink away my tears, as I consider how much emptier my days will be without hearing your bright laughter or your wonderful constant chatter.

I must not let you notice my hesitation. I must not show you my fears.

How I pray that on your new journey you will not encounter insensitive teachers. How I wish the children you meet will never utter hurtful words to you.

Dear Child, you are so tender.

I plant a giant smile on my face to reassure your frightened eyes, eyes that are pleading with me not to leave you.

Come, my child. There is no need to hide behind my gathered skirt. Be brave. Here's a tissue to wipe away your tears. Gently, I smooth your quivering chin.

The school bell rings loudly and I force myself to pull my hand out of your desperate hold as I silently wave good-bye.

Don't worry, dear child. My thoughts will be with you. I'll be here at the end of your day, waiting for you, eager to share in your adventures and discuss all that you learned and gained.

G-d said to Moshe:
"Then I shall remove My hand and you will see My
back, but My face may not be seen."
(Ex. 33:23)

"What do G-d's back, achor, and face, panim,
signify? These are spiritual concepts clothed in
human language.
"G-d, Who is Infinite, is unbounded by time or
space. Throughout his life, finite man strives to
emulate G-d and reach ever-higher levels of
holiness. Panim, face—forward motion—
symbolizes each higher level. His previous level
which he left behind is called achor, back—that
which is behind a person.
"No matter what lofty heights man reaches, there
will always be a panim, an even higher plateau to
which he can aspire. The ultimate panim can
never be attained, for G-d is Infinite and 'My
face will not be seen.' Man does, however, leave
behind the lower stages on his never-ending climb
upwards."

Rabbi Shlomo Hakohen Rabinowitz of Radomsk (1803–1866)

Dear Daughter,

We couldn't have chosen a better day for your wedding. It is warm and beautiful outside, not a cloud in the sky.

Silently, I pray that your future horizons be so clear and that your days be filled with even more warmth and beauty.

Come, my daughter. There is so much to do.

After weeks and months of frantic preparation, the guests will be arriving momentarily. The hall is all set up. The photographer wants to begin taking pictures.

Despite the constant smile on my face, I hope the camera won't capture the lines of worry around my eyes.

I am so happy for you, dear daughter.

I swallow hard to suppress the huge lump that has formed in my throat.

Today, you begin the next stage of your life. You are no longer my little girl; you have grown into a woman.

You are leaving my home to set up your own.

You look so beautiful, dear daughter. Your elegant white gown is adorned with tiny, iridescent pearls. Your delicate tiara resting on top of your ebony curls frames your radiant, pure face.

It seems like just yesterday that I cuddled you in my arms, just moments after you were born. I held you then, my firstborn child, tightly to my chest, determined to never let you go. As I wrapped you cozily in the hospital's soft, white blankets, I vowed to protect you forever from life's coldness and harshness.

And I embrace you now, knowing that in but a short moment, you will leave your childhood behind as you bravely enter into your new, unexplored destiny.

Remember, dear daughter, no matter how mature you grow, whatever your future may hold, my vow to protect you will remain. Wherever you may be, I will always be your mother, always there for you.

Be good to her, dear groom. She is so precious. She is so special.

Be good to her, dear G-d. She is my love.

"Warm yourself by the fire of the sages, but beware of their glowing embers lest you be burnt."
(Avot 2:15)

The Rebbe is compared to a burning coal. Do not keep aloof from your Rebbe; you will become cold. Do not come too close to him; you may be burned.
The same holds true of your relationship with your friends.
And spouse.

The Baal Shem Tov

Dear Spouse,

Today we celebrate twenty-five years of marriage. Years of happiness and joy, years of growth and development, but also years laced with stress and sadness.

As a bride, I remember how I dreamt that our relationship would unfold.

We would never argue with one another. Never would harsh words pass between us.

We would do everything together; never be apart for a night. Never face a crisis in our relationship.

How naive were my thoughts.

Just imagine the intimacy that we now share, only because of all that we've gone through.

Yes, you were always there for me, and I for you, but sometimes from a distance. Sometimes, you took a step back, allowing me to discover myself. You understood when I needed time alone and you didn't stifle me with your tender care.

And that is precisely why we became even closer, vacillating between dependence and independence, between intimate closeness and needed space.

Life showered us with its share of hardships. We each had our own unique set of difficulties to overcome. Each was a stress on our relationship, stretching further apart the elastic bond that ties us together. But after surmounting each challenge, we meant more to each other, and the bond tightened.

As we reached new plateaus of awareness, our relationship deepened just as it became more flexible.

I can only wish us, dear spouse, to experience many more blessed years together. Years filled with growth and development, and years where we become ever closer.

The unsure toddler learns how to walk under his mother's watchful gaze. The dependent child grapples with her first day at school, away from her parents' comforting side. The bride forsakes her childhood home to embark on her new journey of married life. And the elderly married couple's anniversary commemorates years of shared joys and pains.

All of these are landmarks in a person's life; all periods of growth in an individual's personal development. Each event marks a new turn, changing somewhat the direction of each relationship, inviting more freedom and independence. While seemingly outgrowing the former relationship, in truth, each event deepens its very bonds, bringing it to a higher plateau.

Each of these occurrences underlines the delicate balance of providing direction, while allowing for maturation; of demonstrating love and care, without stifling with concern; of offering support, while not crippling with neediness.

In every relationship, at some point, for the best interests of those involved, a space needs to be created, so that each individual can be given the freedom to discover his own growth.

Growth can be painful. Yet the toddler's, child's and bride's mother realizes that for the sake of the child's future happiness, sometimes difficult growing pains need to be suffered as part of her continued development. In life, we often need to "descend for the sake of a greater and higher ascent."[163]

Heart-wrenching though it may be, each descent ultimately leads to greater growth and maturation, which deepens the very relationship it seems to be impeding.

Below, we will explore how these dynamics come to play particularly in marriage, and how the Torah's code of conduct for Jewish marriage positively affects this interplay.

We will further discover how these dynamics are reflected in the cosmic dance of exile and redemption, in the ultimate marriage relationship—between G-d and His people.

THE DYNAMICS OF MARRIAGE

R elationships. A mother cradling her newborn child; their bond is immeasurable. A proud father walking hand-in-hand with his toddler; the joy is evident in their eyes. Two sisters sharing their secrets; their companionship is cherished.

And the love of husband and wife; their attachment is deepest and ever growing.

There are three sights that warm my heart and are beautiful in the eyes of G-d and man: unity among brothers, friendship among neighbors, and a man and wife who are inseparable. [164]

The paradigm of a love relationship is that of husband and wife. Their love surfaces and flowers as it deepens to reveal infinite levels of unity and oneness.

The seeds of this relationship are planted with the introduction of two distinct, unique individuals possessing diversified characteristics and attributes, who often originate from divergent backgrounds, cultures or environments, each possessing dissimilar habits, wants and needs.

Yet with time and nurturing, the seeds grow into a new shape as the partners form a new whole. Peeling away the other's external, the partners unmask each other's essential selves. And in so doing, the two emerge as a new unit; no longer one of *I* and *you*, but as a third dimension of *we*.

As he walks down the road of marriage, man undertakes the never-ending, life-long journey of creating this third dimension, and making it his life. In doing so, he does not suppress his own self, nor does he subjugate his wife's desires, but rather the two selves develop to encompass each other's, forming a third beautiful unified entity—the married couple.

This is the deepest transformation that can occur. Unlike a parent-child relationship in which a parent suppresses his own personal needs, goals or desires for the sake of his child, in the ideal man and wife relationship, the needs, goals and desires become shared. In unison, man and wife define and build a new set of ideals, taking into account and encompassing the unique and special psychological, spiritual and physical demands and desires of the other.

Said Rabbi Moshe Leib of Sassov to his Chassidim: "From a simple peasant, I learned how we must love our neighbor. Drunk in the tavern, I overheard his discussion.

"Ivan: 'Sasha, tell me, do you really love me?'

"Sasha: 'Ivan, I love you dearly.'

"Ivan: 'If you love me, tell me what is bothering me.'

"Sasha: 'How can I know what is troubling you?'

"Ivan: 'If you don't know what is bothering me, how can you say that you truly love me?'"

Concluded Rabbi Moshe Leib: "To love another person means to know what is troubling him, and to share his burden, as though it were your own. That is true love."

For this reason, the first letter of the first verse in the Torah, *"Bereishit bara Elokim," In the beginning, G-d created,* is the second letter of the Hebrew alphabet, the *beit.* The first letter, the *aleph,* cannot be the initial letter of the Torah because its numerical value is one, indicating separation and isolation. In order to convey a blessing, the letter *beit,* whose numerical value is two, was needed. For blessing only comes when there is another. The *beit,* with its duality, symbolizes the couple: man and wife.[165]

Therefore, after embarking on the journey of marriage, every action and thought should no longer be tainted by selfish or personal desires. From now onwards the couple must consider this new transformation, this duality in their lives, which is their source of blessing.

After his wife passed away, the Baal Shem Tov suffered greatly from his loss. Not accustomed to seeing the Baal Shem Tov concerned with worldly matters, the members of his household asked him to explain his obvious anguish.

The Baal Shem Tov replied that he was suffering because he would now have to die and be buried in the ground. He said, "I had hoped to ascend to heaven in fiery chariots [like the prophet Eliyahu (Elijah)], but now, without my wife, I am but half a body, and it is impossible. It is for this reason I suffer exceedingly."

The Hebrew word for love, *ahava*, is numerically equivalent to *echad*, meaning *one*. The sum of both words totals twenty-six, the numerical equivalent of G-d's quintessential Name, the *Tetragrammaton* or *Havaye*. The couple's love expresses a oneness reflective of their quintessential unity, as two halves of the same whole. When the two join together in love and physical intimacy, they reveal and draw down G-d's presence.

"Where there is no union of male and female, man is not worthy of beholding the Shechina, the Divine Presence."[166]

In the beginning of creation, G-d created humankind as one androgynous being, with both male and female attributes, emulating G-d who is One.[167] Only later was Adam divided into both man and woman. But in his original form he was a singular functional being.

"Therefore, shall a man leave his mother and father and cleave to his wife, and they shall become one flesh" (Gen. 2: 24).

The eternal attraction between man and woman reflects his "quest for something lost,"[168] man's urge to discover and become unified with his missing primordial self. Lacking part of his soul powers, each cleaves to his second half. And only through the union of husband and wife can each partner fulfill his full mission and realize his ultimate potential of being created in the image of G-d, Who is singular in His Oneness.

"Whoever lacks a wife, remains without atonement and without life" (*Yevamot* 62b).

The relationship between man and woman can never be static, attaining a pinnacle of awareness and then stagnating. For just as each partner continues to grow personally, the relationship, by definition, must develop, vacillating constantly between ups and downs, electrified by passion and distance, in an incessant rhythm of motion pulsating between intimacy and withdrawal.

For each withdrawal is, in truth, the next stage towards reaching a higher plateau of more profound attachment. Each separation becomes another rung propelling the relationship upwards on the never-ending ladder of love and intimacy.

For this reason, the paradigm of husband and wife is used to metaphorically depict the relationship between G-d and His people, with G-d serving as the groom, and His nation—His bride. No other relationship better exemplifies the cultivation of these deepest levels of dynamic growth.

Parenthetically, for this reason, in our prayers when referring to G-d we often employ the masculine pronoun (whereas when we refer to the Jewish people, we use the feminine). This is not to attribute masculine character traits to G-d, or to confine Him to a particular gender. On the contrary, many traits ascribed to G-d in our prayers are traditionally feminine qualities, such as compassion, mercy, kindness, etc. The masculine terminology, however, is used to elicit this archetypal structure of a husband/wife or groom/bride relationship that defines the most potent relationship capable of being experienced.

"Like a lily among thorns, so is my beloved among the maidens. Like an apple tree among trees of the forest, so is my beloved among the youths. I delight to sit in his shade, and his fruit is sweet to my mouth . . .

"How sweet is your love, my own, my bride. How much more delightful is your love than wine; your ointments more fragrant than any spice. Sweetness drips from your lips, O bride; honey and milk are under your tongue . . .

"For love is fierce as death, passion is mighty. Its darts are darts of fire, a blazing flame. Vast floods cannot quench love, nor do rivers drown it . . ." (Song of Songs, chaps. 2, 4, 8).

While outwardly the Song of Songs is simply a beautiful love song, it actually is the most mystical song of unification of Z'er

Anpin, the male attributes of G-d, and His Bride. It thus contains a hidden holiness, just as the mundane world contains the hidden holiness of the Shechina (the feminine attribute of G-d, and G-d's presence in our world).[169]

This dichotomy between revelation and withdrawal is the ultimate mystery of creation. Only through G-d's withdrawal into Himself, so to speak, could a creation come to be; only by "making room" or a "place" for the world to exist—without being nullified by His existence, or overwhelmed by His revelation—could creation take place.

This original withdrawal and separation, then, ultimately manifests itself as a deeper and subtler mode of revelation. Only through separation, after intimate closeness, can the most profound union occur.

For only after withdrawing and limiting Himself can the greatest revelation occur—G-d forging a relationship with created beings in our physical world.

For this reason, the Hebrew word for holy, *kadosh*, also means separate and set apart. For something to retain its holiness, it must also, at times, be separate. Otherwise, it risks losing its special quality. Likewise, G-d's Kingship, as does the majesty of any king, lies as much in His aloofness from His people as it does in His revelation to them.[170]

Similarly, the holiest sections in the Temple were used rarely and only by specific individuals. The Holy of Holies, for example, was only entered once a year, on Yom Kippur, the most sanctified day of the Jewish calendar, and only then by the High Priest, at precise intervals of the service and after intense preparation.

Interestingly, the Holy of Holies is referred to as none other than the Cheder Hamitot,[171] or bedroom chamber, emphasizing, once again, the metaphorical relationship between G-d and His people as that of bride and groom. This reinforces the hallowed regard in which Judaism holds the intimate union of husband and wife—that, in fact, the Holy of Holies itself is referred to as "the master bedroom."

Furthermore, the holiest vessel in the Temple was the *aron*, the ark, which was hidden behind the *parochet*, an elaborate curtain, in the innermost chamber. The golden *cherubim*, molded in the shapes of a male and female, crowned the ark. When G-d was pleased with His nation the *cherubim* were said to be embracing one another. When G-d was displeased, the *cherubim* would turn away from each other. The *cherubim* underline, as well, the central ideal of a man-woman relationship as a depiction of the truest, deepest love between G-d and His people.

In contrast, in a relationship between parent and child, or between siblings, the love is constant and steadfast. Though this love grows, the disparity between what it was and what it has become never differs radically. Though it deepens, the love was always there, and, normally, always remains.

In a healthy marriage, however, the love between spouses deepens precisely because of its constant transformation and magnetic pull oscillating between distance and passionate attachment. For only after a withdrawal following an intense peak, can husband and wife reach a new plateau of more penetrating and more intense love. Each is able to strip away another outer layer of external self as together they reach a new unity of oneness, both in body and soul.

When love is strong, a man and woman can make their bed on the blade of a sword. When love is weak, a bed of sixty cubits is not wide enough (Sanhedrin 7a).

The laws of Taharat Hamishpacha or Family Purity are in tune with this necessary and natural rhythm in the relationship between man and woman.

Briefly stated,[172] the laws stipulate that a man and woman are forbidden any physical contact with each other from the onset of the woman's menstrual period, for a minimum of twelve days, (or more, depending on the woman's cycle).. After the woman bathes and immerses in the *mikve*, the husband and wife are then, once again, permitted to resume relations.

The Family Purity laws reflect the holiness of the physical union between man and woman, not the negation of it. By ensuring that even the most powerful of physical drives be touched with an awareness and code of holiness, the Torah sanctifies the drives themselves. The physical flesh, then, does not carry any tinge of contempt, but rather has become refined, so it, too, can be vested with the spiritual.

"In order that man should know that he has a Maker, a King, He set rules limiting his union with his wife, as He set rules covering all His gifts to mankind."[173]

Family Purity laws ensure that the innate equilibrium between intimacy and separation be maintained so that each separation leads to a greater unity. The natural pulse of the relationship becomes vivified as the couple explores other modes of attachment besides physical venues. The times of separation demand that man and wife relate on a non-physical plane, and that the couple functions in close proximity, as well as from a distance. This time provides an incentive for developing, forming and nurturing other interpersonal ties[174] that unite them, and will serve them well in life.

"Why did the Torah forbid [intercourse] with the menstruating woman for seven days? Because the husband becomes accustomed to her and tires of her. Therefore, the Torah said let her be impure ... so that she will be dear to her husband as she was at the time she entered the chuppa [the marriage canopy]" (Nidda 31b).

In addition, monotony in marriage is avoided, as each partner becomes dearer and more precious to the other when they consecrate themselves afresh on a monthly basis. After their period of separation, their reunion becomes another *chuppa*, each a little more intimate and profound than its predecessor. Instead of experiencing the emotional pinnacle of marriage as a bride and groom only once, these laws ensure the excitement of courting and union for a lifetime, constantly renewing the marital relationship.

The physical separation between husband and wife at prescribed times, then, provides a counterpoint to the couple's intimate times. Consequently, it leads to a deeper, more meaningful union.

This conjoining is the only opportunity in which man can actually emulate G-d, since it is the only opportunity that he is given to create another life. In his ability to father a child, man emulates G-d's creative powers. Furthermore, this child will, in turn, create more children, generation after generation, until eternity. Thus, by creating a child, and through this child an endless chain, man emulates G-d's power of creation, eternity and endurance.

"Know that the intimate union of man with his wife is holy and pure . . . The male is the mystery of Chochma—wisdom and conception; the female is the mystery of Bina—understanding and development. Pure intimate union can be a means of spiritual elevation when properly practiced. A mystery greater than this is the secret of the Heavenly Bodies—when they unite in the manner of man and woman."[175]

The union of man and woman is the one occasion when G-d provides man with the opportunity to come closest to being G-d-like. As such, these moments are replete with potential for the highest and greatest sanctity, or conversely, the lowest, most depraved immorality.

Submission to a divinely imposed restriction invests the act with sanctity. Through their submission, man and woman acknowledge that the pleasure and power of their union are divinely granted. They must comply with His will, with their personal gratification not being the highest priority. This awareness sanctifies their union, turning their pleasure into a precious gift of G-d, weaving a holy bond that unites husband and wife in all aspects of their lives.

By following G-d's code of conduct, man elicits the Divine, drawing Him into his physical relationship.

By doing so, the Holy of Holies not only resembles the bedroom chamber, but one's own bedroom becomes the Holy of Holies.

TUMA AND TAHARA
LOWS AND HIGHS

Everything has a season; and there is a time for everything under the heavens.

> *A time to be born; and a time to die.*
>
> *A time to plant; and a time to uproot the planted.*
>
> *A time to kill; and a time to heal.*
>
> *A time to wreck; and a time to build.*
>
> *A time to weep; and a time to laugh.*
>
> *A time to wail; and a time to dance.*
>
> *A time to scatter stones; and a time to gather stones.*
>
> *A time to embrace; and a time to shun embraces.*
>
> *A time to seek; and a time to lose.*
>
> *A time to keep; and a time to discard.*
>
> *A time to rend; and a time to mend.*
>
> *A time to be silent; and a time to speak.*
>
> *A time to love; and a time to hate.*
>
> *A time for war; and a time for peace."*
>
> (*Kohelet* (Eccles.) 3:1-8)

Everything in this world has its season. A time for the seemingly positive experiences, and a time for the seemingly negative ones. Life is a never-ending cycle of these low points that emerge into high points, only to revert back again to lows. The lowest points on life's cosmic wheel serve as mere introductions to the next stage of highs, enhancing the highs by accentuating their positions.

For everything there is a season and a purpose. There is a time to toil, and a time to absorb the fruits of one's toil. A time for the mundane six days of the week, and a time for the holiness of the Shabbat.

A time for twenty-nine ordinary days of the month, and a time for consecrating *rosh chodesh*, the New Month. A time for living within this world during the days of the year, and a time to transcend this world during the specified Yomim Tovim, holy days of the year.

A time for the six years of working the land through natural means, and the seventh year of Shemitta, when we consecrate our work, relying on a Force beyond ourselves. Forty-nine years to enjoy our purchases, and a year of Jubilee when all possessions return to their original owners, thereby reminding us of the True Owner of our world.

A time for the season of winter, when the world experiences coldness, barrenness and lifelessness; and a time for the season of summer, when we become warmed, rejuvenated and invigorated.

A time for darkness and night, and a time for day and revelation. A time for sleep and immobility, and a time for wakefulness, energy and vitality.

A time to withdraw, and a time to draw near. A time for exile with its inherent "hiddenness of G-d's face,"[176] and a time of redemption and open revelation of goodness, peace and truth.

Life is full of lows and highs that are part of the natural order of our world. Some of these lows and highs can be defined by the halachic terminology of *tuma* and *tahara*. Loosely translated, *tuma* means impurity, and *tahara* means purity. Nonetheless, these terms have nothing to do with physical cleanliness, but are wholly spiritual concepts.

Tuma would more correctly be defined as an absence of holiness, while *tahara* would mean a state of readiness to receive, or be imbued with, holiness. Though sometimes *tuma* can be caused intentionally by sinning and pushing G-d away from one's life, many forms of *tuma* are inborn in the rhythm of life itself, and have no association with sin, or negativity, at all.

Thus, the severest source of *tuma* is a corpse. Bereft of its *neshama*, soul, to provide holiness and vitality, the body remains in a state of void, and therefore in a state of impurity. Anyone coming in contact with a dead body is likewise considered ritually impure.

Similarly, during sleep, the soul temporarily leaves the body to ascend on high (therefore sleep is considered one sixtieth of death). Upon awakening, the hands, the medium through which the soul departs, are considered *tameh*, impure, until they are ritually washed. Though the hands are not physically dirty, they must be purified since the body has experienced a void of *kedusha*, holiness.

For this reason, as well, many men have the custom to ritually immerse in a *mikve* prior to Shabbat (and are actually mandated to do so prior to Yom Tov[177]) in order to purify themselves for the extra holiness of these holy days. Many Chassidim will likewise immerse daily, before the morning prayer service, as a preparation for the forthcoming state of holiness inherent in communication with the Almighty.

A convert to Judaism will similarly ritually immerse to mark his new status as someone who will now fulfill Divine precepts, and thus prepares for the oncoming additional *kedusha*.

Furthermore, G-d promises that in the era of redemption, "I will sprinkle you with *tahor* [pure] waters," and "I will remove the spirit of *tuma* from the land" (Zech. 13:2). This will be accomplished metaphorically through our immersion into the "knowledge of G-d" that will suffuse creation "like water covers the sea bed" (Isa. 11:9).

The ultimate purpose of *tuma*, or of any concealment of G-d's revelation—a low on life's cosmic wheel—is to achieve a higher level, by transforming it. The lows provide us with the opportunity of churning life's wheel, through our exertion, and effecting an elevation, bringing the world closer to its ultimate perfection.

Thus, each of these descents is a preparation for the ultimate ascent. The real purpose of the descent is, in fact, the ascent. Therefore, though the lows externally appear to be a descent, internally, they are a real part of the ascent itself. For the bottom of life's cosmic wheel portends the top, and thus, not only affect the topmost part, but is an integral part of it.

Sleep furnishes strength for the hours of wakefulness. Winter hibernation provides for the coming spring's vitality.

The weekdays supply the framework for change, development and creativity so that we can absorb the blessing, serenity and peace on the Shabbat. All week long we exert mastery over creation so that on Shabbat we can live in harmony with our world. In the Sage's words, "He who toils on the eve of Shabbat, shall eat on the Shabbat" (*Avoda Zara* 3a).

All year long we function within the reality of nature so that on Yom Tov and Holidays we can function in a manner transcending time and reality. During the six years prior to Shemitta and during the forty-nine years prior to the Jubilee, we live within creation, so that in the special year that follows, we can gain a perspective beyond our reality.

Similarly, throughout the millennia of exile, we have the opportunity to "fill the earth and conquer it" (Gen 1:28), uprooting the evil surrounding us, so that we can attain the era of redemption, when we will nurture the inherent good and reveal the Divine Essence of creation.

If the purpose of exile was only to punish us for our sins, exile's hardships would become lighter with the passage of time.[178] However, the closer we approach redemption, the harsher and darker exile becomes. This is so because the concealment and darkness serve as a preparation for the greater revelation to follow.

It was the holy day of Rosh Hashana. All the Jews were lost in fervent prayers to the Almighty, beseeching Him, once again, for a year of health and prosperity in both material and spiritual needs. Each Jew, in his own way, was enraptured with the prayers, lost in thought, communing with his Father in heaven.

Moshe, a simple and honest farmer, was trying his best, to keep up with the congregational prayers. At first, he, too, cried out intensely to G-d for all his innermost wants and needs. But as the prayers wore on, and the day grew longer, Moshe began to tire of the long service. Not understanding much of the meaning of the prayers, and having difficulty reading their Hebrew words, Moshe's mind began to wander and his stomach began to grumble, persistently reminding him just how hungry he was.

Soon, soon, we will be finished, Moshe assured his empty stomach and his aching feet. But the prayers continued unabated.

Then Moshe recalled the hearty pot of cholent that his wife had put up on the low fire to cook the previous night. Its succulent juices, tender meats and vegetables, and perfect blend of spices tasted their best after extended hours of slow cooking. Now, every time his stomach sent a rumbling message to him, he reminded himself that patience was the key to a delicious cholent and the wait was worth its while.

Indeed, Moshe looked around the large shul and convinced himself that that must be precisely what all the other worshippers were contemplating. Ah, he finally understood why the congregants were taking their time, patiently chanting their prayers, swaying to and fro. They, too, are hungry! Only they remember the wholesome meal that awaits them, and are just letting it cook a little longer.

But the prayers droned on . . . and on . . . hour after hour, with no end in sight.

Finally, Moshe became frustrated and pleaded: "G-d, Alm-ghty, I realize that the longer the cholent cooks, the more succulent it tastes. But enough already! How long must we wait? The cholent is surely tasty enough, just as it is!"

We, too, beseech our Father, "While we realize that the longer and harder the exile cooks, the better the revelation of the redemption that awaits us, but enough already! The exile is sufficiently cooked by now!"

Exile provides the opportunity for us to uncover the mantle of divisiveness and separation from G-d, and reveal the G-dly core in all of creation. It allows us to reveal our deepest dimensions, as we struggle for our very survival and for the triumph of good over evil. For this reason, our Sages commented, "Performing good deeds for merely one hour in our world is worth more than all the days of the World-to-Come" (*Avot* 4:17).

Though painful to endure, exile is a descent for the sake of a future and greater ascent. Just as the toddler's first falls and scrapes, or the child's heart-wrenching first separation from her mother, the period of exile is intended to be a learning and growing experience.

Since we are in a state of exile, this concept is presently beyond our comprehension. However, in the era of redemption, we will palpably experience how our service in exile was beneficial, and necessary for our individual and collective development. So, though now exile seems like a painful innovation, in the era of redemption, we will see why this lowly descent was needed for us and for the world at large.

We will then understand why G-d's "hiding His face from us" (Deut. 31:17)[179] was not cruel. But, like a mother prodding her child to development, it was a necessary distancing for the sake of achieving a greater, more profound and more comprehensive union.

Therefore, the mundane weekdays stand in contrast to the holy Shabbat; the twenty-nine days of the month, in contrast to *rosh chodesh*; the six-year cycle of working the land, in contrast to Shemitta; and the long hardships of exile, in contrast to the ensuing redemption. These are all inherent lows in life's cycle.

Similarly, a woman's *tuma* during *nidda* (a woman who is menstruating has the status of *nidda* until she immerses in the mikve) is a built-in component of her natural monthly cycle. Her status of *tuma* demonstrates her descent from a peak level of *kedusha*, when she has the ability to conceive a new life through her union with her husband.

The status of *nidda* is not meant to imply sinfulness, degradation or inferiority. On the contrary, it emphasizes, in particular, the great level of holiness inherent in woman's G-dly power to create and nurture a new life within her body, and the great holiness of a husband and wife's union, in general. Since a woman possesses this lofty potential, she also bears the possibility of its void; hence her status as *tameh*. Since she experienced "the touch of death," so to speak, with the loss of potential life as reflected by her menstruation, she enters this status of *nidda*.[180]

Her descent into the status of *nidda*, just as other inborn cycles mentioned above, is for the purpose of her higher ascent through the purification of the *mikve*. The *mikve* prepares her for the new status of *tahor*, when she once again can receive *kedusha*—though every month on an increasingly higher level—through her union with her husband, and through her G-dly power to create life.

We can now examine a perspective on the woman's monthly cycle as an introspective process in our relationship with G-d. We will explore how a woman, through her cycle, can sensitize herself and her husband to improving their spiritual service. We will then continue this theme to elucidate the inner meaning of the *mikve* as a constant process of purification and ascension, leading to the ultimate state of union between husband and wife, and between G-d and His people.

THREE PHASES OF ATTACHMENT

Until now, we have examined how a woman's monthly cycle parallels the ongoing stages of development in a couple's relationship. We discussed how a separation period can be utilized to develop other, non-physical, bonds, thereby enhancing the couple's overall closeness.

Furthermore, as mentioned, the distance also provides a pause in the relationship so that each partner can evaluate whether their goals are self-serving, with their own pleasure being of paramount importance, or whether each one is sensitive to, and in tune with, the other.

On a deeper level, since the Jewish people metaphorically are compared to a "wife," and G-d to a "husband," this cycle also parallels phases of spiritual development, in our relationship with our cosmic Groom. Thus, the monthly cycle is also symbolic of the stages that we experience in our quest for Divine closeness.

A woman who is in tune with her monthly cycle, and with her emotional and spiritual psyche—and a husband who is in tune with his wife's biological, psychological and spiritual self—can use the month's various phases as a barometer for evaluating where they stand in their relationship with the Creator. As we will see further, each stage prods man to ask himself whether his goals are self-serving, or in accordance with the will of His Divine partner.

Just as each stage symbolizes a specific form of growth in the spousal relationship, as well as in the individual-to-G-d relationship, each also reflects a cycle of development in the cosmic rhythm of exile and redemption involving the Jewish people and G-d.

Interestingly, the word indicating a woman's impure status, *nidda*, is composed of the words *nod Hay*, or *nod Hashem*—G-d wanders. On a cosmic scale, the *nidda* cycle reflects the exile cycle of the Jewish people during which G-d Himself "wanders" and descends, so to speak, with us throughout our sojourn.[181]

For the Jewish people are compared to the moon. Just as the moon waxes and wanes every month, so, too, the Jews undergo stages of concealment and renewal throughout their experience of exile and redemption. *Rosh chodesh*, the holiday of the revelation of the New Moon, is also a special holiday for women, in reward for not participating in the sin of the golden calf.

On an inner level, *rosh chodesh* reflects the monthly cycle of separation and renewal inherent in a woman's biological makeup. After total concealment, *rosh chodesh* marks the first citing of the sliver of moon, when it once again begins to reflect the sun's rays. Metaphorically, *rosh chodesh* symbolizes the moon's renewal and purification process as it once again "unites" with the sun by receiving and reflecting its light.

Thus the union of sun and moon on *rosh chodesh*, a woman's holiday, reflects the union of man and wife after her period of *nidda* is completed.[182] This union of sun and moon, and husband and wife, corresponds, as well, to the future, ultimate and deepest union to be experienced between G-d and His people in the era of redemption. During this time the "banished wife," the Jewish people, will once again be welcomed in their homeland where, together with their Groom, they will unite in the matrimonial home.

"In that era there will be neither famine nor war, neither jealousy nor strife. Blessings will be abundant, comforts within the reach of all. The one preoccupation of the whole world will be to know the L-rd. Jews will be very wise, and will know the things that are presently concealed, and will attain an understanding of their Creator . . ."[183]

In order to fully implement the growth potential inherent in the monthly cycle and in the laws of *nidda*, the various phases of this cycle and their symbolism must be analyzed.

Halachically, there are three distinct stages to a woman's monthly cycle. The first begins with the onset of the menstrual flow and continues until its cessation, for a minimum of five days. This stage begins the period when a woman is considered *tameh*.

The second is a preparatory seven-day period, during which no blood is seen, although the woman is still considered ritually impure. During these days, a woman counts seven blood-free days in anticipation for her immersion in the *mikve* at its conclusion.

The final stage begins after immersion in the *mikve*. At this point, a woman is considered *tahor*, ritually pure, and intimate relations between husband and wife are permitted until the next reappearance of blood.

Symbolically, the first stage resembles the spiritual service termed "submission."[184] During this phase, the focus is on the distance between us and our partners, or us and G-d; and encourages our desire to come closer. Emphasis is placed on becoming aware of the impurity in our lives, however subtle, and initiating changes in our behavior to remove this negative barrier and distance.

This stage initiates the *tuma*, or "descent," in our relationship with our spouses, and spiritually, with G-d. In order to transform this descent into an ascent, we need to be attuned to those areas of our lives in which we can incorporate positive change. Becoming aware of the disparity between where we are, and where we know we could be, increases our desire and determination to reach our spiritual destination. Thus the distance itself serves as motivation, pushing us to achieve our goals.

We find a similar concept, where the negative is turned into positive, echoed in the laws of repentance.

Repentance is so powerful that when an individual repents genuinely, even his prior intentional sins become merits. While we can understand that sincere regret can remove the taint of sin, how can it turn the spiritual blemish into a merit? However, since our repentance comes about because of our sincere regret over this sin, the sin itself has become, in retrospect, something positive. Since it was the impetus for change, the sin does not merely become neutralized, but, incredibly, is transformed into merit.

"In the place where penitents stand, even the [wholly] righteous cannot stand" (*Berachot* 34b).

Similarly, this descent into *tuma*—for the couple, on a personal level, and for the Jewish people, on a cosmic level—becomes the impetus for a greater spiritual awakening and awareness, if imbued with the correct mindset. Therefore, a couple that attains this awareness, and acts upon it, can improve their interpersonal relationship, as well as spiritual standing, during this phase of "submission."

Rabbi Shneur Zalman of Liadi, known as the Baal HaTanya, wanted to bless his chassid Reb Yekusiel Liepler with long life.

Reb Yekusiel replied, "But not with peasant years—the years of one who has eyes but does not see, ears but does not hear. Such people do not see the Divine and they do not hear the Divine. Their years are dead years."

The submission stage urges us to sensitize ourselves so that our years remain alive.

During the second phase of the monthly cycle, a woman is still considered *tameh*, although no blood is seen. Every day during this seven-day period, a woman is required to make a halachic *bedika*, examination for any sign of blood.

The spiritual service during this time is called "separation." This phase symbolizes the introspection and change that a couple incorporates into their lives. It reflects how a couple will implement the newfound sensitivity, and submission to a higher Will, gained from the first phase.

Therefore, they will make regular *bedikot:* introspective reviews of their thoughts and behavior, to rid themselves of any negative aspects. Since the couple yearns and counts towards the end of the seven-day period, when the wife will immerse and become spiritually pure, these days are goal-oriented. While rectifying the past, by scrutinizing their current state, the couple also awaits the long-expected conclusion of the seven days.

From a macrocosmic perspective, this period alludes to the mission throughout the close to two millennia of exile, waiting for the "seventh" era of eternal goodness. During these long years of exile, the focus is on introspection, examining our activities and motives, and cleansing ourselves of negative character traits and behaviors.

Reb Shmuel Betzalel Sheftel, known as the Rashbatz, was one of the early teachers of Rabbi Yosef Yitzchak Schneerson, the sixth Rebbe of Lubavitch. He used to compare people whose spiritual lives were not motivated, ignited and set into motion by their Torah study, to portraits—devout and learned, perhaps, but utterly inert.

Knowledge and Torah study must spur us to action, to incorporating positive change into our life.

At the conclusion of the second stage, a woman immerses and begins her new status of *tahor*, and its concurrent spiritual service, which is termed "sweetening." It is the climax of the cyclical experience, affording the couple with the opportunity to unite in flesh and spirit.

On a personal level, this stage resembles the closeness to the Creator that we feel after reaching a spiritual high. After removing the negativity from our lives, we have achieved a certain triumph of spirit. Like the euphoria felt after pushing oneself beyond one's limits, this stage celebrates the human capacity for triumphing over wicked adversaries.

On a universal scale, this third stage represents the ultimate union between mankind and our Creator, which will transpire in the future era of redemption, after the world's evils have been vanquished and man's service is complete.

After successfully completing the stages of submission and separation, which cultivate an awareness and sensitivity to spirituality; and after implementing this appreciation by separating oneself from the evils of the world; we can then exult in our triumph and victory in the consummation of our relationship with our Creator. This phase reflects the ultimate destination of the journey of the Jewish people, who await the ultimate union of messianic proportions.

"It is well known that the Messianic Era, and especially the Era of the Resurrection of the Dead, signifies the fulfillment and culmination of creation, the purpose for which the world was originally created" (Tanya, chap. 36).

On a universal level, this stage lasts for eternity. Nevertheless, on a personal level, the monthly cycle is continuous, constantly beginning anew and returning to the first stage of *tameh* and submission. But our subsequent starting point is from a constantly higher level of spiritual sensitivity and growth. So, in climbing our metaphorical spiritual ladder, we never begin from the bottom rung, but neither do we ever reach the very top.

For, "there is no man on earth who does only good and does not err" (Eccles. 7:20). As human beings, who possess an unbounded, infinite soul, each of us can tap into our unlimited capacity for development of our infinite potential. Even the greatest individual can strive for a still greater level of perfecting himself.

Indeed, the *nidda* cycle reminds us never to placate ourselves with our present spiritual rung; never to be smugly self-satisfied with our current accomplishments, no matter how grand; but to aspire to greater and greater heights.

At the same time, the *nidda* cycle also cautions us not to become embittered with our present reality, for its purpose is merely a prelude for the next, redeeming phase.

"The ultimate purpose of creation is the lowest world. For such was His will, that He derives pleasure when the forces of evil are subdued and darkness is transformed into light" (Tanya, chap. 36).

The female's unique biological, emotional and spiritual makeup has enabled women to excel in their determination even in the most difficult of times. Throughout our long exile, it has always been women who have been encouraging their husbands and families to remain resolute, to see beyond the darkness. Women have provided the steadfast *emuna*, faith and strong resolve.

Examples of this determination are numerous. From the righteous women in Egypt who prepared their tambourines during the hardships of the exile, so certain were they of their redemption; to Queen Esther[185] bringing salvation to her people through her own personal self-sacrifice during the reign of the Persian Empire; to Yehudit, who placed herself in mortal danger to kill the Greek general, Holifornus, and bring victory to her people; to Chana, during the era of Greek dominance, who demonstrated tremendous faith and strength in encouraging her seven sons not to bow to idolatry despite having to pay for such resolve with their very lives; and even up until the ashes of Auschwitz; woman's faith has remained unwavering.

Day after day, the Bluzhever Rebbe, Rabbi Spiro, saw new arrivals being rounded up to be sent to the gas chambers. He watched as weak mothers, clutching infants just days old, were forced to line up while their newborns were barbarically torn from their arms.

One skeleton of a mother, in obvious anguish, approached the German guard in charge, begging for a sharp knife. Seeing this, Rabbi Spiro frantically ran over to her, to stop her from injuring herself or her child, and to encourage her that no matter how bleak our fate appears, we may never lose hope and give up.

With a sadistic grin, the German guard restrained Rabbi Spiro and handed the woman the knife, anticipating a gruesomely entertaining scene.

Holding the knife in her trembling hand, the woman placed her baby on the ground, unbundled him and loudly declared: "G-d, You have given me a beautiful child. He is now eight days old and I am returning him to You, perfect, as You desired.

"Blessed are You, our G-d, King of the universe, Who has sanctified us with His commandments and commanded us regarding circumcision."

Then, in the depths of Auschwitz, this heroic Jewish woman proceeded to circumcise her baby.

In fact, this is precisely why, when presenting the Torah to the Jewish people, G-d instructed Moshe to address, first and foremost, the women.

"Moshe ascended on High, and G-d called to him saying:

"So shall you say to the house of Yaakov and relate to the children of Israel" (Ex. 19:3).

"So shall you say—in this manner and in this order.

"The house of Yaakov—these are the women, speak to them softly.

"The children of Israel—these are the men. Explain to them the harsh punishments and the details of the laws." (Rashi, ad loc.)

First tell the women, the carriers of the faith,[186] the ones who, for all times until eternity, will transmit the message of strength, determination and resolve. And then, afterwards, explain the details of the various laws—to the men.

Perhaps women have this strength to face the difficulty of the darkness because of their innate ability to see beyond the gloom, as reflected in their biological and spiritual makeup alluded to in the laws of *nidda*. Realizing that the light is sure to emerge, that the good is sure to succeed, that these spiritual descents are sure to lead to higher ascents, they intuitively sense that the darkness is merely a prelude to a greater and better time.

"If a man sees that painful sufferings come to him, let him examine his deeds . . .

"If he examines his deeds and finds nothing amiss, let him see whether the cause is his neglect of Torah . . .

"If he still finds this is not the cause, he may assume these are sufferings of love, as it is written, 'For whom G-d loves, He corrects' (Prov. 3:12).

"If the Holy One, Blessed be He, loves a person, He crushes him with sufferings" (*Berachot* 5a).

In order to prod him further.

The darkness itself will enhance the ensuing light. Therefore the highs and lows, the ups and downs, the descents for the sake of ascents, all need to be seen as passing obstacles, however difficult, intended to strengthen our resolve, and not to deplete it.

ETERNAL
WATERS

After the conclusion of her status of *tuma*, before the new stage of *tahara*, a woman must immerse in the mikve. This immersion is the intermediary between these two phases, vesting the woman with her new status, enabling her to transcend her present level and attain a higher degree of purification.

In this chapter's final part, we will explore the spiritual significance of mikve waters, and how they affect the individual who immerses in them.

Water.
Clear, natural.
Cleansing, refreshing.
Purifying, hydrating.
The essence of rebirth.

Water.
Flowing, mobile.
Changing shapes, adapting forms.
Flexibility, fluidity.
The prototype of impermanence.
The transition of the individual.

Water.
The embryonic liquid,
The source of life.
Quenching thirst,
Sustaining life.
Flowing from the life-giving waters—
Of Eden,
The primeval womb of creation.

Anything undergoing a fundamental process of transition must pass through a state of void before it can emerge as a new entity. To make a radical step forward, we must first annul the previous frame of reference. Then, like a vacuum, this state of non-being draws in a new and loftier level of existence.

Before a seed sprouts, it must first be planted in the ground, where it disintegrates. Only after this void, can it grow into a healthy tree. To metamorphose into something greater requires the intermediate stage of void or nothingness.

The *mikve* resembles this intermediary state of void that facilitates the emergence of the new stage of *tahara* from its prior state of *tuma*. "*Tevilla*," immersion in the waters of the *mikve*, accomplishes this transition. *Tevilla* is composed of the same Hebrew letters as the word "*bitul*," self-nullification.

Bitul entails freeing oneself from the imprisonment of one's own ego to experience transcendence from the petty entanglement and never-ending selfish demands of one's own negative inclinations and self-centered identity. It involves breaking loose from the shackles of self-importance to experience the freedom of spiritual expression, and the sense of joy in the infinite unity of all reality.

Immersion in the *mikve* represents this concept of *bitul*.

Rabbi Moshe Leib of Sassov: In order to pour liquid from one vessel to another, the vessel containing the liquid must be on top, and the receiving vessel must be below. Similarly, in spiritual matters, only those who feel lowly or humble will learn from others.

The *mikve* is made up of natural, fluid water. Water symbolizes impermanence. While solids remain in their unchanging, frozen state; water, the prototypical liquid, readily takes on different shapes and forms.

Tasteless, water has no clearly defined and restrictive characteristic; nevertheless, it is the essence of all liquids. It is the foremost component of all foods, precisely because of its adaptability. Its life-giving and thirst-quenching power derives precisely from its simplicity.

The ego in man represents permanence. Water, on the other hand, represents a dynamic progression and flow closer to the Divine Will.

Therefore, immersion in the *mikve* is in water. Water, or *"mayim"* in Hebrew, has at its root the word *"mah,"* or *"what."*[187] Immersion in the *mikve's* waters is meant to change us, to spur us to ask the ultimate question of "what?" What am I? What is my true worth? What is my real existence? For what purpose am I here?

Having been inspired by the students of a certain Rebbe, a businessman by the name of Chaim Moshe decided to pay a visit to their teacher to gain insight and inspiration from his Divine service.

Upon entering the Rebbe's study, the man introduced himself.

The Rebbe asked him, "What are you?"

Chaim Moshe explained that he did business in the various villages and larger surrounding cities.

"What are you?" repeated the Rebbe.

Unsure what the Rebbe was asking, this time Chaim Moshe replied more particularly, explaining the exact nature of his business, the products he sold, where he purchased and how he gained profits.

"And what are you?" the Rebbe continued to probe.

A baffled Chaim Moshe remained silent. "I don't understand the Rebbe's inquiry," he finally managed.

"You are explaining to me what you do, your occupation, your business dealings. What I am questioning, though, is not what you do, but rather what are you? What are you accomplishing with your life that is meaningful? Is the focus of your life your business or your Creator?"

The waters of the *mikve* beckon us to replace the *"ani,"* the *"me"* and its egotistical slant, with *"ayin,"* nothingness (a rearrangement of the same Hebrew letters). This *ayin* is the awareness that "there is nothing other than G-d," that Divinity and G-dly spirituality is the only meaningful reality.

When we are ready to substitute the *"ani"* with *"ayin,"* we emerge from the waters with a new realization that allows us to experience a rebirth of our true selves. Having subjugated our static egos to the Divine Will, we've made room and opened ourselves up to perceptive growth. We leave the waters with a newfound consciousness, effectively capable of responding to the existential question of *"mah."*

This realization frees us from the confinement of viewing the world as orbiting around ourselves, and permits us to embrace the freedom of Divine expression. Contrary to popular thought, by removing our egos from the picture, we don't emerge as a non-entity, but rather become empowered and confident to develop and discover our true selves.

In the little, silly village of Chelm, Motti had a dilemma. He was about to immerse in the mikve, as was the weekly custom before Shabbat. He feared, however, that since, under the waters of the mikve, everyone is unclothed and looks exactly the same, he might forget who he was. For in the pool of the mikve, there are only similar bodies, and how would Motti identify himself?

Motti was deep in thought, perplexed with this problem until he came up with a brilliant solution. He would tie a red string around his big toe. That way, while in the waters of the mikve and even after he left, he would know that the individual with the red string on his toe was indeed Motti.

Satisfied, Motti went to the mikve's bathhouse and confidently prepared to immerse in the mikve. Once inside the waters, Motti periodically glimpsed at his large right toe, strung with the red string, and silently gave praise to the Almighty for making him so bright, that he thought of such brilliant solutions to help him remember that he was himself. He pitied other men who had absolutely no way of knowing who they really were.

After some time, Motti emerged from the waters and began dressing. To his utter horror, when he looked down at his right toe, he saw that the red string was missing. Now he was in a real quandary: he couldn't be Motti, because Motti had a red string to help identify himself. Yet if he wasn't Motti, then who, indeed, was he?

The waters of the *mikve* are meant to nullify the individual who entered, so that the one who leaves does so as a remade person.

For this reason, the *mikve* must contain a minimum of forty *seah*[188] (the equivalent of about two hundred gallons of water), in order that "He shall cover all his flesh in water" (Lev. 15:16).

The largest human body has a volume of twenty *seah*. However, something that is mixed with twice its volume is considered nullified.[189] Therefore, the *mikve* must contain minimally forty *seah* of water, to "nullify" our sense of self, so that when we emerge, we experience a spiritual rebirth.

For this reason, as well, we are commanded *"Verachatz,"* "wash," with the waters of the *mikve*. *Rachatz* is phonetically related to *raatz*,[190] "break down," and *lachatz*,[191] "crush." Purification in the *mikve* is meant to break down the ego and crush the selfish sense of self.

Therefore, the waters of the *mikve* must be natural, collected without passing through or over anything capable of being defiled. When immersing in the *mikve*, we are re-establishing our link with mankind's perfected state.

All the waters of the world have their source in the original river that emerged from Eden.[192] By immersing ourselves in these undefiled, naturally gathered waters, we reconnect to our source and our perfected original state, in Eden.

Thus, the Hebrew letters of *mikve* can also be rearranged to spell *"komah,"* rising and standing upright. Liberated from the weighty shackles of self-importance, and reconnected to his source, man rises to greater heights and grows towards Divine goals. While his egotistical self may be broken, he has freed himself to develop his potential.

Furthermore, this concept of connecting and reconnecting to one's source is clearly observed in water creatures.[193] Animals of the sea, while varied and diverse like land creatures, differ from the latter in that they are constantly connected to their source of life—the water—and submerged within it.

On the other hand, land creatures, while connected to the earth and their source of sustenance, nevertheless can be apart from it for long periods. For a fish to leave the sea, however, is antithetical to its existence. [194]

Similarly, by submerging ourselves in the *mikve*, which originates from the waters of Eden, we remind ourselves that, like water creatures, we must remain connected to our source, the G-dly dimension of existence, which is true reality. This realization gives rise to the individual's rebirth, so that he embraces dynamic change in his quest to reunite with his original pure state and Divine source.

During the era of Roman domination over the Land of Israel, religious expression and the study of Torah was suppressed and punished with cruel tortures—often with death.

The Jewish leaders, at extreme personal risk, continued teaching Torah and encouraging their people's adherence to its mitzvot.

Rabbi Akiva explained: "A sly fox wishes to lure a prize fish from its home in the sea.

"The fox persuasively reasons, 'Look around you at all the dangers lurking in the deep waters: the fisherman's nets, the larger fish searching for a meal, the rampant pollution. Why not leave these waters behind? I'll help you establish a better life, here, on the firm, solid ground, where the dangers of the sea aren't ever-present and all encompassing.'

"Replies the wise fish, 'True, there are many dangers in the sea, and I must maintain a vigilant guard at all times. Nevertheless, if I abandon the sea and its life-sustaining waters, I will surely die.'"

Says Rabbi Akiva: "The Jew, as the fish in the water, must be immersed in his soul's nourishment—the Torah and its mitzvot. Though at times the dangers of Torah study and the fulfillment of its precepts threaten our very life, without it—like the fish without its water—we would all surely perish."

The waters of the *mikve* remind us to connect to our true source, and encourage us to experience spiritual rejuvenation and rebirth through them.

Therefore, the *mikve* hints to the embryonic womb, the place of birth. The forty *seah* of the *mikve* waters represent the forty days needed for an embryo to take human form. Halachically, the embryo has no status, nor is it discernible, until forty days after conception.[195]

Similarly, the earth was remade and purified by the forty days of rain during Noah's flood, similar to the forty *seah* of the *mikve*'s waters. Cleansing the world from the defilement of its inhabitants, Noah's water gave rise to a new world, in closer harmony with its Divine source.[196]

The waters of Noah were not meant as a punishment for the world, but, like the waters of the *mikve*, served as a cleansing and purifying agent, giving birth to a world with less lust and poised to discover its Creator. Therefore, the waters are called *"mei Noach,"* the waters of Noach. The word *noach* also means peacefulness and consolation, and alludes to the positive facet of these waters, that they were not strictly punitive, but redemptive. These waters erased negativity and brought a fresh awareness, sensitivity and consolation to creation.

Similarly, after the sin of the spies, the Jews of the wilderness needed to wait forty years before meriting entering the Land of Israel. These forty years of wandering represented the rebirth of the nation, with a new generation which would recognize and implement their G-dly mission.

Furthermore, the forty *seah* of the *mikve* hints to the birth process of creation as a whole. The world was created through ten utterances, which descended through four stages or worlds. Thus, the ten utterances multiplied by the four worlds totals forty phases in the birth of the world. The forty *seah* of the *mikve* evokes the image of, and brings us back to, the primeval state of the creation, or birth, of the world.

For the world in its original state was covered with water: "G-d's spirit hovered over the face of the water" (Gen 1:2). Only on the second day were the waters divided: into upper waters, representing the male dimension, and lower waters, representing the female dimension of all of reality.[197]

On the third day,[198] creation underwent a new *mikve*, a gathering of waters, with the division of sea from earth. This *mikve* represents the feminine waters, and the original "womb" of creation. From this womb, the world and man would be born and formed.

Therefore, immersion in the *mikve* represents rebirth and entry into the new status of an undefiled world. We emerge, cleansed of our ego, as an infant, completely removed from impurity or defilement, untouched. We have been born anew, divorced of our restrictive selfish selves, subject only to G-d's creative powers.

For this reason, a *mikve* must be built in the ground,[199] in order to resemble a grave, the other end point in the cycle of life. When immersing completely in water, we place ourselves into an environment in which it is impossible for us to live—a place without air. Momentarily, we enter into the realm of non-living, so that when we exit, we do so as an innocent newborn. [200]

As such, we transcend the limits of time, entering a zone where past, present and future converge in one instant—the instant of the here-and-now. In that moment, we are free to give birth to a new identity.[201]

Thus, the *mikve* waters also allude to the waters of purification that G-d will sprinkle on us to remove the "spirit of impurity,"[202] in the era of redemption. It represents the rebirth of creation, as a whole, when all humanity will attain the perfection and purity for which it was originally destined.

"They shall not hurt or destroy . . . for the earth shall be filled with the knowledge of G-d, like waters cover the sea" (Isa. 11:9).

The foretaste of this renewal is the waters of the *mikve*. These waters allude to the future waters of knowledge that will encompass all of mankind with a new awareness. Listening to the message of the *mikve* provides us with a foretaste of this era, now. It allows us, at least temporarily, to remove the ego-centered shackles of exile and experience a glimpse of the future reality when the true unity of all existence will be obvious.

Women, who are in tune with their own spiritual rebirth and renewal, and who, generally, are more intrinsically connected to the concept of *bitul*, can more fully experience the lesson of the *mikve* and grasp the deep message of its still waters.

Mikve.

A gathering of water.
A gathering of past.
And future.
Into the absolute present.
The only instant of time,
Where man has control.
And places his hope,
In the hands of G-d.

Mikve.
A gathering of waters.
Upper waters—
Rain.
Lower waters—
Springs.
From creation's masculine elements,
And from its feminine ones.

Mikve.
A gathering of waters.
Untouched, undefiled, natural.
A direct link,
To the original waters,
Of the world's perfected state.
A world yet unborn,
Emerging from the Garden of Eden,
Subject only to the creative powers of G-d.

Mikve.
A gathering of water.
Representing rebirth, cleansing.
A minimum of forty seah,
Forty days for the embryo,
To take shape in a form.
Forty days of Noah's flood water,
To cleanse and purify the world.
Forty years in the desert,
To experience an entire generation's rebirth.
Forty seah, double the volume,
Of the largest human body,
To nullify the ego—
The essence of spiritual purification.

For Further Reflection

- How do the mitzvot of the Jewish woman make our home into a *mikdash me'at*—a microcosm of the Holy Temple?
- Is the world of materialism and physicality antithetical to the world of spirituality and transcendence? Explain.
- A relationship entails going beyond what you rationally understand for the sake of another. Give examples from your own life of how your sacrifices strengthened your relationships.
- How can you make Shabbat a day of inner peace and harmony for yourself? For your friends or family?
- What is selfish love? What is real love?
- Why do human beings marry?
- How can we develop mutual respect in a marriage?
- The Talmud (*Kiddushin* 2b) speaks of a man finding his wife as looking for his "lost half." What are the implications for this idea vis-à-vis the man-woman relationship?

Section Three

TIME
Feminine Influence
The Role of Women in the Celebration and Formation of the Holidays

❧ Rosh Hashana
   Chana's Prayer: A Guide to Touch the Divine
❧ Chanuka
   The Paradox: Women in the Miracle and Celebration of Chanuka
❧ Purim
   Esther: A Paradigm of Self-Sacrifice
❧ Pesach
   Miriam's Tambourines: Vision and Courage
❧ Shavuot
   Ruth, Mother of Mashiach
   Nitzevet, Mother of King David: The Bold Voice of Silence
❧ Tisha B'Av
   A Feminine Journey: The Era of Redemption

Rosh Hashana

CHANA'S PRAYER
A Guide to Touch the Divine

Rosh Hashana, the beginning of the new year, is a holy, spiritual time when prayer plays a prominent role. In the Haftara of Rosh Hashana, we read about the experience and perspective of Chana, a woman who taught us how to pray. Through one woman, the inner dimension of prayer emerges for all future generations of both men and women.

Recalling the Rosh Hashana services of our childhood inspires in many of us an aura of reverence and holiness. As we awaited the blowing of the shofar, or as we glanced at the faces of the adults surrounding us, the spirituality was palpable in the atmosphere.

Growing older, special tunes or melodies have become our favorites while others evoke a special feeling inside us. At some point, we may be touched by something greater than ourselves, yet emanating from deep within, inspiring appreciation and awe of our Creator.

The Essence of Rosh Hashana

The major theme of the Rosh Hashana liturgy is the acceptance and recognition of G-d's sovereignty over creation. This consciousness serves as the basis of all of Judaism. Moreover, the very essence of reality is dependent on this dynamic.

G-d, as it were, expresses his desire to interact with our reality as Sovereign of the Universe.

We, in turn, express our awareness that our perfection, as well as the perfection of all creation, is dependent on our submission to the all-encompassing unity of G-d. Hence our prayer, "Rule over the entire world in Your glory" (Rosh Hashana Liturgy), expresses our recognition that the very essence of our being is dependent on its recognition of its Divine origin.

Praying for Material Concerns

Although several of the Rosh Hashana prayers deal with G-d's sovereignty, we also petition Him for the specific needs of the individual or for the well-being of the Jewish people and of all humanity. Among several examples, we ask:

And may we be remembered before You in the Book of Life, Blessing and Peace and Good Livelihood and Goodness and Salvation and Comfort and Good Decrees . . . for Life and Goodness and Peace. (Rosh Hashana Liturgy)

Is it appropriate on the day when we focus on the essence of our relationship with G-d to sprinkle our prayers with personal requests for mundane needs?

Furthermore, the *Zohar* censures someone who focuses on their own needs. "A person who makes personal requests during the Days of Awe resembles a parasitic leech crying, 'Give, give!'" (*Tikkunei Zohar* 22a).

How can this statement be reconciled with the repeated requests for personal needs, interspersed throughout the Rosh Hashana liturgy by the great Rabbis of the Holy Assembly (who authored these prayers approximately 2,200 years ago)?

Prayer in General

The above difficulties regarding our Rosh Hashana prayers apply to the mitzva of prayer in general.

Prayer is a Biblical obligation. Although the specific times of prayer, as well as the text of the liturgy, were formulated by the Talmudic sages, the basic obligation is Biblical.

The sages derive this obligation from the verse: "And now Israel, what does G-d ask of you? Only to fear G-d, to go in His path and to love *and serve G-d with all your heart and soul*" (Deut. 10:12).

The Talmud[203] explains that serving G-d with our heart refers to the act of prayer. Prayer is considered a service of the heart because it is the expression of a deep and heartfelt emotional bond with our Creator. Prayer is not simply reading a text, but rather a *service* that needs to be worked on with *all our heart and soul* to experience this connection and transcendence.

However, Maimonides specifies that the Biblical obligation of prayer includes the requirement of beseeching G-d for our specific, personal needs.

"The obligation of prayer is such that a person implores and prays every day in the following manner: One begins by stating the praise of G-d, *afterwards he asks for his needs,* and then he concludes with praise and thanksgiving to G-d for the good and abundance that He has bestowed upon him." 204

If the essence of prayer is the expression of our innermost bond with G-d, why is it necessary, in fact obligatory, to request personal, mundane needs?

Furthermore, on Rosh Hashana, when we are renewing our relationship with G-d, how can we possibly ask for personal desires?

Haftarat Chana

The key to a proper understanding of the Rosh Hashana prayers, as well as prayer in general, is appropriately found in the *haftara* of the day. The *haftara* records a prayer that was recited on Rosh Hashana by Chana, the prophetess

In the year 2830, during the era of the Judges, Elkana from the tribe of Levi lived in Ramatayim Tzofim. Elkana was married to two wives, Chana and Penina. The childless Chana silently suffers humiliation from her more fortunate rival, Penina, who has mothered several children.

According to some commentaries, Penina "provoked Chana bitterly to irritate her," not out of malice and spite, but precisely to cause her to feel such acute pain that she would resort to intense prayers.

Elkana takes his family on a yearly pilgrimage to Shilo, site of the Mishkan, the temporary spiritual center preceding the Temple. Solemnly, Chana enters the holy Mishkan, offering heartfelt prayers for a child.

Many laws of prayer are derived from Chana's conduct, most notably, reciting the *Amida*, the climax of our prayers, silently: "Only her lips moved, but her voice was not heard."

Eli, the High Priest, unaccustomed to such prayers, "thought that she was drunk."

An interesting exchange ensues between Eli and Chana.

Eli reprimands Chana: "How long will you be drunk? Sober up!"

Chana responds: "No, my lord, I am a woman of sorrowful spirit; I have drunk neither wine nor spirits, but have poured out my soul before the L-rd."

Eli concludes: "Go in peace; and may the G-d of Israel grant your request."

The following year a son, Shmuel, was born to Chana. When Shmuel is weaned, Chana brings him to the Mishkan to be taught by Eli. Young Shmuel grows up to become Shmuel Hanavi, the great, fearless prophet who coronated the first kings of Israel, King Shaul and King David.

Questions

There are some glaring questions on this story:

i) Eli, the High Priest and one of the Judges, was wise and experienced in dealing with people. Why did he judge Chana so harshly without investigating her real motives?

ii) The Torah never dwells on the negative (for example, when discussing animals that are *tahor* [pure] and *tameh* [impure], the Torah uses extra words to write *"asher eino tahor he"* [which are not pure] just in order to avoid using the word *tameh*). Why is it necessary to record Eli's obvious misjudgment? What are we to learn from Eli's conduct?

iii) What is the deeper connection and relevance of this story to Rosh Hashana (other than that it possibly occurred on Rosh Hashana)?

Eli and Chana's Conversation

To address these issues, we need to closely examine the conversation between Eli and Chana.

When questioning Chana, Eli asks, "How long will you be drunk? Put away your wine from you."

Eli did not actually believe that Chana was intoxicated, or he would have been required to remove her immediately from the premises out of respect for the holiness of the Mishkan. Eli's words must be understood figuratively.

Eli was asking Chana, "How long will you remain intoxicated by your own desires? How long will you remain so absorbed in your own needs, drunk with your own wants? Ask for your needs, but don't become obsessed with them."

To this, Chana responds: "No, I am not drunk with personal concerns. My prayers are not selfish. I have poured out my soul from the core of my being."

Chana's response sheds light on why we experience physical desires.

On a Simple Level

A Jew's most basic and innate desire is to fulfill his mission in life. To do this, we need health and financial means in order to focus on the meaningful and spiritual dimension. As we pray for health or material sustenance, it is not an end to itself but rather our means to serve G-d.

Chana did not pray solely for the pleasures and *nachat* a parent derives from a child. She wanted to play her part in bringing into the world another Jewish soul who would dedicate his/her life to G-d.

On a Deeper Level

A verse in Psalms (107:5) reads, "Hungry and thirsty, their soul longs within." Simply, this means that an individual who is thirsty or hungry longs for sustenance.

The Baal Shem Tov provides a novel explanation. "Why are they hungry and thirsty? Because 'their soul longs within.' Their soul seeks a bond with the G-dly energy contained in the food and drink." [205]

Man's purpose is to refine this material world and give expression to its innate G-dliness. All physical matter has a specific G-dly purpose and our Divine service causes this to be realized. Every individual is assigned a corner of physical reality to uplift.

Through every mitzva, physical matter becomes elevated. Say a *bracha* (blessing) on kosher food and you have given expression to its Divine purpose, unifying it with its source. Desire something physical and you are experiencing your soul's deep longing to unite "your" corner of physical reality with its G-dly intent.

Should man not elevate those aspects of physical reality which he was meant to, "his soul longs within," for not having completed his mission.

Chana, too, wanted to sanctify her son to G-d. The purpose of her requesting a son was not for personal reasons. She "poured out her soul"—her request was initiated from deep within her being.

Haftarat Chana and Rosh Hashana

Rosh Hashana focuses on G-d's sovereignty and creation's acceptance of His Kingship. G-d did not desire to remain in the spiritual spheres, but wanted a relationship with human beings in our physical world.

Physical desires are a manifestation of this truth. We cannot serve G-d properly when we lack physical necessities. Furthermore, fulfilling the mitzvot depends on the specific physical items associated with any given mitzva. Our attraction to the physical is an expression of our soul's yearning to facilitate the G-dly mandate of *dira betachtonim,* a dwelling for G-d in our physical realm.

So ask for material blessings on Rosh Hashana, as well as throughout the year. But as you do, listen to Chana's inner message. Meditate on G-d's sovereignty over creation. Reaffirm your mandate by asking for the material items necessary to realize your personal goal of transforming reality into an expression of G-d's unity.

At the same time, remember Eli's dialogue. Eli's questioning teaches the necessity of introspection during prayer. Requesting material blessing is appropriate and commanded. But experience Eli, the High Priest within you, confronting you about your motives for these desires.

Chana's Second Prayer

This leads to Chana's second prayer, recited after Shmuel's birth (1 Sam., chap. 2) giving praise and thanksgiving to G-d. This prayer refers to a new era of Mashiach when there will be no conflict or dichotomy between the material and the spiritual, since Divinity will openly permeate all reality.

In this second prayer, the ultimate direction and purpose of all our work becomes apparent. "The adversaries of the L-rd shall be broken . . . and He shall give strength to His king, and exalt the horn of His anointed." His anointed refers to Mashiach and describes the culmination of creation, when reality will be visibly imbued with Divinity.

Experiencing Chana's Message

On Rosh Hashana, the anniversary of mankind's creation, experience the message of one woman—Chana, the prophetess, who revealed the inner dimension of prayer and many of its basic laws, as well as the interface between our most essential physical and spiritual needs.

Chanuka

THE PARADOX

Women in the Miracle & Celebration of Chanuka

Chanuka represents a special time for the Jewish people, when light and right won over the dark and evil forces of the world. We celebrate the freedom of our people to observe their religion and, in a deeper sense, we renew our own commitment as we face the challenges of our own times. Women played a prominent role both as victims of the harsh decrees issued against our people, as well as in their ultimate victory and salvation.

The scene is the Jewish family home one Chanuka evening. The bright Chanuka lights illuminate the darkness as the family gathers together, drawn to the glow of the lamps.

Although Chanuka represents the freedom of the entire Jewish people from Greek assimilation and subjugation, perhaps less well known is that for women, in particular, Chanuka signifies a more intimate and personal freedom. It represents the Jewish woman's freedom from personal violations against her purity and integrity.

Interestingly, however, the Chanuka scene in most of our minds is of the family gathered around as the father (and son) lights his *menora,* while the wife and daughters stand passively watching on the sidelines.

Do the rituals, festivities or laws of Chanuka in any way reflect or pay tribute to women's personal salvation and victory from the hands of the Greeks?

Women's Obligation

Ordinarily, women are exempt from time-bound, positive mitzvot, due to their time constraints as mothers and wives. But in three separate sources in the Talmud, women are mentioned as obligated to keep specific time-bound, positive mitzvot on account of their particular involvement in those commandments.

One of these obligations is the Chanuka lights. The reason is as follows:

i) The decrees of the Greeks were on all Jews but, even more so, specifically on the women. The Greeks decreed that on the night of her wedding, every woman would first be violated by the local governor. Thus, when the miracle of Chanuka came about, though it was a salvation for all Jews, women especially encountered a very personal freedom.

ii) Furthermore, the miracle of Chanuka happened through a woman—the beautiful widow Yehudit (Judith) bravely killed the Greek general Holifornus after intoxicating him with her wine and cheese. This victory was a turning point for the Jews.

Another woman to impact upon the war was the daughter of Matityahu. At her wedding, before all the prominent guests, she stood up and ripped off her gown. Her brothers, thoroughly embarrassed and outraged by her actions, wanted to kill her for her immodesty.

She reprimanded them, "Why does seeing me like this bother you, yet knowing that immediately after my wedding I will be taken by the Greek general, does not?!" Her words aroused her brothers to battle the Greeks.

Thus, women's stronger connection to Chanuka is twofold. Through the violation of Jewish women, the Greeks were personally attacking her purity and integrity. Furthermore, the salvation came about through women and, therefore, its victory is all the more meaningful for them.

Women's deeper connection to the Chanuka victory should be reflected in the laws of Chanuka; that in some aspect, her participation or involvement should be more intense than man's.

The *Shulchan Aruch* (sec. 675) states that a woman may light the Chanuka lights even for the men in her household.

Similar to the laws of Shabbat candles, the Chanuka candles are not an obligation placed on individuals but rather on the family as a whole, which any adult can perform. Unlike the *menora*, Shabbat candles have been specifically entrusted to the woman to light on behalf of her family. The Chanuka lights, however, have not been entrusted specifically to either the husband or the wife. The mitzva applies to both.

Why Women Don't Light the Menora

Nevertheless, even if women are entrusted *equally* with this mitzva, how is their *stronger* connection to the miracle represented?

Furthermore, the custom amongst most of us is that a wife and daughters do not light the Chanuka lights at all. How can this be understood, especially in view of women's deeper connection to Chanuka?

Various commentaries provide explanations on why women do not light the *menora*. These include the fact that from the Torah's perspective, the concept of a marriage is one in which the union is so strong that the two submerge into one unit. Therefore, "*ishto kegufo*," husband and wife are considered as one, and the husband's *menora* includes in it his wife's.

This explanation, however, does not answer why a single daughter does not light her own *menora*, or why the husband, and not the wife, takes the leading role.

Another answer given is that the *menora* was lit outside of the home and it was not considered modest or respectful for a woman to go outside at night amongst the males. This custom, although inapplicable today, has remained.

Others see a more plausible reason being that many women in the past may have been woefully unlearned and perhaps unable to make the proper blessings. In sensitivity for their fellow sisters, all women refrained from lighting and thereby avoided embarrassing these illiterate women.

The above explanations supply the practical reasons behind this custom. These do not, however, address women's stronger, intrinsic connection to Chanuka.

Working While the Lights Are Burning

In the laws of Chanuka (*Shulchan Aruch*, sec. 670), women are singled out as being prohibited from working while the candles are burning (or in some places, during the entire Chanuka holiday) due to their inner connection to the miracle of Chanuka.

What is the deeper meaning of this custom? How does refraining from work show women's deeper connection to Chanuka?

To understand this, we need to first appreciate the concept of work in general. All Jews are commanded to abstain from any type of creative work on the holy Shabbat. This is because the holiness of the day penetrates and permeates every aspect of our lives. Doing work profanes this holiness.

Why then is work permitted on some holidays, including Chanuka?

According to the mystical traditions, the spirituality embodied in the holiday of Chanuka is a far greater spiritual light than many of the other holidays, and even of Shabbat. The spiritual light of Chanuka is essentially associated with the future, with the Messianic era. This spirituality does not permeate our reality at this time, because it is too high and too intense.

While the spirituality generated on Shabbat and Yom Tov is intense, it is not too lofty to be absorbed and directed into our reality. Therefore, in our realm of reality, we abstain from all work on these days.

However, the spiritual light generated by the holiday of Chanuka is too intense and concentrated to be absorbed in our reality of exile. Rather, it is as if it hovers over our existence. Since it doesn't penetrate our realm of reality, it does not affect us by prohibiting us from work.

Women, however, are prohibited from working while the candles are burning.

Though the holiness of Chanuka does not permeate or have a connection to all of existence, it does have an inner connection to women.

Since the Greeks' subjugation and decrees against the Jewish people touched women in a more intimate way—personally, to their very core—the spiritual salvation of Chanuka and its light and holiness also touches them in a deeper way. This deeper, inner spiritual connection is what caused the victory of Chanuka to come about specifically through a woman.

Absorbing the Message

Women do not customarily light the Chanuka lights, since lighting is not the main element of the *menora*. The essential point of Chanuka and of its candles is absorbing and integrating the holiness generated by this light.

For the various reasons mentioned above, the ceremonious part of the holiday—the actual lighting of the *menora*—was left to the men.

Women's connection, however, lies far deeper. It is an inner connection—touching their essential selves.

Women's refraining from work reflects their ability to absorb the spiritual light and holiness of the holiday. They react in a manner similar to Shabbat and Yom Tov, during which work is forbidden due to the immense degree of spirituality. Women's connection to Chanuka is in essence a connection of the future, to the Messianic era, when these lights and intense spirituality will be readily incorporated within our reality.

A woman has a taste of that reality every night of Chanuka—as she refrains from work—while she watches and absorbs the message of its glimmering candles.

Purim

ESTHER

A Paradigm of Self-Sacrifice

A lthough each of the Jewish holidays has unique qualities and characteristics, there is only one that will be celebrated in the era of the redemption. This is the festival of Purim.[206] The superiority of Purim over the other holidays stems from the strong attachment to G-d that the Jewish people attained during the prelude to the miracles of Purim. This was accomplished through the courageous and pious efforts of the heroine of the Megilla, Esther.

A superficial study of the Book of Esther *(Megillat Esther)* reveals almost a fairy tale—an orphaned Jewish girl meets her prince-in-waiting.

The *Megilla* was recorded during the fourth century B.C.E.,[207] when the Jews were subjects of the Persian Empire. To compose it in a way that would be inoffensive to the Persian King, much of the inner workings had to be concealed between the lines, visible only to the discerning eye.

A careful read reveals a grotesque tragedy befalling a righteous woman. Esther's personal plight is the most gripping component of the *Megilla*. In order to indulge an alcoholic king's pleasure, Esther is coerced into undergoing a twelve-month beauty treatment in a harem.

As Esther's turn to meet the king approaches, she is hoping against hope not to become the First Lady of a world empire. But she is chosen. Esther is crowned queen and placed in the royal palace, the stage of the Persian Empire, infamous for its gluttonous passion and depraved, pleasure-seeking ways.

Esther, or Hadassa (called so because of her sterling spiritual beauty),[208] abhorred life in this defiled society. Commentaries[209] point out that Esther was originally radiantly beautiful, but after living in a constant state of revulsion,[210] her complexion developed a greenish pallor. Even so, her inner beauty shone through, entrancing all who met her.[211]

A Double Tragedy

The tragedy of Esther's life, however, runs far deeper. Esther was not only a refined Jewish girl forced to live with a gentile king, a terrible aberration in its own right. Esther was, in fact, already *married*!

Not only was Esther married, she was—and remained—married to the leader of the Jewish people, Mordechai.[212]

Yet, amidst the agony of being forced to live such a conflicting double life—as the wife of the holy Jewish sage[213] and simultaneously as the queen of a vulgar king—Esther maintained her piety masterfully.

A close examination of the narrative, with the aid of Midrashic and Rabbinical sources, exposes Esther's true ordeal and conduct within the hedonistic Persian palace.

Life in the Palace

The *Megilla* relates that Vashti, King Achashverosh's (Ahasueres) first queen, was executed by orders he gave while drunk. He became lonely and sought a new queen, ordering that all the pretty, young maidens be gathered to Shushan, the capital city of the Persian Empire.

When the young women were congregated, they were assigned to Hegai, guardian of the women. He allocated cosmetics and ointments to the incumbents, who were beginning their twelve-month beauty treatment. He also appropriated supplies that might enhance the women's attractiveness for their future appointment with the king. The girls asked for a variety of jewelry and clothing.[214]

The *Megilla* records that Esther didn't ask for anything to enhance her beauty since she had no desire to impress the king. She secretly tried to decrease her chances of charming Achashverosh so that she would be rejected and sent home to her family.[215]

Esther made only one request—for seven maidservants. The Talmud[216] explains that Esther asked specifically for seven so that she could keep Shabbat. She rotated her seven maids daily so that the maid serving her on Shabbat, seeing her perform no work, assumed that Esther did no work on the remaining days of the week.[217] Esther was thereby able to observe Shabbat while still masking her identity as a Jewess, as per Mordechai's instructions.[218]

In fact, Esther's compliance with all of Mordechai's requests is attested to by the verse: "Esther continued to do Mordechai's bidding, just as when she was raised by him" (Esther 2:20).

The commentaries use these words as proof that the immorality and decadence of the king's palace did not prevent Esther from living a full Jewish life according to the training she had received from Mordechai. She observed Shabbat and the holidays, avoided non-kosher food, and even faithfully adhered to the laws of family purity,[219] visiting the *mikve* regularly so that she could join her husband, Mordechai, when she was permitted to him.

This double life required much cunning. To be a clandestine, religious Jewess who maintained veiled relations with her husband, while simultaneously attending to the dazzling palace lifestyle, wasn't simple. No wonder the Talmud asserts that Esther's royalty refers not only to her queenly clothing and position, but to her royalty of spirit.[220] In the midst of the world's center of depravity, the holy prophetic spirit clothed Esther.

Salvation through Pain

Considering Esther's saintliness, there emerges a perplexing question. G-d, who orchestrated all these events, certainly could have contrived a less traumatic means to save His people from Haman's wicked plot of annihilation. Even if Esther's conduct was permitted according to Jewish law,[221] what purpose was served by degrading the refined Esther? In fact, Mordechai discerned Divine intervention from the very unusual set of circumstances leading to the coronation of his wife.[222]

To understand why the miracle had to be performed in this unusual way, we have to analyze what initiated the entire chain of events.

The first tragic turn of fate for the Jewish people occurred when Haman persuaded the King to issue a law calling for the annihilation of the Jewish people. In truth, however, this was the consequence of the errant behavior of the Jews.

The Party

At the onset of the *Megilla*, in the year 371 B.C.E.,[223] King Achashverosh threw an extravagant party for all his subjects. Achashverosh was celebrating the third anniversary of his ascension to the throne. He celebrated this anniversary with an annual feast, but in this third year, he had multiple reasons for celebration. He had completed the building of his magnificent throne; he had finally secured his reign;[224] and he had taken Vashti as his queen.[225]

It is ironic that precisely at a feast celebrating her queenship, Vashti angered her drunken husband and was executed by him.[226] Unwittingly, she paved the way for Esther to be chosen as queen and to save her people.

In accordance with Achashverosh's invitations, citizens from throughout the one hundred and twenty-seven provinces came to Shushan to partake in the celebrations. And what a sight they beheld!

The affair was so lavish that resplendent golden goblets were used for the occasion. No cup was used more than once and no two goblets were alike. Yet, as magnificent as these utensils were, they dimmed in comparison to a select group of prominent vessels.[227] These were the holy vessels that had been used for the priestly service in the Beit Hamikdash (Holy Temple) that had been looted and razed almost seventy years earlier by the Babylonian King Nebuchadnetzer.

Achashverosh, too, was elegantly dressed. He adorned himself in special robes woven from pure golden threads and the finest colors of linen fabric. Besides their splendor, his garments were unique in that they had been worn before—by the Jewish High Priest in his services in the Beit Hamikdash.[228] At his feast, Achashverosh dared to don these holy, priestly robes and use these holy utensils.

This was, in fact, one of Achashverosh's main reasons for celebration. He was ecstatic that the ominous prophecy of Jeremiah,[229] promising the Jewish people's return to the Land of Israel after a seventy-year period of exile, would not occur. He therefore audaciously used the vessels and garments from the Holy Temple.

Mordechai detected these underlying reasons behind the celebrations. He warned the Jewish nation not to participate. However, apprehensive of appearing as ungrateful citizens, few

Jews heeded Mordechai's directive.[230] And so, the holy nation of G-d attended these degrading celebrations.

Chilul Hashem: Affronting G-d

To participate in an event extolling a Jewish future outside of the Holy Land was a disgrace to the Jewish people and an affront to G-d. By resigning themselves to life in exile, in essence, the Jewish people were acquiescing, and even celebrating, their separation from the Holy Land, from the Holy Temple and from G-d. This was a *"chilul Hashem,"* a flagrant desecration of G-d's Name.

Chilul Hashem, publicly disgracing G-d, is considered the ultimate detachment. Since *chilul Hashem* is a transgression of severe magnitude, it can be rectified only through the perpetrator's death. *Teshuva*, repentance, alone cannot erase the taint caused by *chilul Hashem*, but only when *teshuva* is accompanied by death does true atonement occur. The inner essence of the soul, which has never been disconnected from G-d, must be touched by the awesome experience of death to obtain forgiveness.

Husband-Wife Bond

An analogy to this concept would be of a husband-wife relationship. Suppose the husband offends his wife slightly. When he apologizes for his insensitivity, his thoughtlessness will be forgiven.

The husband, in this situation, has not terribly hurt his wife. She understands that her husband sincerely loves her, but has hurt her due to carelessness. Only the superficial, outer layers of their relationship have been affected. Inside, each is aware of the other's deep love. The apology reveals a deeper aspect of the relationship so that the insult is seen for what it is, a careless remark.

However, were a husband to publicly shame his wife and deliberately disgrace her, the apology that was sufficient in the former case is no longer adequate. Such a serious offense requires a correspondingly more earnest show of regret.

Since the husband has shown utter disregard for his wife, he will have to reveal a much deeper aspect of their relationship to prove his love. He may have to expose a hidden part of himself, in order for his wife to truly forgive him.

The husband-wife metaphor can be applied to the relationship between G-d and the Jewish people. There are certain sins that we consciously commit. While these sins disturb and disrupt our bond with G-d, they do not penetrate to the very core of our relationship. For sins of this nature, repentance—demonstrating true regret—is sufficient.

By publicly profaning G-d's Name, however, an individual creates a tremendous breach in the relationship. To repair this deep rupture, the very essence of the bond between the individual and G-d must be exposed. This rectification requires the revelation of the inner essence of one's soul, which is, and always remains, united with G-d.

Mesirat Nefesh: Self-Sacrifice

This revelation can be accomplished only through the process of *mesirat nefesh*, self-sacrifice. Life itself is one's dearest possession. By being willing to sacrifice this most precious possession, one demonstrates that nothing is more significant than the relationship and bond with G-d. His very life loses its value, when contrasted to the relationship with his Creator.

When Haman decreed the annihilation of the Jews, he was unwittingly giving the Jews the opportunity to repair their breach with G-d. Haman succeeded in issuing his decree, in order to bring about the rectification for the *chilul Hashem*. Unbeknown to Haman, he served as a tool to reunite G-d with His People.

The response of the Jewish people to Haman's decree caused this reconciliation. For an entire year—from the time that the decree was publicized until it would take effect—the Jews lived in a constant state of danger. Although they could have saved themselves by converting to the Persian religion, not one of them considered this avenue of escape. To the Jews of Persia, maintaining a bond with G-d was more valuable than life itself.

This self-sacrifice was sufficient to atone for the first level of *chilul Hashem*. At this level, the sin committed is a desecration of G-d's name by demonstrating a public disregard for G-d's Torah. The Jews rectified this deficiency in their service by being prepared to die, rather than renounce Judaism.

On a deeper level of *chilul Hashem*, however, a Jew not only desecrates the *Torah* of G-d but he publicly disgraces the *people* of G-d. We may suggest that death, alone, does not atone for one who publicly humiliates the *children* of the Almighty.[231]

The *chilul Hashem* caused by the Jews of Persia involved this latter level. They did not transgress any Torah precept at Achashverosh's feast. In fact, the commentaries note that Achashverosh had tables of kosher food set especially for the Jews. The crime of the Jewish people wasn't an affront against the Torah; it was an affront against the *Jewish people.*

By participating in the celebrations, the Jews were insinuating that they were no longer the Chosen People. For this crime, they required more than the atonement received when one sacrifices one's life for Torah. A higher level of self-sacrifice, a sacrifice *for the Jewish people*, was required.

For this the Jews needed Esther.

Mesirat Nefesh: Sacrificing the Soul

In the usual process of *mesirat nefesh*, one sacrifices physical life for G-d or His Torah. Although one's physical existence ends, his spiritual existence continues.

Moreover, dying for the sake of G-d strengthens one's connection with Him. By displaying an absolute love for G-d, an individual attains a higher spiritual state in the World-to-Come. For this reason, righteous saints often prayed to merit to die "*al kiddush Hashem*," for the sake of G-d.[232] Ultimately, it may be a spiritually pragmatic calculation to sacrifice one's worldly existence for a greater unity with G-d for all of eternity.

The highest level of *mesirat nefesh,* however, occurs when the self-sacrifice makes no sense. This ultimate level is experienced when the individual sacrifices not merely his physical body, but the most sacred of sacred, his *spiritual self* as well, for the sake of the Jewish people. Esther, due to her sublime soul, was chosen to fulfill this ultimate level of self-sacrifice, thereby completing the atonement needed for her people.

When Mordechai requested that Esther plead with King Achashverosh to save the Jews from the wicked decree of Haman, Esther agreed. She, a married Jewess, would voluntarily submit herself to the non-Jewish king in order to attempt to rescue her people.

Heroically, Esther replies to Mordechai, "*ka'asher ovaditi ovaditi*"—"whatever I will lose [by this act] I will doubly lose" (Esther 4:16). The commentaries analyze this unusual wording as implying that through her petitioning the king, Esther would suffer a double loss.

First, since voluntarily approaching the king was considered like an act of adultery, she would lose her husband, Mordechai.[233] Second, and most important, by knowingly committing the serious transgression of adultery, she would forego her spiritual future. Yet Esther wasn't thwarted by these considerations.

The righteous Esther was prepared to follow the instructions of Mordechai, the tzaddik of her generation, to reject the Torah in order to save her people. In her mind, she didn't anticipate any spiritual benefit from her heroic actions. On the contrary, she assumed she was surrendering her spiritual life because of her impending sin. Nevertheless, she was willing to sacrifice everything, even her eternal life, for her people's salvation.[234]

Spiritual death for the sake of the Jewish people, the children of G-d, is a level of *mesirat nefesh* that reveals the deepest core of the soul. It exposes the part of the soul most intimately connected to G-d—in fact, utterly united with Him.

Dying for the Sake of Love

To illustrate, let us return to the metaphor of a husband-wife relationship. When one spouse is prepared to give up his or her life to save the other, then this is the ultimate self-sacrifice. The spouse realizes that upon death, there will no longer be any relationship. Nevertheless, the love for one's spouse is so great that one is willing to forego the pleasure of the very relationship, for the sake of the other.

Likewise, Esther's actions demonstrated that her love for the Jewish people was so intense that she was willing to relinquish her spiritual future for them. By displaying such a love for the Jewish people, whose essence and core is one with G-d, Esther was showing a love for G-d. Ultimately, by sacrificing everything for the Jewish people, Esther was sacrificing everything for G-d.

Through this supreme self-sacrifice by the pious representative of the Jewish people, Esther was able to obtain atonement for their sins and annul the decree calling for their annihilation.[235]

Due to Esther, the Jews were finally able to celebrate appropriately, in the festivities of Purim each year.

After-thought

In our personal lives, we are not called upon to renounce our spiritual existence. Most of us are not called upon to sacrifice even our physical existence for the sake of the Torah or the Jewish people.

All of us, however, in our daily struggles and challenges are called upon to sacrifice some of our self-gratifying instincts for our more sublime, G-dly desires.

This, too, is hinted to in the *Megilla*. When Achashverosh threw his lavish party, his desire was *"La'asot kirtzon ish va'ish"* (Esther 1:8)—"to fulfill the will of every man and man." The Talmud[236] explains that this "man and man" refers both to the righteous Mordechai and the wicked Haman. Achashverosh erroneously believed that he could satisfy them both.

Chassidic teachings explain that within each and every individual there lurks a personal Haman, the base and selfish instincts of man. Within us all, there is also a Mordechai and an Esther, namely, our G-dly soul, the source of our desire to reach beyond the confines of our finite selves to achieve a higher truth. Man has been blessed with the freedom to choose between "man and man."

We can tap into the power of Esther's enormous self-sacrifice by acting with more resolve in overcoming our daily "Hamans" to achieve more "Mordechais." This capacity, exemplified by Esther, enables us to bring the ultimate redemption, a time when our closest and deepest relationship with G-d will become manifest.

Pesach

MIRIAM'S TAMBOURINES

Vision and Courage

O ur Sages teach that: *"In the merit of the righteous women, our forefathers were redeemed from Egypt."* Despite the bleakness of their situation, the women of that generation strengthened their faith in a better future. Pesach is the time when we relive the Exodus just as we tap into that strength, faith and energy.

Bitter was the daily fare of the Jewish slaves in their Egyptian exile. What began as forced labor steadily degenerated into acts of unspeakable brutality and horror, culminating in King Pharaoh's decree to murder all newborn male infants and his bathing in Jewish children's blood.

While the physical labor was back-breaking, the spiritual toll was similarly exacting. The family unit was shattered; wives separated from husbands who were forced to remain at their work sites in far-away fields.

Subjected to such unrelenting malice, the people were demoralized and depressed, stripped of any vestige of dignity or self-respect. Amidst the daily terror, feeling the burning whip searing their raw flesh while trying to fill impossible daily quotas, it seemed useless to hope for a better tomorrow.

The Jewish nation's heart had become too dulled, their minds too numbed and their bodies too worn to muster any faith.

One group of slaves, however, did not succumb, but carried in their heart an inextinguishable spark of optimism. They retained their human dignity; they continued to believe in a better life.

Encouraging their families daily with superhuman strength, they remained confident that their prayers would be answered.

This group of slaves was the Jewish women.

"In the merit of the righteous women of that generation, our forefathers were redeemed from Egypt."[237]

After an exhausting day of excruciating labor, the women would polish their mirrors and use them to beautify themselves for their husbands.[238]

At night, the women would sneak out to the men's camps, bringing hot, nourishing food. They would heat the water in the fields and bathe their husband's wounds.

The women spoke soft, soothing words. "Do not lose hope. We will not be slaves to these degenerates all our lives. We have G-d's promise that He will have mercy on us and redeem us" (*Bereishit Rabba*, chap. 27).

Many women conceived during these visits, subsequently giving birth to the children who would ensure the continuity of the Jewish people.

How did these Jewish women discover their reservoirs of hope amidst a hopeless situation?

The women had a leader and a teacher to emulate.

Her name was Miriam.

The Talmud comments (*Ta'anit* 9): "There were three excellent leaders for Israel. They were Moshe, Aharon and Miriam."

While Moshe and Aharon were leaders for all the people, "Miriam was the teacher of the women" (*Targum Micha* 6:4).

She was a teacher who led by example.

From where did Miriam derive her wellsprings of courage and vision?

Miriam's name has two meanings, both exemplifying the qualities of her character.

Miriam as Bitterness

The first, from the Hebrew root *mar*, means bitterness.

Miriam was born at the time that the oppression of the exile had reached its nadir. "And they [the Egyptians] embittered [from the root *mar*] the lives of the Jewish people with hard work" (Ex. 1:14).

Born into the worst period of servitude, Miriam felt the bitterness and ache of her people. Her earliest years were formed by the heartbreaking reality of the Jewish exile.

Witnessing the murders and torment, she shed rivers of tears with her brethren, praying incessant prayers, and hoping beyond hope for a better future.

Being personally exposed to the decrees of the wicked Pharaoh, no one could understand the bitterness of the exile better than Miriam.

Miriam as Rebellion

The other meaning of Miriam's name is rebellion (from the root *meri*).

Despite being born into the most difficult period of oppression, Miriam rebelled from her earliest age against the slave mentality engulfing her people.

Though she felt their pain acutely, she would not succumb to fear or despair. Though she was exposed to abject cruelty, she would not yield to moral corruption or apathy. Bravely and resolutely, she defended her convictions.

The Midwives

We are introduced to Miriam just as the new Pharaoh ascends the Egyptian throne. "There arose a new king over Egypt . . . And he spoke to the Hebrew midwives, the name of one was Shifra and the name of the other Pua.

"And he said, 'When you act as a midwife to the Hebrew women and see them on the birthing stool, if it is a son, you shall kill him, but if it is a daughter, she shall live.'"

Despite this decree, "The midwives feared G-d and did not act as the king of Egypt commanded them . . . And it came to pass because the midwives feared G-d that He made them Houses..." (Ex. 1:8-17).

Rashi explains that the names of the midwives mentioned were the professional names for Yocheved and Miriam.

Yocheved (Miriam's mother) was called Shifra because she was expert in beautifying (from the root *shafar*) and cleansing the newborn. Miriam, though still a child, was expert in cooing (from the root *pa'a*) to the newborn and calming a crying infant with her soothing voice.[239]

According to the Midrash,[240] Miriam was called Pua due to another episode. "She revealed her face brazenly [from the root *hofiya*] against Pharaoh, pronouncing, 'Woe to this man, when G-d avenges him!'

"Pharaoh was infuriated with Miriam's comment and wanted to have her killed. But Yocheved appeased him, 'Will you pay attention to her? She is but a child who doesn't realize to whom she is speaking, or what she is saying!'"

Miriam was only five years old at this time. Despite her tender years, she valiantly stood up to the mightiest ruler on earth, audaciously rebuking him for his cruelty to her people.

This was Miriam, the rebel.

Rebelling against the status quo, fighting against apathy and cruelty. Bravely, she and her mother disregarded Pharaoh's edict to murder the infant boys, even providing food and necessities for their survival.[241]

G-d repaid these valiant women by granting them "Houses"— from their descendants issued the dynasties of Priesthood, Levites and Kingship. Such positions of leadership could only be filled by the descendants of such women who would pass on their moral strength and convictions, enabling them to prevail over any acts of immorality or injustice.

Miriam's Confidence

Another incident in Miriam's childhood also reflects her strong character and ability to stand up against the status quo, and, despite the bleakness of the moment, find enduring faith in a more promising future.

The Talmud relates (*Sota* 12) that when Pharaoh decreed that all newborn baby boys be cast into the Nile River, Amram, Miriam's father, decided to divorce his wife.

As the preeminent leader of the generation, Amram was setting an example for all others. If no children would be born, innocent babies would not be killed.

All the men of the generation followed Amram's example, divorcing their own wives.

Observing this, Miriam approached her father, saying: "Father! Your decree is worse than Pharaoh's. Pharaoh only decreed against the males, but you are decreeing that our people should be bereft of both males and females!

"Pharaoh is a wicked man and therefore it is unlikely that his decree will stand, but you are righteous and your decree will be carried out.

"Furthermore, Pharaoh is only doing evil in this world. The murdered infants are innocent and have a portion in the World-to-Come. But your decree will deprive them of the next world, for if a child is never born, how can he gain a portion in the future world?[242]

"You must remarry Mother. She is destined to give birth to a son who will set Israel free!" (*Bamidbar Rabba, Naso*, chap. 13).

Miriam was six years old when she confronted her father. Her words made such a profound impact on him that he brought her before the Sanhedrin (Jewish Supreme Court) to repeat her petition.

The members of the Sanhedrin responded to Amram, "You forbade [us to remain married to our wives], you must now permit."

He said, "Should we return to our wives quietly?"

They answered, "And who will let all the Jewish people know [to likewise remarry their wives]?"(*Pesikta Rabosi* 43, 27).

Amram put his wife on a beautiful *chuppa* (bridal platform). Aharon and Miriam danced and sang before her, as before a bride. Miriam sang repeatedly, "My mother is destined to give birth to a son who will set Israel free!"

Though Yocheved was one hundred and thirty years old, her youth miraculously returned and she became beautiful as a fifteen-year-old. Even the ministering angels joined with them, singing, "joyous mother of children" (Ps. 113:9).

After seeing this, the rest of the Jewish men also remarried their wives. An entire generation was transformed, all due to the courage and vision of the young Miriam, who had the confidence to speak her mind and declare her prophecy.

Standing at the River

Shortly after, Yocheved gave birth to a son and saw that "he was good."

At the moment that Moshe was born, the entire house was filled with the holy light of his Divine radiance.[243] Amram kissed Miriam on her head and said to her, "My daughter, your prophecy has been fulfilled!"

The happiness of the moment was shattered, however, with the realization that this male child would be taken to be killed.

"And when Yocheved could no longer hide him, she took for him an ark made of reeds . . . and put the child in it and laid it in the rushes by the river's bank. And his sister [Miriam] stood far away, to see what would be done to him" (Ex. 2:3-4).

When they took Moshe to the river, the disheartened Yocheved hit Miriam on the head and said, "My daughter where is your prophecy now?" (*Shemot Rabba* 1:22).

But Miriam remained stubbornly resolute.

She stood by the river to see not *if*, but *how* her prophecy would unfold.

She, too, felt the pain and bitterness of her baby brother's being torn away from her family. But at the same time, she was filled with her spirit of rebellion—she would not succumb to hopelessness.

This was Miriam. She encompassed the dual qualities of feeling the intensity of pain while at the same time rebelling against its overpowering hold to discover a seed of faith and yearning, deep within.

In the thicket of the bushes, Miriam stood watch over her brother's fledgling life. It was she who witnessed Batya, the daughter of Pharaoh, come to bathe in the Nile River. Upon discovering the basket at the edge of the river and hearing the woeful cries of the infant within, Batya decided to rescue the child.

It was a self-assured Miriam who then suggested to Batya that she would bring the baby to a Hebrew wet-nurse. Unbeknownst to Batya, Miriam brought Moshe back to his own mother.

Moshe remained in his home, absorbing the crucial spiritual nourishment of these tender years until he was weaned. Only after being equipped with his parents' love and teachings was Moshe transferred back to the palace to begin his role as leader and redeemer.

Miriam was there, standing watch on the bank of the Nile, as her entire nation's future hung in balance, dependent on the precarious fate of an infant floating in a small basket in that mammoth river. But never did her faith in the redemption of her people falter. As the leader of the women, Miriam imbued this quality in their aching hearts. And it was this quality that empowered the righteous women to be the channel for bringing the redemption.

The Women's Song

We are now many decades later, on the shores of the Red Sea.

Moshe has grown, and has returned from Midian as the divinely appointed redeemer of his people. G-d had performed the wondrous Ten Plagues to punish the Egyptian's cruelty and free His people from their oppression. The people have marched triumphantly out of Egypt. Then, as they were being chased by a recalcitrant king and his army, G-d miraculously split the sea, saving His people and drowning their enemies.

Finally, after hundreds of years in exile, their enemies had been utterly thwarted and the Jews experienced a complete, miraculous salvation. The Jewish people's ordeal in Egypt was over! Their servitude had come to an end and their redemption was palpable.

Standing at the shores of the Red Sea, the Jewish people, under the direction of their leader, Moshe, begin to sing *Az Yashir*, a song expressing their ecstatic gratitude and thanksgiving to G-d.

And as Moshe and his nation conclude their song, something inexplicable happens.

"And Miriam the prophetess, the sister of Aharon, took a tambourine in her hand; and all the women went out after her with tambourines, dancing. And Miriam answered them, 'Sing to the L-rd . . .'" (Ex. 15:20-21).

Moshe and the men sang their song. And then Miriam and the women rose to sing their song.

The men sang with their voices. And the women sang with voice, tambourines and dance. The women's hearts were full of a greater joy and their song was more comprehensive.

Tambourines of Faith

What was the women's contribution to the singing? Why did Miriam and the women's singing surpass the men's song?

Rashi (Ex. 15:20) explains how the women had these tambourines with them. "The righteous women of that generation were confident that the Holy One Blessed be He would make for them miracles, so they prepared tambourines and dances."

When the Jewish people left Egypt, they left hastily. So hastily, in fact, that they were not even able to finish baking their bread, and it baked flat on their backs as matza. The women were not concerned about their physical sustenance; they were certain that G-d would provide. They lived in a higher dimension, beyond the natural reality. Yet despite their hurriedness, the women took the time to prepare, well in advance, something that they felt would be essential.

After hundreds of years in bitter exile—after witnessing acts of utter barbarism, after shedding rivers of tears as their babies were torn from their arms, after seeing their children cemented alive into brick walls to fill missing quotas—what did these women prepare while still slaves in Egypt?

What was on the minds of these women who had seen affliction beyond the human breaking point? What was in the hearts of these women who bore too much anguish to fathom? What do their worn, tired, tortured and beaten bodies carry?

Tambourines.

Instruments with which to sing and praise their G-d.

Engulfed in misery, the women did not lose their vision. Mourning their children's deaths with their feminine sensitivity more keenly than any of their male counterparts possibly could, the women found the strength to fortify themselves not to lose hope.

The women found *meri*, Miriam's spirit of rebellion. They would rebel against depression that would have been a natural outgrowth of such circumstances. They would rebel against apathy. They would rebel against hopelessness.

Amidst their agony, the women prepared tambourines. They fanned the spark of yearning within their worn souls until it grew into an overpowering, inextinguishable flame of faith.

As bitter as their lives became, their faith grew stronger.

Certain beyond a shred of doubt that their G-d would remember them, their only concern was being adequately prepared to sing with the appropriate expressions of joy for the miracles that were sure to occur!

This was the strength of Miriam. A feminine strength born out from bitterness; a faith sown amidst despair.

This was the strength of the women who left Egypt, equipped with tambourines and dances of joy and faith.

And this is the strength of all women.

Shavuot

RUTH

Mother of Mashiach

It is customary in many communities to read the Book of Ruth on the holiday of Shavuot since Ruth was the ancestor of King David, whose birthday falls on Shavuot. In addition, the Book of Ruth describes Ruth's sincere devotion and self-sacrifice in joining the Jewish people and accepting the Torah, qualities which are essential for all of us to emulate in following the Torah's path. Ruth's experience parallels the collective experience of the Jewish people in accepting the Torah at Sinai.

Conflicting images come to mind when we consider Ruth. We picture Ruth in all her glory, the great-grandmother of the illustrious King David, the forebear of Mashiach, the royalty to surpass all royalties. Ruth, a woman well advanced in years,[244] sitting beside the throne of King David, the fruit of her great self-sacrifice.

Yet, we also ponder a very different image. Ruth, a convert stemming from the selfish and cruel nation, Moav.[245] Ruth, the descendant of an incestuous union between Lot and his eldest daughter, after they fled from the immoral land of Sodom and were spared G-d's wrath.

Beneath these conflicting images, a deeper lesson awaits discovery. By reviewing the story of Ruth we will discover how, from her murky origins, she came to be the ancestress of the saintly Mashiach.

The Background

This unusual story begins in the famine-stricken Land of Israel during the historical period of the Judges, approximately in the Jewish year 2787 (973 BCE).[246] The scene is a barren country, its parched fields yielding only scorched, dying grains. The people of Israel are dejected, drained of almost any hope of extracting themselves from their dismal predicament.

In the midst of this desolation, we are introduced to the prominent[247] and wealthy Elimelech, and his pious wife, Naomi. Together with their two sons, Machlon and Chilion, the parents resolve to abandon their land and people in search of a better future.

Though they have deserted their brethren, Elimelech and Naomi cannot leave behind their people's suffering, as one tragedy after another befalls the couple. In the neighboring land of Moav, the family loses its fortune. Elimelech dies. His sons marry the princesses of Moav,[248] Machlon marrying Ruth, and Chilion marrying Orpa. Soon after these marriages, Machlon and then Chilion tragically die.[249] The once esteemed Naomi is now a penniless, childless widow, a stranger in a foreign land.

The Return

Naomi realizes her serious mistake in forsaking the Holy Land[250] and is determined to return. When the mourning period for her sons ends, Naomi immediately begins her long and arduous journey back to her land and her people.

Ruth and Orpa faithfully begin to accompany her, but Naomi discourages them. She urges them, instead, to return to their parents' homes, and to the affluent palace life. Orpa agrees, exchanging her failing, elderly mother-in-law for a new and hopeful future back with her own people.

Ruth, however, remains impervious to all of Naomi's persuasions. She is determined to share a common destiny with Naomi whatever the future holds. In her famous heroic words, Ruth declares: "Wherever you will go, I will go. Where you will lodge, I will lodge. Your people are my people. Your G-d is my G-d. Where you die, I will die" (Ruth 1:16-17).[251]

What a profound commitment Ruth is making. After living as the wife of Machlon, Ruth has tasted Judaism and identifies it as a true way of life. Her youth as a gentile princess seems to her a life devoid of morals and values. Ruth has a monumental goal ahead of her. She obstinately clings to this objective and stands by it with every fiber of her being.[252] Nothing, not even her own mother-in-law's urgings, can persuade her to relinquish what she adamantly believes to be a life of truth.[253]

Ruth possesses the strength of character to follow what her spiritual intuition believes essential, regardless of the personal outcome. She was severing all ties with her past world in order to accompany a destitute, withered woman in her journey to her nation and her people. And yet, those very people may well reject her and her mother-in-law. She is trading a life of certain opulence and prestige for a life of possible poverty and disgrace.[254] Yet she understands the Jewish way to be the path of truth and remains steadfast in her convictions.

Ruth's monumental decision, however, involved more than a materialistic sacrifice alone.

Moabite Converts

After the Jewish people had left Egypt and were traveling towards the land of Israel, they asked various nations for permission to pass through their lands and to purchase food and drink. Many nations were sympathetic and graciously consented. The nations of Ammon and Moav, however, responded cruelly and maliciously, forbidding the Jews to even pass through. Because of this complete lack of compassion, G-d forbade any Jew to marry a convert from these two nations.

Most people understood this law as applying to a male or female Moabite convert. Only the learned scholars grasped the implications of the Biblical restrictive "Lo yavo Amoni u'Moavi bikhal Hashem"—"An Ammonite or Moabite may not enter the congregation of G-d" (Deut. 23:5) as referring exclusively to a male Ammonite or Moabite convert while permitting a female Ammonite or Moabite convert.[255] Only in later generations (in the period of King David) was this rule clarified to the masses: that it was permitted to marry a *female* Moabite convert.

With this information, we can appreciate that when Ruth chose to accompany Naomi to a Jewish destiny, she was surrendering not only her Moabite past, but, she assumed, her Jewish future as well. The masses (and possibly Ruth, herself) believed that a Jewish man was forbidden to marry Ruth because she was a Moabite convert.[256] Ruth's accompaniment of Naomi showed utter self-sacrifice; she would become a social outcast from the very nation that she sacrificed so much to join.

This was the immense inner strength of Ruth. She understood all that she was relinquishing, yet she chose the path of Judaism.

Continuing the narrative, we see the outcome of Ruth's determination.

Life in the Holy Land

Ruth and Naomi approach the Holy Land. People snicker and stare in astonishment, shocked by Naomi. Can this wrinkled, barefoot woman, lacking even a parasol to shield her fine features, be the same affluent and revered noblewoman who deserted them in their desperate times, abandoning the Land of Israel on her extravagant horse-drawn chariots?[257]

People are not certain how to respond. Perhaps Naomi should be ostracized for forsaking her nation. Or perhaps she deserves sympathy and compassion in light of her misery and degradation. And what of Ruth? Is she a genuine convert? Is her status as a Jewess legitimate?

The famine had recently ended[258] and the first crops were ripe for harvesting. The initial curiosity over Ruth and Naomi begins to wane. As people become preoccupied with their own harvesting, Naomi and Ruth are no longer the center of attention.

Life goes on. Ruth and Naomi subsist with what little they have. But in time, that too is exhausted. Aware of the extensive laws of charity in the Torah, Ruth requests permission from her mother-in-law to glean among the leftover ears of corn from the local fields, as was customary for the poor. Reluctantly,[259] Naomi allows her regal daughter-in-law to garner grains as would any common beggar.

The Meeting

As Divine Providence would have it, Ruth is directed to the field of the illustrious Boaz, leader of the generation. Boaz is also Naomi's nephew,[260] the son of Elimelech's brother. Boaz returns to his fields after his wife's recent passing,[261] at the precise moment that Ruth is gleaning there.

Though unaccustomed to casting more than a glance at the paupers in his field, Boaz's attention is drawn to Ruth. He marvels at her proficiency in the laws of charity,[262] restricting her gleaning to only two individual ears of corn, whereas most beggars hoarded whole sheaves of the fallen grains. He admires her modesty and the special, chaste way in which she bends to the ground.[263] He is awed by her general refinement of character, and wonders who this unusual woman could be.

Speaking with his workers, Boaz learns that this woman is his close relative through marriage. He approaches Ruth and graciously invites her to continue reaping in his fields.[264] He charitably offers her lodging with his maidservants, and welcomes her to glean as much as she desires without limiting her in any way. Boaz also instructs his servants to be especially generous to Ruth.

By the conclusion of the harvest season, Ruth is able to amass a sizable amount of grain from Boaz's fields. At last, after weeks of strenuous labor, the final day of harvesting arrives. Ruth is invited that evening to Boaz's thanksgiving party, celebrating the first abundant harvest since the onset of the famine. Before leaving to attend the dinner, Naomi—in a tone of grave importance—instructs Ruth to follow an incredible plan. Ruth obligingly undertakes to follow every step of the astounding instructions.

Midnight Encounter

That evening after the festive meal, Boaz retires to the threshing floor where he is accustomed to sleep during the harvesting season.[265] As he falls into a deep sleep, Ruth stealthily sneaks in, uncovers the blanket from Boaz's feet and reclines at the side of his feet. When Boaz awakens in the middle of the night, he discerns the form of a woman and orders her to identify herself. In her demure manner, Ruth explains who she is and proceeds to demand that Boaz fulfill his obligation to her, the penniless Moabite convert, by taking her hand in marriage!

In this bewildering episode, Ruth, through the instructions of Naomi, was alluding to the Jewish law of *yibum*, levirate marriage.[266] This law states that if, in a valid marriage, the husband dies childless, his nearest of kin is required to marry the deceased's widow (if both he and the widow consent) in order to perpetuate the name of the deceased. If either party is disinclined, the nearest of kin is obligated to perform a ceremony, *chalitza*, involving the removal of his shoe, which is what Ruth was alluding to by uncovering Boaz's feet. Ruth, now, is requesting Boaz to live up to this responsibility.

There were two possible reactions from Boaz to this surprising proposal. He might appreciate the sincerity and pure motives of Ruth, and agree to marry her; or more plausibly, he might become infuriated and offended by Ruth's brazen behavior and severely reprimand her for acting in such a fashion.

Ruth had already been ostracized by many for being a Moabite convert previously married (possibly without prior conversion) to someone who had deserted the Jewish people. If Boaz were indeed to perceive the proposal in a negative light, she would face public disgrace and total ostracism. Any chance of integration into normal Jewish communal life would be lost.

Ruth was an intelligent woman, capable of foreseeing the implications of her actions. Yet when Naomi advised her to execute this potentially scandalous plot, we see no hesitation on the part of Ruth. Why? And from where did Ruth acquire this courage to disregard her own plight even if it entailed being cursed by the leading sage of the generation?

The Sacrifice

To gain a deeper perspective, we have to look back several centuries in time to Ruth's ancestor, the daughter of Lot.[267] In fact, Ruth's connection with Lot's daughter, the mother of Moav, is more than one of simple ancestry. Sources from Kabbala teach that the soul of Lot's eldest daughter was reincarnated in Ruth. It was from Lot's eldest daughter that Ruth acquired the strength to implement her seemingly audacious behavior.

The Torah records[268] that when G-d became angry with the corrupt inhabitants of Sodom, He sent an angel to destroy the city. Through the interventions of his righteous uncle, Avraham, Lot and his daughters were rescued. They were unaware that only the inhabitants of Sodom were killed. Lot's daughters believed that, as in the days of Noah, the members of their family were the sole survivors on earth. To them, the destruction of Sodom spelled the end of human life.

Lot's eldest daughter did not hesitate to take a bold step that she felt was essential for the survival of humanity. She intoxicated her father and then had relations with him while he slept. Her motive in lying with her father was solely to perpetuate mankind, and the act was performed with the purest of intentions.

Although she had the rashness to cohabit with her own father, her motives were sincere. Therefore, she ultimately received great rewards for this incestuous act. Many generations later, her descendant, Ruth, converted to Judaism and mothered Israel's ruling dynasty, beginning with her great-grandchild King David, and culminating with Mashiach.

It was from Lot's daughter that Ruth acquired the fortitude to disregard her personal shame for the sake of mankind, and, more specifically, the Jewish people. Naomi had disclosed to Ruth that the future of the Jewish people would rest on this bizarre, midnight meeting with Boaz. Through her prophetic powers, Naomi had informed Ruth that the union between Boaz and Ruth had the capability of bringing the light of Mashiach into this world.

Ruth, confronted with possible personal doom on the one hand, and the potential of bringing a great Divine light into the world on the other, did not hesitate. There was no room in her mind for considering her personal, albeit spiritual, welfare when it came to heightening holiness in the world at large, and bringing mankind to its utmost completion.

Boaz, the leader of the nation, perceived this purity and grandeur of character when Ruth came with her demand. He realized all that Ruth was risking by laying at his bedside in the dark of night. He appreciated the courage it required.

It was from this meeting that Boaz acquired a new perception of Ruth. Now he could discern that Ruth was more than the modest, righteous and learned woman that he had noticed in his fields. She was even more than an extraordinary woman who jeopardized everything to become a part of the Jewish nation.

Here was a woman of self-sacrifice, devoid of any selfish aspirations, including spiritual ones. Ruth was willing to forego her entire self, even if this might involve being cursed by the sage of the time, in order to do something that had the potential of intensifying G-dly light for mankind. Only a person of such stature had the capability of becoming the forebear of Mashiach.

Mashiach has the task of "fighting the war of G-d" (Rambam, *Hilchot Melachim* 11:1), by combating common perceptions that creation lacks a G-d. Mashiach will convince the Jewish people, a "stiff-necked" nation, to return to a spiritual life of Torah. Mashiach will not be affected by present-day norms or societal pressures. His consciousness will only be concerned with magnifying G-dly awareness among his people.

Only someone of Ruth's caliber could merit to mother a soul of such quality.

Epilogue

Boaz did indeed follow the laws of levirate marriage by marrying Ruth. He attempted to publicize through this marriage, as well, a clarification of the law that female Moabite converts (as opposed to male Moabite converts) were permitted in marriage.

On the night of the consummation of their marriage, Ruth conceived a child, later named Oved. Boaz was eighty years old at the time.[269] Unfortunately, he did not live to see the birth of his child. The day following Boaz and Ruth's first union, Boaz died.[270]

Many ignorant people understood this to be a sign from heaven that G-d was affronted by his forbidden marriage to a Moabite convert.[271] Only in later generations, in the latter part of the life of King David, did people finally appreciate that G-d had extended Boaz's life specifically for this union.

Boaz's son, Oved (appropriately named—*oved* means "one who continuously serves," and he served G-d, doing His will), had a son named Yishai, who was the father of King David. Ruth lived to old age and was able to see her great-grandchild, David, ascend the royal throne and wear the crown of the king of the nation of G-d. Ruth was finally beginning to be rewarded with seeing the fruits of her labor.

Ruth's ultimate reward, and the reward of the entire Jewish people, is yet to come . . .

Shavuot

NITZEVET, MOTHER OF KING DAVID

The Bold Voice of Silence

Many communities read the Book of Ruth on the holiday of Shavuot, since Ruth was the ancestor of King David, whose birthday falls on Shavuot. This chapter tells the story of young David's life and the vital role played by a hidden heroine, his mother, Nitzevet.

Save me, O G-d, for the waters threaten to engulf me...
I am wearied by my calling out and my throat is dry. I've lost hope in waiting. . .
More numerous than the hairs on my head are those who hate me without reason. . .
Must I then repay what I have not stolen?
Mighty are those who would cut me down, who are my enemies without cause. . .
O G-d, You know my folly and my unintended wrongs are not hidden from You. . .
It is for Your sake that I have borne disgrace, that humiliation covers my face.
I have become a stranger to my brothers, an alien to my mother's sons.
Out of envy for Your House, they ravaged me; the disgraces of those who revile You have fallen upon me. . .
Those who sit by the gate talk about me. I am the taunt of drunkards. . .
Disgrace breaks my heart and I am left deathly sick.
I hope for solace but there is none, and for someone to comfort me but I find no one.
Instead they put gall into my meal and give me vinegar to quench my thirst. . .
(Psalm 69)[272]

This Psalm describes the life of a poor, despised and lowly individual who lacks even a single friend to comfort him. It is the voice of a tormented soul who has experienced untold humiliation and disgrace. Through no apparent cause of his own, he is surrounded by enemies who wish to cut him down; even his own brothers are strangers to him, ravaging and reviling him.

Interestingly, this is the voice of the mighty King David, righteous and beloved servant of G-d, feared and awed by all.

King David had many challenges throughout his life. But at what point did this great individual who possessed such sterling personal qualities feel so alone, so disgraced and so undeserving of love and friendship?

What caused King David to face such intense ignominy, to be shunned by his own brothers in his home ("I have become a stranger to my brothers"), by the Torah Sages who sat in judgment at the gates ("those who sit by the gate talk about me"), and by the drunkards on the street corners ("I am the taunt of drunkards")? What had King David done to arouse such ire and contempt? And was there no one at this time in his life that would provide him with love, comfort and friendship?

The sages explain that this Psalm, in which King David passionately bares these deepest burdens of his soul, refers to the time from his earliest childhood onwards up until his being coronated as king.

David was born into the illustrious family of Yishai, who served as the head of the Sanhedrin (Jewish Supreme Court) and was one of the most distinguished leaders of his generation. Yishai was a man of such greatness that the Talmud observes that "Yishai was one of only four righteous individuals who died solely due to the taint of the serpent" (*Shabbat* 55b),[273] i.e., because he was a human being, not due to any sin or flaw of his own. David was the youngest in his family, which included seven other illustrious and righteous brothers.

Yet, when David was born, these very upstanding and prominent family members greeted his birth with absolute derision and contempt. As David describes quite literally in the Psalm, "I was a stranger to my brothers, a foreigner to my mother's sons. . .they put gall in my meal and gave me vinegar to quench my thirst."

David was not permitted to eat with the rest of his family, but was assigned to a separate table in the corner. He was given the task of shepherd because "they hoped that a wild beast would come and kill him while he was performing his duties" (*Sifsei Kohen, parshat Vayeishev*) and for this reason was sent to pasture in dangerous areas "full of lions and bears" (1 Sam. 17:34-36).

Only one individual throughout David's youth felt pained over his unjustified plight and felt a deep, unconditional bond of love for the child whom she alone knew was undoubtedly pure.

This was King David's mother, Nitzevet bat Adel, who felt the intensity of her youngest child's pain and rejection as her own.

Torn and anguished by David's unwarranted troubles, yet powerless to stop the degradation, Nitzevet stood by the sidelines, in solidarity with him, herself shunned, as she, too, cried torrents of tears, awaiting the time when true justice would surface.

It would take twenty-eight long years of assault and rejection, suffering and degradation, until that justice would finally begin to take root.

David's Birth

Why was the young David so reviled by his brothers and nation?

To understand the hatred directed to David, we need to investigate the inner workings behind the events, the secret episodes that aren't recorded in the book of Prophets but hinted to in midrashim.[274]

King David's father, Yishai, was the grandson of Boaz and Ruth. After several years of marriage to his wife, Nitzevet, and after having raised several virtuous children, Yishai began to entertain personal doubts about his ancestry. True, Boaz was the leading Torah authority in his day, but his grandmother, Ruth, was a convert from the nation of Moav.

During Ruth's lifetime, many individuals were doubtful about the legitimacy of her conversion. The Torah specifically forbids a Moabite convert,[275] since this is the nation that cruelly refused the Jewish people passage through their land, or food and drink to purchase when they wandered in the desert after being freed from Egypt.

Boaz and the sages understood this law as forbidding the conversion of male Moabites (who were the ones responsible for the cruel conduct), while exempting the female Moabite converts. In Boaz's marriage to Ruth, he was hoping to clarify and publicize this Torah law, which was still unknown to the masses. (See chapter on Ruth for more detailed explanations on this topic.)

Boaz died the night after his marriage with Ruth. Ruth conceived and subsequently gave birth to their son, Oved, the father of Yishai. Some rabble-rousers at the time claimed that Boaz's death verified that his marriage to Ruth the Moabite had indeed been forbidden.

Time would prove differently. Once Oved, and later Yishai and his offspring, were born, their righteous conduct and prestigious positions proved the legitimacy of their ancestry. It was unquestionable that men of such caliber could have descended from a forbidden union.

However, later in his life, doubt gripped at Yishai's heart, gnawing away at the very foundation of his existence. Being the sincere individual that he was, his integrity compelled him to action.

If Yishai's status was questionable, he was not permitted to remain married to his wife, a veritable Israelite. Disregarding the personal sacrifice, Yishai decided the only solution would be to separate from her, by no longer engaging in marital relations. Yishai's children were aware of this separation.

After a number of years had passed, Yishai longed for an offspring whose ancestry would be unquestionable. His plan was to engage in relations with his Canaanite maidservant.

He said to her, "Prepare yourself for tonight. With this union, I will be freeing you, conditionally. If my status as a Jew is legitimate, then you are freed as a proper Jewish convert to marry me. If my status, however, is blemished and I am a Moabite convert, I am not giving you your freedom, but as a *shifcha Canaanit*, a Canaanite maidservant, you may marry a Moabite convert."

The maidservant was aware of the anguish of her mistress, Nitzevet. She understood her pain in being separated from her husband for so many years. She knew, as well, of Nitzevet's longing for more children.

The empathetic maidservant approached Nitzevet and informed her of Yishai's plan, suggesting a bold counter plan.

"Let us learn from your ancestress and replicate their actions. Switch places with me tonight, just as Leah did with Rachel," advised the maidservant.

With a prayer on her lips that her plan succeed, Nitzevet took the place of her maidservant. Though Yishai remained unaware of this switch, that night Nitzevet conceived.

After three months, Nitzevet's pregnancy became obvious. Incensed, her sons wished to kill their mother and the illegitimate fetus that she carried. Nitzevet, for her part, would not embarrass her husband by revealing his plan. Like her ancestress Tamar,[276] who preferred to be burned alive rather than embarrass Yehuda, Nitzevet chose a vow of silence. And like Tamar, Nitzevet would be rewarded for her silence with a child of greatness who would be the forebear of Mashiach.

Unaware of his wife's behavior, but having compassion on her, Yishai ordered his sons not to touch her. "Do not kill her! Instead, let the child that will be born be treated as a lowly and hated servant. In this way, everyone will realize that his status is questionable and, as an illegitimate child, he will not marry an Israelite."

From the time of his birth onwards, Nitzevet's son was treated by his brothers as an abominable outcast.[277] Noting the conduct of his brothers, the rest of the nation assumed that this youth was a treacherous sinner full of unspeakable guilt.

On the infrequent occasions that Nitzevet's son would return from the pastures to his home in Beit Lechem, he was shunned by his townsmen. If something was lost or stolen, he was accused as the natural culprit, or, in the words of the Psalms, ordered to "repay what I have not stolen."

Eventually, the entire lineage of Yishai was questioned, as well as the basis of the original law of the Moabite convert. People claimed that all the positive qualities from Boaz became manifest in Yishai and his illustrious seven sons, while all the negative character traits from Ruth the Moabite clung to this despicable youngest son.

This same hated youth was later crowned as the venerated King David.

King David's Coronation

We are first introduced to David when Shmuel (Samuel) the prophet is commanded to go to Beit Lechem to coronate a new king to replace the rejected King Shaul.

Shmuel arrives in Beit Lechem and the elders of the city come out to greet him. This was an unusual and unexpected visit, since

Shmuel had stopped circulating throughout the land. The elders were visibly nervous and feared that the prophet had heard about a grievous sin that was taking place in their city.[278] Perhaps he had come to rebuke them over the despicable behavior of Yishai's despised shepherd boy, living in their midst.

Shmuel answered, however, that he had come in peace and asked the elders, and Yishai and his sons to join him for a sacrificial feast. As an elder, Yishai was invited to the feast, but when his sons were inexplicably also invited, they worried that perhaps the prophet had come to publicly reveal the embarrassing and illegitimate origins of their brother. Unbeknownst to them, at this feast, Shmuel would anoint the new king of Israel.

> When they came, Shmuel saw Eliav (Yishai's oldest son) and he thought, "Surely G-d's anointed stands before Him!"

> But G-d said to Shmuel, "Don't look at his appearance or his great height, for I have rejected him—G-d does not see with mere eyes, like a man does. G-d sees the heart!"

> Then Yishai called Avinadav (his second son) and made him pass before Shmuel. He said: "G-d did not choose this one either."

> Yishai made Shamma pass, and Shmuel said, "G-d has not chosen this one either."

> Yishai had his seven sons pass before Shmuel. Shmuel said to Yishai, "G-d has not chosen any of them." At last Shmuel said to Yishai, "Are there no lads remaining?"

> He answered, "A small one is left; he is taking care of the sheep."

> So Shmuel said to him, "Send for him and have him brought; we will not stir until he comes here."

> So he sent for him and had him brought—he was of ruddy complexion with red hair, beautiful eyes, and handsome to look at.

> G-d said: "Rise up, anoint him, for this is the one!" (1 Sam. 16:6-12)

The Small One, Left Behind

As Shmuel laid his eyes on Yishai's eldest son, Eliav, he was sure that this was the future king of Israel. Tall, handsome and distinguished, Shmuel was ready to anoint him, until G-d reprimanded him not to look at the outside but to the inside.

A short while after this coronation feast, David was instructed by his father to visit Eliav at the battlefield. A war with the Philistines was imminent, and Eliav lashed out in anger at David.[279] This tendency to anger disqualified Eliav now from the throne.

No longer did Shmuel make any assumptions of his own, but he waited to be told who was to become the next king. All the seven sons of Yishai had passed before Shmuel, and none of them had been chosen.

"Are these all the lads?" Shmuel asked. Shmuel prophetically chose his words carefully. Had he asked if these were all Yishai's *sons*, Yishai would have answered affirmatively, that there were no more of *his sons,* since David was not given the status of a son.

Instead, Yishai answered, "A *small* one is left; he is taking care of the sheep." David's status was small in Yishai's eyes. He was hoping that Shmuel would proceed and allow David to remain where he was, out of trouble, tending to the sheep, in the faraway pastures.

Shmuel ordered that David immediately be summoned to the feast. A messenger was dispatched to David, who, out of respect for the prophet, first went home to wash himself and change his clothes. Unaccustomed to seeing David home at such a time, Nitzevet inquired, "Why did you come home in the middle of the day?"

David explained the reason and Nitzevet answered, "If so, I, too, am accompanying you."

As David arrived, Shmuel saw a man "of ruddy complexion, with red hair, beautiful eyes and handsome to look at." David's physical appearance alludes to the differing aspects of his personality. His ruddiness suggests a warlike nature, while his eyes and general appearance indicate kindness and gentility.[280]

At first, Shmuel doubted whether David could be the one worthy of the kingship, a forerunner of the dynasty that would lead the Jewish people forever. He thought to himself, "This one will shed blood as did the red-headed Esav" (*Bereishit Rabba* 63:8).

G-d saw, however, that David's greatness was that he would direct his aggressiveness towards good causes. G-d commanded Shmuel, "My anointed one is standing before you, and you remain seated? Arise and anoint David without delay! For he is the one I have chosen!"[281]

As Shmuel held the horn of oil, it bubbled, as if it could not wait to drop onto David's forehead. When Shmuel anointed him, the oil hardened and glistened like pearls and precious stones, and the horn remained full.

As Shmuel anointed David, tearful weeping could be heard from outside the great hall. It was the voice of Nitzevet, David's lone supporter and solitary source of comfort.

The twenty-eight long years of her silence in the face of humiliation were finally coming to a close. At last, all would see that the lineage of her youngest son was pure, undefiled by any blemish. Finally, the anguish and humiliation that she and her son had borne would come to an end.

Facing the rest of her sons, Nitzevet exclaimed, "The stone that was reviled by the builders[282] has now become the cornerstone!" (Ps. 119:33)

Humbled, they responded, "This has come from G-d; it was hidden from our eyes."

Those in the hall cried out in unison, "Long live the king! Long live the king!" Within moments, the once-reviled shepherd boy became anointed as the future king of Israel.

Nitzevet's Legacy

King David would meet many more trials until he was acknowledged by the entire nation as the new monarch to replace King Shaul (Saul). During his long, forty-year reign as king and throughout his life, King David faced many more challenges.

King David's righteous disposition would assist him in dealing with these ordeals. Many of his positive qualities were inherited from his illustrious father, Yishai, after whom he is fondly and respectfully called *ben Yishai,* the son of Yishai.

But it was undoubtedly from his mother's milk that the young David absorbed strong values and the courage to face his adversaries. From the moment he was born, and during his most tender years, it was Nitzevet who, by example, taught him the essential lesson of valuing every individual's dignity and refraining from embarrassing another, regardless of the personal consequences. It was she who displayed a silent but stoic bravery and dignity in the face of the gravest hardship.

Undoubtedly, it is from Nitzevet that King David absorbed a strength born from an inner confidence to disregard the callous treatment of the world and find solace in the comfort of his Maker. It was this strength that would fortify him to defeat his staunchest antagonists as well as his most treacherous enemies, as he valiantly fought against the mightiest warriors on behalf of his people.

Nitzevet taught her young child to find the strength to follow the path of his inner convictions, irrespective of the cruelty that might be directed towards him. Her display of patient confidence in the Creator that justice would be restored, gave David the inner peace and solace that he would need, over and over again, in confronting the formidable challenges in his life. Rather than succumb to his afflictions, rather than become the individual who was shunned by his tormentors, David learned from his mother to stand proud and dignified, feeling consolation in communicating with his Maker in the open pastures.

She demonstrated to him, as well, the necessity of boldness to passionately defend one's convictions. When the situation would call for it, personal risks must be taken while pursuing the right path. Without her bold plan, the great soul of her youngest child, King David, the forebear of Mashiach, would never have descended to this world.

The soul-stirring Psalms composed by King David in his greatest hours of need eloquently and poetically describe his suffering and heartache, as well as his faith and conviction. The book of Psalms gives a voice to each of us, and has become the balm to sooth all of our wounds, as we, too, encounter the many personal and communal hardships of exile life.

As we say these verses, our voices join with Nitzevet's, with King David's and with all the voices of those past and present who have experienced unjustified pain, in beseeching our Maker for that time when the "son [descendant] of David" will usher in the era of redemption and true justice will suffuse creation.

Tisha B'Av
A FEMININE JOURNEY
The Era of Redemption

Tisha B'Av marks the saddest time of the year, when our nation reached an all-time spiritual low with the destruction of our First and Second Temples as well as our exile from our homeland. Yet, as sad as Tisha B'Av is, hidden within this time period is the greatest potential for our Redemption.

For this reason, the great master Rabbi Levi Yitzchok of Berditchev explained that Shabbat Chazon (the Shabbat prior to Tisha B'Av) means the "Shabbat of Vision," since our souls perceive a vision of the Third Temple.

Each of us has the ability, at this time, to tap into that power of redemption—a feminine power.

Come with me on a journey.

A journey of souls.

Together, let us embark on an expedition to a destination beyond our present reality. There we will encounter a different time and a different people. Though unfamiliar to us, it is a place that each of us has the power of making his very own.

Whether man or woman, for a moment, let us experience the feminine journey.

Come with me...

To a land where the sword is no longer a weapon of war, since peace is all-pervasive.

Where a muscled fist makes no impact, only the power of communication and persuasion.

Where there are no ravages of battle, only the shelter of the family.

Where the darkness has been dispelled by a singular light suffusing the entire night.

Where there are no acts of dominance and suppression, only acts of kindness and charity.

Where harsh rebuke is not used against negative characteristics, only pointed praise, which elicits a wellspring of hidden qualities.

Where the power of a tear is subdued by the power of a smile.

Where divisiveness is dissolved by the bonding of unity.

Where the accomplishments of the mundane weekdays are absorbed by the harmony of the eternal Shabbat.

Where the joy of giving far surpasses that of receiving.

Where we are no longer judged by what we do, but rather by what we are.

Throughout the close to six millennia of history, we have been on a masculine journey. Collectively and personally, mankind had a mission—rectify the world, vanquish the evil, fight against the darkness, suppress the negative and dominate the ill will. The tools we used had to break, discard and subdue the husks of negativity which surrounded us. Humanity was involved in a struggle, a spiritual war, against evil.

We were in a world that only could appreciate aggressiveness. You got the lion's share if you were self-centered, screamed the loudest, and pushed and pulled the hardest. Destruction, domination and suppression were rampant.

"G-d of vengeance, L-rd, G-d of vengeance, appear!

"Rise up, judge of the earth, give the arrogant their just deserts!

"How long shall the wicked, O L-rd, how long shall the wicked exult?

"Shall they utter insolent speech, shall all evildoers vaunt themselves?

"They crush Your people, O L-rd, they afflict Your very own;

"They kill the widow and the stranger;

"They murder the fatherless, thinking, G-d does not see it, the G-d of Yaakov does not pay heed." (Ps. 94: 1-7)

But now, we are experiencing a foretaste of a very new journey—a feminine journey. It is no longer one of dominance, but rather revelation; no longer one of war, but peace; no longer one of exile, but redemption.

At this time, our paramount mission is to reveal the inner essence in all creation, uncover the inner good inherent in all people, discover and bring out the Divine core in all reality. We no longer need to discard, fight or rid ourselves of evil and negativity, because it will be nonexistent.

This war is not fought with bullets, but rather with education and communication. We no longer destroy, we rather imbue with goodness. There will be no fists of destruction, no swords of battle, no tyrannical dictators or domineering superpowers. And no pain or sadness.

Our weapons are acts of kindness and goodness, acts of charity and humility. We illuminate the darkness with spiritual light. We battle the indulgence in materiality, by exposing its source as a Divine blessing. We are victorious, through our smiles, through our unity and peace, through our empathy and care.

"And the L-rd passed by. There was a great and mighty wind, splitting mountains and shattering rocks by the power of G-d; but G-d was not in the wind.

"After the wind, an earthquake; but the L-rd was not in the earthquake. After the earthquake, fire; but the L-rd was not in the fire.

"And after the fire, a soft murmuring sound.

"When Eliyahu heard it, he wrapped his mantle about his face and went out and stood at the entrance of the cave. Then a Voice addressed him" (1 Kings 19: 11-14).

G-d was neither in the loud and angry winds, nor in the mighty earthquakes or fierce fires. G-d appeared in the soft, still, murmuring sound.

This is the essence of the feminine journey. The quiet, soft voice.

While the wind, earthquake and fire may represent the masculine saga and the aggressive male talents employed throughout the millennia—both for bad and good—the soft, murmuring sound exemplifies the feminine motif.

In the past, the traditionally male qualities were valued due to their need to fight evil. This was our mission, at that time. However, in the era of redemption, the feminine qualities will reign, because of their inherent capacity to reveal the inner good and discover the G-dly unity in all of creation.

The feminine voice is heard not because of its fierceness, but because of its message; not because of its volume, but because of its character; not because of its power, but because of its passion.

Therefore, the feminine journey epitomizes the era of redemption, where the feminine soul qualities will prevail. Indeed, our sages have described this era as one where "woman will supersede man" (Jer. 31:21); her innately feminine soul powers will supersede the male's.

It is not a journey about working from without, but from deep within. It is not about externals, but rather inner space. Not about struggle, but harmony. Not about commanding, but communicating. Not about doing, but being. Not about influencing, but receiving. Not about hard goals, but empathy and nurturance. Not about the career ladder, but the family unit.

It is a time when the soft, still voice will be heard.

For this reason,[283] referring to this era, it states, "Then will be heard...in the cities of Judah and in the streets of Jerusalem...the voice of the groom and the voice of the bride" (Jer. 33:10-11).[284]

Throughout the ages, the bride's role in the marriage ceremony was one of complete passivity, and her voice was silent. In this future era, though, her voice will be heard. Her intuitive, inner qualities will be valued and sought after.

The feminine journey is not about a gender issue, or about struggles for equality. It is rather a change in our perception, our value system and our life's goals—for both man and woman. It is not a battle of the sexes, but rather an internalization and empowerment of the feminine qualities. As such, it is something that both men and women are experiencing a foretaste of now, as each incorporates more and more of the feminine perspective into their lives.

It sounds like a dream? It is a dream. But one that is materializing before our very eyes.

The changes occurring throughout our society can be seen as a backdrop for this era of peace, prosperity, education and communication. Though we certainly haven't yet reached this idyllic period, numerous developments occurring in the last couple of decades point in this direction, and include the following, to cite but a few:

In geopolitics, the collapse of the Iron Curtain, and the crumbling of communism and tyrannical leaders are major events giving a preview of world peace. The use of the military for humanitarian purposes—to distribute foods and medicines in needy countries and for defending the rights of the underprivileged, women and children—demonstrates a new perspective of looking beyond our self-centered goals to see others as part of the global enterprise.

The existence of a global village, with a sophisticated network of communication at our fingertips, is a foretaste of world unity.

The move from an industrial to an information society brings man to using his mind over his muscle and encourages him to seek depth and meaning in intellectual and spiritual pursuits.

In most sectors of the workforce, communication and interpersonal skills, as opposed to only hard, goal-oriented know-how, have become recognized as vital business commodities.

Family has taken on new importance as people seek to share with their children and develop meaningful relationships. The American dream is no longer to merely accumulate personal wealth and prosperity, but to seek spiritual fulfillment and meaning in life.

In our educational systems, schools are, more and more, realizing their vital role of not only training professionals, but of shaping personalities; not only imparting skills, but developing character.

Ecological sensitivities train us to appreciate the inherent G-dly gifts in our physical world and elicit our efforts to preserve and pass them on to our children. Environmental action is, furthermore, based on the conviction that one small deed can make a disproportionately huge impact in the world.

Thus, the setting in which we live our lives is not changing; rather, we, collectively, are changing our approach and perspectives as we become more conscious of the G-dly life force permeating our lives. This is what the era of redemption and the feminine journey is all about.

Indeed, all along, through her secret role, the deeper dynamics of her soul powers, and, consequently, the inner dimensions of her special mitzvot, women have been entrusted with the mission of bringing this unique era upon us.

So, in truth, we need to listen to the quiet, soft voice emanating from deep within, which prods us to develop our innately feminine spiritual qualities—for ourselves, for our families and for humanity.

This is the feminine journey. This is the soft, still voice.

It starts as a seemingly unrealistic dream. It develops into an abstract ideal. It emerges as a universal goal. It becomes a personal mission that impacts upon the way we think and feel, and, more importantly, upon the way we behave.

And, then, ultimately, it becomes reality.

For Further Reflection

- How can challenges strengthen our faith and vision?
- How have women taken a prominent role in the formation or celebration of the holidays?
- What is the greatest expression of self-sacrifice? Share an example of it from your own life.
- What is self-confidence?
- What motivates us to want children?
- How can hardships bring out our strongest qualities?
- How can we rebel against the bitterness that life throws our way?
- Are there any positive ramifications to the long purification process of exile?
- What is the "feminine journey"?

Section Four

IMAGERY
The Feminine Realm
A Mystical Look at the Feminine Elements in Reality

❀ Two Forms of Universal Energy—Two Modes of Being
  ❧ A Cosmic Inhale and Exhale—Ratzo V'Shov
  ❧ Outer and Inner—the Concept of "Kav and Reshimu"

❀ Malchut: The Feminine Sefira
  ❧ Sefirot in Kabbala
  ❧ Malchut, the Feminine Sphere and Bat, the Daughter
  ❧ Malchut and the Feminine Shabbat
  ❧ Malchut as the Feminine Womb
  ❧ Malchut as Speech and Communication
  ❧ Malchut as Mitzvot and the Woman of Valor
  ❧ Malchut, the Final Sefira

TWO FORMS OF UNIVERSAL ENERGY
Two Modes of Being

"The whole universe functions according to the principium of masculine and feminine."
(The Arizal, *Eitz Chaim* 11:6)

"All that the Holy One Blessed be He, created in His world, He created male and female."
(*Bava Batra* 74b).

A COSMIC INHALE
AND EXHALE

Ratzo V'Shov

The doctor and his team of nurses surround the laboring woman. One wipes her furrowed brow with a damp cloth. The other grasps her clenched fist. Anticipation palpably fills the sterile, white room, but for now, only labored breathing can be heard.

A tremendous final effort, and then utter stillness envelops the room. The shallow moment feels like eternity until the baby's long-awaited wail pierces the silence.

A large smile, then a gentle, soft laugh breaks across the tired woman's features. The moment of tension has passed.

The newborn shrieks louder, and with each wail a greater blissfulness fills the room. The baby's cry signifies vitality, health and vigor. Great expectations await this child!

Gently the baby is hushed, swaddled and tenderly cradled in her mother's arms. As the mother's chest calmly rises and falls, baby's does too, and the only sound now is the contented breathing of both.

With each tender inhale and exhale of her child, mother gains newfound appreciation for the miracle of her baby. Each inhale and exhale is a testimonial and a tribute to life itself.

But a few floors down, in the corridors of the same building, a very different scene is unfolding.

Here my aged grandmother lies motionless on the sterile sheets of the hospital bed. Her labored breathing complements the soft beeping of the heart-monitoring machine.

My grandmother's face is slightly wrinkled; yet her eyes are fully focused and attest to her years filled with experience and shared wisdom. She is surrounded by her many children and grandchildren.

A tear rolls down the cheek of one adult child, while a younger one clasps her grandmother's fragile hand, and yet another softly sings words of prayer. All eyes are focused on the matriarch of the family.

Each one has his own thoughts. One reminisces about a special, private moment shared with this elderly woman. Another, her sage words of advice that were to change the direction of his life. While yet a third, her open home, filled with hand-baked delicacies and her equally open ears, perpetually ready to listen.

My aged grandmother, like the members of her family encircling her, is aware that the end is but moments away. Each laborious breath attests to its imminent arrival. She gazes intently, poring into the eyes of each of her loved ones. An inner contentment and peace passes over her features. Her breathing becomes softer and softer.

And then her chest falls and rises no longer.

With her final exhale, the legacy of this cherished family matriarch has come full circle.

Breath, the inhale and exhale, marking life itself. From the first breath to the last, the constant inhale and exhale signifies vitality.

Take a moment to experience it. Breathe deeply. Fill your lungs with the fresh, pure oxygen. This inhale represents your very inner, core essence, your very being in life. It signifies who you are.

Now, release it; let it all out. Witness your breath exiting and meshing with your surroundings. This represents your doing in life, your impacting on the outside world and accomplishing.

Your inhale is self-preservation, defining your own boundaries of self. Your exhale is your universal imprint on the society and world around you.

All beings and any life force experience this duality of inner and outer; inner parameters and boundaries versus outer affects and imprints. Who it is and what it does. The protection of its inherent boundaries, and its reaching out to the world.

The greater a life force, the more evident is its inhale and exhale.

Indeed, all creation, say the Kabbalists, is characterized by this to and fro movement, called *"ratzo v'shov"* (running forth and drawing back) or *"mati v'lo mati"* (reaching and retreating).

The heart contracts and expands; the lungs exhale and inhale. On a deeper level, the body sleeps, extinguishing its active faculties in order to rejuvenate. The earth enters an interlude of night and winter in order to vivify itself with the necessary energies for its more outward-oriented dawn of spring.

The same is true of the flow of vitality from G-d to His creation. This flow also comes in flashes of running forth and drawing back, reaching and retreating.

In fact, the more elevated the bestowal, the more intense is the withdrawal preceding it. Both revelation and its preceding concealment, then, are two faces of the same reality and reflect the innate pendulum of life.

Furthermore, the microcosm is reflected in the macrocosm. Each breath of life—each protective withholding of boundaries as well as each outer exertion—reflects the Divine balance and flow to creation.

An allusion to this is seen in the creation story of mankind. Original man was created as a "two-sided being." Having been created in the Divine image, man, too, had a masculine and feminine aspect.

"And G-d created man in His image, in the image of G-d He created him; male and female He created them" (Gen 1:27).

G-d then split this being into two distinct beings. From then on the divided halves of the Divine image seek and yearn for each other, creating an eternal tension that draws them back together, this time as separate individuals.

While every man and woman is his or her own unique being, each recognizes something in the complete transcendental persona of the other that is missing in his or herself. Seen within this context, the Divine analogue is once again made whole upon the uniting of the two, particularly within the context of marriage.

The masculine and feminine dichotomy is not simply two genders within a species. Each reflects, rather, subtle forms of

Divine energy that are constantly being renewed within the process of creation.

In its most abstract form, the feminine energy reflects internal energy, the withdrawal and inhale of the cosmos. The masculine energy reflects projective energy, expansiveness and revelation, or the cosmic exhale of all creation.

This is not to say that all women have only characteristics of this elusive inner trait, or all men of this powerful external trait. While it is true that a woman is generally more characterized by her feminine energy and a man by his masculine energy, the energies of both are found in each other.

This is true because ours is a world of integration, where there are no absolutes, but rather things blending, sharing and balancing each other. So, in everything male there is at least a small bit of female, and likewise in all things female, there is some male. As a result, every aspect of creation shares in this duet of masculine and feminine.

However, to be attuned to her inner self and her feminine self, a woman would need to discover what and how to use her feminine energies productively and positively. The same holds true for a man.

The Torah encourages the awareness of these equally important, yet different, arenas of masculine and feminine energies. We are encouraged to learn how to integrate these qualities in our lives, on a personal as well as on a cosmic level. In fact, upon closer analysis, each of the gender-divided mitzvot of the Torah is fashioned based on these boundaries.

OUTER AND INNER

The Concept of "Kav and Reshimu"

What are the masculine and feminine forces of the universe, and how do these energies express the distinctive roles or character traits of man and woman?[285]

As with any concept, the best way to understand this duality is to examine it at its roots.

Just as our conscious mind reflects the hidden subconscious chambers of our soul, by the same token, our physical world mirrors a hidden spiritual universe. All the qualities, characteristics, textures, feelings and thought processes of all the various items and issues of our concrete world are but a glimpse of what lies beyond in the spiritual realm of the cosmos.

A deeper, fuller and holistic perception of the realities of our world, then, can be attained by seeing them at their cosmic, underlying foundation.

Kabbala[286] explains that in the beginning:

"A simple Divine light filled the entirety of existence...When there arose in His simple will the desire to create the worlds, He contracted His light, withdrawing it to the sides and leaving a void in its center to allow for the existence of the worlds. He then drew a single line of His infinite light into the void to illuminate the worlds..."

G-d is neither male nor female. G-d is also not infinite nor finite; not spiritual nor physical; neither heaven nor earth; neither active nor passive. For G-d is beyond and above all limiting descriptions and constraints.

In creating a world, however, G-d conceived of, and utilized, two complementary, yet distinct, forces.

According to Kabbala, the act of creation can be defined as an act of "tzimtzum" or concealment, contraction and withdrawal. Originally a simple or omnipotent "presence" of G-d was all that existed.

This presence, however, precluded the creation of a world such as ours, a world filled with self-defined, independent and finite existences. Our world is complex and multi-dimensional. Objects have their own physical boundaries and parameters. Beings assert their right to be independent individuals, choosing and acting on their own volition. We live in a world that in its every breath screams its self-identity—to the point, sometimes, of even excluding or denying its Creator.

Such a world could not have come to be, and would by definition be totally absorbed and swallowed up within the all-inclusive presence of the original, simple and all-encompassing Divine light.

Therefore, according to the *tzimtzum* doctrine, to allow for the potential of a creation, G-d "contracted" His light or presence, thereby creating a "void" or space within which His infinite being is not apparently manifest.

He then projected into this void a singular line, or in Kabbalistic terminology, a *"kav"* of light. This *kav* is the flow of Divine energy sustaining and energizing every level of reality according to its distinctive needs, ability and vitality.

However, this *kav* is not the only source of Divine vitality for all of creation.

Even after G-d's contraction of Himself in the *tzimtzum*, there still remained a vestige of Divine energy in the world. This residual light or remnant of G-dliness is called, in Kabbalistic terminology, a *"reshimu."* It is a G-dly force that doesn't contradict finiteness, but to the contrary, is its very source.

While the *kav* represents new, powerful Divine light descending on creation, the *reshimu* represents a more subtle Divine vitality that always remained within creation. The *kav* breaks the boundaries of our natural world to impose Divinity on creation; the *reshimu* nurtures the G-dliness already inherent within creation.

And so, we have two modalities for the manifestation of Divine energy in creation: the outer versus the inner.

The *kav* coming from beyond imposes its rule and direction on the world. It represents the masculine forces of the G-dhead, and G-d's power of infinity, revelation and expansion.

And then there is the *reshimu*, the G-dly energy already inherent within creation, which always was and is. It represents the feminine energies of the G-dhead and the Divine potential of finite   self-expression,   of   concealment,   limitation   and definitiveness.

We access the *kav* by doing; we uncover the *reshimu* by being.

Two genders for the Creator and His light. The imposing force versus the nurturing energy. The force of control versus one of cultivation. Authority versus dialogue. Linear as opposed to parallel. The outer as opposed to the inner. The cosmic exhale as compared to the cosmic inhale.

Or, on a practical day-to-day level, the masculine forces versus the feminine.

Just as the Creator uses these two forces, so does each of us employ both the masculine and feminine dynamics in the many facets of our daily lives.

From the perspective of the Kabbalists, our mission in life is to return the full Divine energy to our world, just as it had been before the "void" was created.

We accomplish this in two ways. One involves drawing new energy via the *kav* to our world, while the other means discovering the *reshimu*, or the Divinity already present within the world's very finiteness and physicality.

We are in a male mode when we go outside of our physical selves and beyond the confines of our material existence in order to impose a higher truth upon our world and ourselves.

When we seek to nurture the Divine power in what already is, and become sensitized to the potential of our inner essence, we are using our feminine dynamic.

In fact, on closer and deeper analysis, the duality of within and without is present even within the *kav* itself, just as it is within all aspects of creation.

The *kav*, too, is made up of two distinct components, a more outer and a more inner dimension. In Chassidic terminology, "*sovev*" is the transcendental nature of the *kav* while "*memaleh*," its imminent nature.

On a practical level, these contrasting natures can better be understood through a metaphor.

There are some teachers who impart the facts, raining down the information until it affects their students. This is the transcendental process. The information is being compressed so it is now within the grasp of the pupil, but it still remains somewhat aloof, outside of the student's sphere. He knows it not on his own, but through the teacher.

Other educators emphasize imparting skills, so that the knowledge need not remain outside the student's sphere, but becomes an actual part of his thought process and experience.

While in the first example, a greater quantity and more powerful information may be transmitted, in the second process the student is opened up to understanding a world of his own, precisely because it comes from within.

The transcendental Divine light is transmitted through an outward process, and it hovers above the inner consciousness of creation, while the imminent one penetrates to deep within.

Similar allusions of outer and inner are found as well throughout the body of Torah literature. In the *Zohar* we have depictions of the "King" and the "Queen"; in the Talmud, descriptions of "Hakodesh Baruch Hu," or the Holy One Blessed be He, and the "Shechina," or feminine Divine presence.

These analogies represent the two faces, so to speak, of G-d, the aspect that transcends our world and the one that imbues it. The masculine "nature" of G-d that hovers above the activities of our world and the feminine one that, like a weeping mother, accompanies and attends to every pain and need of her child.

Creation itself is evolving from a masculine expression to a more feminine one. Its ultimate purpose will be realized with the Messianic era, which is characterized as "a feminine time period."

World redemption is the time when the forces of imposition will be overcome by the forces of nurture. When compassion will overcome dominance and we will cultivate rather than coerce. It is a time of being rather than doing. An era in which peace, rather than war, will pervade. And an epoch representing a utopian way of living, attuned to our inner selves, or in the words of the sages, a time when "the feminine will supersede the masculine."

Until that time, however—and to get us to that experience—we need to discover these two cosmic modalities of expression, which were born with the first breath of creation itself.

MALCHUT
The Feminine Sefira

I n Chassidic thought, physical matter or processes reflect their spiritual origin, and not vice versa. Thus, the feminine or masculine modes can be defined as they manifest themselves in our physical world in accordance with their origin in the spiritual worlds.

SEFIROT
in Kabbala

In Kabbala, anthropomorphic metaphors and analogies using terms that describe physical objects or processes to explain or denote spiritual ones are employed regularly. It must be cautioned that these metaphors are not meant to be taken literally but are merely used to make these concepts more comprehensible. Needless to say, spiritual terms can in no way have any physical or material connotations.

This chapter makes extensive use of Kabbalistic terminology and analogies, and as such may be challenging for the uninitiated reader.[287]

This chapter often employs the Kabbalistic term *sefira*, or in plural, *sefirot*. *Sefirot* describe the flow of Divine light into creation through the medium of a particular attribute. There are ten *sefirot* or Divine conduits, attributes or emanations through which G-d created the world (and continues to animate it). Since G-d Himself transcends description or definition, He utilized these ten attributes to enable man to relate to Him. These *sefirot* also reflect man's mirror image of the Divine as they are, as well, the source of man's soul powers.

The ten Divine *sefirot*, and the ten corresponding human soul powers are divided into two categories of *sechel*, intellect and *middot*, dispositions. *Sechel* comprises the first three of the ten *sefirot*: Chochma, conception; Bina, elaboration; and Daat, integration. These are sometimes referred to as Mochin, Intellect, or Immot, Mothers, because they "give birth to" and are the source of the *middot*.

Middot, dispositions, comprise the next seven *sefirot*, which correspond to the seven days of creation and include: Chessed, kindness; Gevura, severity or restraint; Tiferet, harmonization; Netzach, endurance; Hod, majesty; Yesod, foundation; and Malchut, royalty. In the human being, the *middot* are affected by the *sechel*, which dictates to the individual where his affections should lie and what his dispositions or reactions should be. The first three dispositions, Chessed, Gevura and Tiferet, or *ChaGaT*, are the principal attributes. The next three, Netzach, Hod and Yesod, or *NeHY*, are their branches, and Malchut is the outlet. This chapter focuses primarily on Malchut, which is considered a feminine *sefira*.

MALCHUT

The Feminine Sphere &
Bat, the Daughter

The Ineffable Divine Name, the *Shem Havaye*, (in Greek termed Tetragrammaton), is G-d's holiest of names and was pronounced by the High Priest only on the holiest day of the year, Yom Kippur. This name, consisting of a four-letter combination, yud-hey-vav-hey, represents the creative and sustaining Divine force.

In Kabbalistic works, the four letters of *Havaye*, among other things, are interpreted as an allusion to and depiction of the descent of G-d's Infinite light to infuse and imbue the corporeality of the physical world. [288]

The first letter, the *yud*, is the smallest letter of the Hebrew alphabet and, in shape, is a mere, simple, non-descriptive point. It symbolizes the flash of illumination, the seminal wisdom or the point of inspiration. This *yud* represents the first of the ten *sefirot* or Divine conduits in the creation of our world, called Chochma, or wisdom. It is the first creative activity of G-d and the initial Divine instrument of actual creation.

The next letter, the first of two *hey*s, has both form and dimension. Its expansion of the *yud* in both breadth and length represents Bina, comprehension and development. While the *yud* of Chochma is the initial flash of inspiration, the *hey* of Bina receives this concentrated and compact point. The potential of Chochma is thus brought out from its intensely concentrated, intuitive flash by *bina*. Bina elucidates, expands and differentiates the details of the inspiration through its development.

Nevertheless, the light of illumination in Chochma (represented by the *yud* of *Havaye*) and its elucidation and expansion by Bina (represented by the *hey*) still remain abstract and, as yet, unrealized. The concept of Infinite light is a potential power that needs to be, but has not yet been, actualized.

This two-letter, *yud-hey*, combination of *Havaye* represents the "hidden worlds," as it was conceived in the Divine Mind. These concealed worlds are those that remain united with Him, having no existence apart from Him. An analogy would be the fish of the sea, which cannot exist outside of, or apart from, their element.

The second two-letter combination, *vav-hey*, represents the "revealed worlds," the actual created worlds, including our physical material world. The revealed worlds appear to exist independent of the Creator.

The *vav* in shape extends downwards and represents the descent of the Divine light to lower worlds that appear to be apart from the Infinite.

The final *hey*, like the first, again represents expansion and dimension. It is the creative power exercised and manifest in the created world.

The first combination of G-d's name *(yud-hey)* indicates intellect, which is internal and united with its thinker. Hence these letters are united with the Thinker in the "concealed worlds."

The second combination *(vav-hey)* is the extension of the process initiated in the first letter and relates to "speech," separateness and revealed worlds. Just as speech reveals the ideas in conception and communicates to the outside world, these letters represent the illumination of Divine light into the physical world, which appears distinct from the Creator.

In the metaphorical terminology of Kabbala, Chochma, represented by the *yud*, is also called *Abba*, father. Bina, represented by the *hey*, is also called *Ima*, mother. Metaphorically, the seed of *Abba* is implanted in the womb of *Ima*, where the condensed seminal seed is received, developed, expanded and finally externalized.[289]

The progression then continues from the concealed worlds to the revealed worlds through the medium of the *vav-hey* combination.

The *vav*, numerically equivalent to six, represents the next six emotive *sefirot* from Chessed until Yesod. These six *sefirot* are also called *Ben*, the son, and represent the masculine mode. They channel, implement and apply the original wisdom and understanding. These *sefirot* bring the Divine illumination further down towards our physical reality through their various attributes.

The final *hey* of *Havaye* represents the final *sefira* of Malchut, royalty or kingship. Unlike the other *sefirot*, it remains in a state of being rather than activity. It represents the feminine mode and is also called *bat*, the daughter, or *nukva*, the female.

The potential from the original *yud*'s flash of illumination emerges into manifest reality and substance as a world and creatures that have come into being through the *hey* of Malchut. It is only then, when finite creatures appear through the Divine attribute of Kingship, that the original Divine Will and intent of "desiring a relationship here with the lower world," becomes manifest.

For no matter how great and grand a king may be, by definition, he is not a king unless he has subjects who acknowledge, and subject themselves to, his sovereignty. Consequently, man is a partner in G-d's original plan of creation, since only through his acceptance of G-d's Kingship is the original Divine intent actualized.

Thus, in Malchut, the potentiality is finally realized.

While Bina is considered the Supernal Mother, Malchut is the Nether Mother. The seed of the original *yud* of Chochma becomes externalized and expanded in the womb of Bina, represented by the first *hey*, but remains like a concealed fetus.

The Light continues its descent with the next six *sefirot* represented by the *vav*, as the concealed becomes implemented in the womb of Malchut, the final *hey*, from where it emerges into manifest being.

Thus, Malchut, the Nether Mother, is identical with the Shechina, the Divine Presence in our world, or the weeping Mother that accompanies her children, the Jewish people, along their exile trek.[290]

MALCHUT
and the Feminine Shabbat

Malchut, portrayed by the *hey* of *Havaye*, represents the feminine sphere that is directed inward.

In contrast, the six emotive *sefirot*, or the *vav* of *Havaye*, represent the six outward modes of direction in a three-dimensional world of north-south, east-west, up-down—the masculine modes of extension.

As such, these six *sefirot* also represent the six days of the creation and the six days of the week, excluding the feminine day of Shabbat.

Malchut, the last *sefira* that manifests itself in this world, represents the feminine, harmonious Shabbat. Unlike the six *sefirot* whose direction is outward, it represents the internal, inner mode. It is the axis or focal point at the center of the six directions.

While the masculine quality is characterized by a flurry of activity, Malchut and the feminine represent the state of being.

Internal, inner-bound, Malchut is the center that draws all six points together. The Shabbat, represented by the feminine Malchut, [291] is appropriately called *Shabbat Hamalka,* the Shabbat Queen.

During the six days of the week we are busy doing and accomplishing, but on Shabbat we channel and direct the blessing into all our activities.[292] The feminine Shabbat is, thus, the unifying and harmonizing force that absorbs spirituality from the six masculine days of the week.

On Shabbat, we are no longer in a state of activity or creation, but in a state of *menucha*, rest, receiving and directing blessing from the whole week.

For this reason, Shabbat is called the "source of all blessing," causing the flow of blessing to suffuse all our spiritual and material lacks from the past as well as the coming week.

So, too, in our physical world, a woman, as the representation of Malchut, is the source of blessing for her home and her family.

In her merit, material and spiritual beneficence is drawn down for her family.

Just like the feminine Shabbat, she directs and harmonizes blessing into her environment. As our sages note, "Blessing only comes to a man's household for the sake of his wife" (*Bava Metzia* 59a).

Furthermore, man accomplishes his mission through his various activities. Woman, on the other hand, is in a state of being. Man does, while woman is.

And, like the *sefira* of Malchut, through her being, woman directs the flow of Divine light into her world.

MALCHUT
as the Feminine Womb

In Kabbalistic terminology, the human body is used as a paradigm to depict the functions of each of the *sefirot*.[293] For example, Chessed, gratuitous and unlimited benevolence, is depicted by the right hand, while the left hand depicts Gevura, severity or restraint. Malchut is likened to the female womb.

Malchut exerts no influence of its own, *per se*, since it is the last and "lowest" of the ten *sefirot*, which "has nothing of its own other than what the other *sefirot* pour into it" (*Eitz Chaim* 6:5, 8:5). Malchut receives the light of all the other *sefirot*, and channels and directs a united light into the world, harmonizing all of the diverse attributes of the other *sefirot* within it and projecting the *sefirot* downward into creation.

Malchut, then, is the connecting link. The Divine emanations and attributes are forged together to project a focused light into our functional world.

Accordingly, Malchut cannot have any characteristic or definition of its own, in order to enable it to unify and project the other lights downward into our world. Would it possess its own characteristics, they would inhibit the processing of other characteristics. For example, the characteristic of severity is antagonistic to, and thus precludes the characteristic of, mercy. Malchut, therefore, has no unique, individual characteristic so that it may encompass all the *sefirot* within it to project a more balanced light into the world.

Nevertheless, Malchut is the very instrument through which the entire creative plan comes into being. Therefore "nothing occurs among the lower beings unless it be through Malchut,"[294] which is referred to as the "architect through which the whole creation was made" (*Pardes Rimonim* 11:2).

The womb, too, is the feminine, open, empty vessel that receives the masculine seminal flow. But in addition to receiving, it nurtures, develops and completes something much greater. The seminal potential becomes a viable life force only through the openness, care, nurturance, love and development from its initial conception in the mother's womb.

Similarly, this innate receptiveness, even to the point of emptiness, is personified by the twofold role of Malchut, royalty, and specifically a *melech*, a Jewish monarch. On the one hand, the king used to be the embodiment of grandeur and achievement, widely respected and honored. On the other hand, he was the personification of humility, constantly aware of his nothingness in the presence of the true King of Kings. In this way, the king opened himself up to the Divine influx, which he would share in turn with others.

For this reason, King David, the personification of human royalty, describes himself as "poor and needy." Even though King David hailed from the wealthiest and most distinguished families of Judah, nevertheless, he considered himself poor. Just as a pauper has nothing of his own, but relies on the generosity of others, so, too, King David realized that his whole grandeur was truly an undeserved gift from his Creator.

The Jewish concept of monarchy, then, is one where a king's entire essence, definition and grandeur is predicated upon his acting as a representative of his Creator.

"The honor of the king's daughter is from within" (Ps. 45:14).

For this reason, each woman is considered a *"bat Melech,"* a daughter of royalty, whose entire source of honor, definition or praise is her quintessential inwardness. Due to her predisposition to receiving, there is no strongly expressed, outwardly directed sense of self to block or interfere with her receiving, and then directing, this light into her environment.

As the embodiment of the feminine, Malchut is also compared to the moon, which emanates no light of its own, but rather reflects the light of the sun.

Interestingly, women have been likened to the moon in many ways. In one metaphor, just as the moon waxes and wanes each month, a woman, physiologically, undergoes a monthly cycle of rebirth and rejuvenation as her body renews its capability for receiving and housing potential life.[295]

Furthermore, *rosh chodesh,* the monthly mini-holiday acknowledging the sighting of the new moon and commemorating the beginning of a new Jewish month, is a holiday entrusted to, and celebrated specifically by, Jewish women.

Knesset Yisrael, the Jewish people, or G-d's collective, cosmic bride, also have been metaphorically compared to the moon because of their continual experience of highs and lows, revelations and suppressions, in their receiving the flow of Divine light.

"An extra measure of Bina, *understanding, was endowed to women" (Nidda* 45:2).

A woman, as the physical representation of Malchut, is thus more inclined to receiving a greater measure of understanding and intuition. Since her perception is not impeded or tainted by a particular distinctive spiritual characteristic, her intuitive understanding provides a balanced and focused perspective on life.

Physiologically, woman develops and expands the seminal flash, bringing it from its potential into actual being. Spiritually, too, a woman nurtures the illumination of spirituality from its external, outward approach, directing it inward into her home and environment.

MALCHUT
as Speech and Communication

Speech has also been used to depict the concept of the feminine Malchut.[296] Through speech or the "Ten Utterances" of G-d, creation came into being, enabling G-d's sovereignty to be felt by seemingly distinct created beings. Through this speech, the "hidden worlds" evolved into revealed worlds with the creation of physical reality.

Therefore, Malchut is called the revealed or manifest world, and is also considered the Mouth of G-d, by which the world came into actual being.

The underlying concept of speech is that the hidden, unexposed thought becomes communicated to the outside, revealed world. The thought no longer remains a seminal point or even an elaborated concept within the mind of its originator, but is communicated to others, to be manifest in reality.

So, too, Malchut channels and elicits the original illumination (represented by the *yud*), its elaboration and development (represented by the first *hey*) and its implementation through the various attributes (represented by the *vav*) into actuality (represented by the final *hey*).

Interestingly, on a sociological and psychological level, women, representing the feminine Malchut, generally excel in the domain of speech and communication. It has been noted how men report while women "rapport," developing the ideas and original dry information as they elaborate, convey understanding and relate it to one another.

Thus, the powers to communicate, to nurture and to empathize are all areas in which women, as the feminine representation of the *sefira* of Malchut, really shine.[297]

Furthermore, as creation continues to evolve towards its ultimate intent, when G-d's sovereignty will be felt over all of creation in the era of redemption, the sphere and qualities of Malchut become increasingly more dominant.

In our own day and age, as we approach this era, these feminine qualities of empathy, nurturing and team playing, otherwise termed "soft skills," are becoming more and more sought after and appreciated by both men and women. This holds true in the work force as well as in interpersonal relationships.

The ideal male is no longer the commanding, hard, goal-driven individual, but has, rather, absorbed the traditionally feminine qualities of sensitivity, supportiveness, communication and empathy.

MALCHUT

as Mitzvot
and the Woman of Valor

The *vav* of *Havaye* and its masculine mode represent Torah study. Malchut and the feminine mode represent mitzvot, which elicit the Divine Will into this physical world by utilizing and consecrating the physical aspects of reality. [298]

While the effects of Torah study remain in the realm of thought and the masculine domain of the *vav*, mitzvot bring that Divine thought down into our world through actual practice. The Thought thus becomes transformed into the Will. As the Divine Will becomes a part of our creation, even the most mundane, material aspects of creation are utilized for G-d's will.

That is how, for example, a crude piece of animal hide can become holy, as it is made into parchment for a Torah, mezuza or tefillin scroll. Similarly, food becomes elevated when used to celebrate Shabbat, the holidays, or even when a blessing is said over it, or when the energy derived from its consumption is utilized for the performance of mitzvot. This principle holds true for all mitzvot, since they are performed specifically with physical objects or our physical bodies.

While men, as the *vav*, are associated with the domain of Torah study, women, as the *hey* of Malchut, are associated with the domain of mitzvot. [299] Though she is obligated to study Torah, and though man is commanded to perform mitzvot, each is represented by their respective, primary domains. For a woman, the abstract knowledge gains relevance and becomes translated into practice within the realm of her home and environment through her performance of mitzvot.

"Heed, my son, the instruction of your father, and cast not off the teaching of your mother" (Prov. 1:8).

The Oral Torah[300] is considered the "teaching of your mother," while the Written Torah is considered the "instruction of your father."

The Written Torah,[301] which represents Divine Chochma (or the *yud*, as mentioned above), is indistinct and hidden. The Written Torah also encompasses the 613 Mitzvot, but in a concealed manner. The Oral Torah clarifies and elucidates the mitzvot.

For example, the mitzva of Shabbat, in the Written Torah, is expressed in the Torah as "And you shall do no work."[302] An elaboration, however, of what constitutes or defines work is not provided. The Oral Torah, ,on the other hand, explains the thirty-nine forms of work and describes in precise detail what may or may not be performed on Shabbat.

The same is true for all the other commandments, which are only revealed, explained and understood through the Oral Torah.

Therefore, the Oral Torah is termed metaphorically, "the teaching of your mother." In reality, each of the particular limbs, sinews and attributes of a child are included, in great concealment, in the seed of the father. Nevertheless, only after being implanted in the womb of the mother does this potential develop into a manifest state when the mother finally gives birth.

Similarly, the 248 positive mitzvot and the 365 negative mitzvot emerge from their concealment only through the medium of the Oral Torah, called "the teaching of your mother."

This is also one of the meanings of "A woman of valor is the crown of her husband" (Prov. 12:4). The Oral Torah is termed a "woman of valor," who gives birth to, or develops, the Divine Will concealed within the Written Torah. This Will, as expounded by the Oral Torah and its *halachot*, laws, are more sublime than the original Divine Chochma. For the Written Torah is only revealed through the Oral Torah.

Just as the crown rests atop the head, and therefore ranks higher than it, so, too, the Oral Torah, referred to as the "crown of Torah," is, in a way, loftier than the Written Torah since it contains the Divine Will and brings it to manifestation.

In a practical sense, too, "a woman of valor is the crown of her husband." She brings out the potential in her husband, children, home and environment, in general, revealing its spiritual goodness and beauty.[303]

MALCHUT
The Final Sefira

The *sefira* of Malchut as the *hey* of *Havaye* represents the last and final link in the flow of Divine light into our physical world.

As such, it is identified with the Shechina, the Divine Presence in our world, also called the mourning Mother, who accompanies and weeps with her children throughout their difficult journey in exile.

As the last *sefira*, Malchut absorbs the light of the other *sefirot* and projects a unified, directed light into the world. Therefore, Malchut is compared to the Shabbat, which absorbs and directs the blessing from the entire workweek. Internalizing the accomplishments from the outwardly directed, six days of the week, the feminine Shabbat draws the blessing inward into our world.

Similarly, Malchut is compared to the womb in its capacity to receive the seminal flow, and nurture and develop it into a complete and healthy child.

As such, it is also likened to the moon, that receives and reflects the light from the sun.

Furthermore, as the *sefira* most connected to the realm of actuality, Malchut represents the practical mitzvot and the Divine Will that implements the Divine Thought into concrete action.

For this reason, Malchut is associated with the Oral Tradition, "teachings of your mothers," which elaborates and expands upon the Written Torah, explaining its practical implementation.

Similarly, Malchut is considered the Mouth of G-d and is likened to speech or communication, bringing creation, through His utterances, to its final, created completion.

These representations and imagery all allude to Malchut's feminine mode. Therefore, Malchut is termed *nukva*, the female, or *bat*, the daughter, due to its intrinsically feminine qualities and functions.

"The beginning is wedged in the end" (*Sefer Yetzira* 1:7).

The ultimate intent of creation is actualized only through Malchut, the final *sefira*. Though it is the last of the *sefirot*, it is only through Malchut that the purpose of creation comes to fruition. Nothing occurs without the instrument of Malchut. For only Malchut has the ability to accomplish G-d's original Divine purpose of establishing a relationship with physical beings in this created, lower world.

So, too, in the succession of the six days of creation, woman was created last. She, too, represents this ultimate end that was wedged in the beginning of G-d's original plan. Only through woman and her feminine attributes of Malchut can creation realize its ultimate intent and mission, when "G-d will be King over all creation; on that day, G-d will be One and His Name will be One."[304]

For Further Reflection

- ❧ What is masculine energy?
- ❧ What is feminine energy?
- ❧ With what qualities are women gifted? And men? Are generalizations justified?
- ❧ How does the concept of "*kav* and *reshimu*" relate to men and women and their respective roles and relationships?
- ❧ In the merit of righteous women we will be redeemed—why is this?
- ❧ How is a woman metaphorically similar to the *sefira* of Malchut?
- ❧ A woman of valor is the crowning glory of her husband. Why is this so?
- ❧ How has studying feminine imagery in Kabbala helped you in relating to your role as a Jewish woman? What have you learned?

Section Five

VISION
Feminine Mandate
The Woman's Role

- ❧ Attuned to the Inner Self
  —the Role of Selflessness
- ❧ Through the Eye of a Needle
  —the Role of Harmony
- ❧ Working from Within
  — the Role of Cultivator
- ❧ Women of Royalty
  —the Role of Humility
- ❧ The Creation Story
  —the Role of Redeemer
- ❧ Acting Like a Sole
  —the Role of Faith & Acceptance

ATTUNED
TO THE INNER SELF
The Role of Selflessness

At his grandson's brit mila (circumcision) celebration, the great Chassidic Master, Rabbi Levi Yitzchak of Berditchev (1740-1810), recounted the following episode:

"This morning, I arose very early to prepare myself to perform the brit milah of my dear grandchild. At daybreak I opened the window and saw a penetrating darkness in the heavens. As I wondered about this blackness, it was made known to me that this very day a prince of Israel, the holy tzaddik, Rabbi Moshe Yehuda Leib of Sassov, had passed away.

"As I mourned for that master, I heard a voice cry out: 'Make way for Rabbi Moshe Yehuda Leib!'

"When Rabbi Moshe entered the celestial realms, the tzaddikim formed a joyous circle around him. Suddenly he heard a voice reaching from one end of the world to the other. Intrigued, he followed it until he found himself at the gates of Gehinom (Purgatory).

"Without waiting for permission, Rabbi Moshe entered Gehinom. The guards there saw him walking back and forth, as if looking for someone, and thought that he had surely come by mistake. Politely, they asked him to ascend to the place that had been prepared for him in Gan Eden.

"Rabbi Moshe said nothing. The guards repeated their request, but he was silent and did not move. They did not know whether to drive him out or permit him to remain. The guards decided to confer with the Heavenly Court. But even the court was puzzled, for never since the creation of the world had a tzaddik descended into the fires of Gehinom of his own will. The heavenly court called Rabbi Moshe before the Throne of Glory.

"Rabbi Moshe began: 'Master of the World, You know how great is the mitzva of pidyon shevuyim, the redeeming of captives. I have busied myself with this mitzva my entire life. Never have I differentiated between wicked captives and righteous ones. All of them were equally beloved to me, and whenever I learned of their plight, I tried to redeem them, and had no peace until I had succeeded. Now that I entered the World of Truth, I found many captives here, too. I wish to fulfill this mitzva here, as well.

"'I will not leave Gehinom until I have fulfilled this mitzva. So dear are Your commandments to me that I have observed them no matter what the place or time or penalty might be. If I can bring these wretched captives out into freedom, good; if not, I would rather remain with them in the fires of Gehinom and suffer with them than to sit with the righteous and bask in the light of the Divine Presence!'

"Rabbi Moshe pleaded his case, his face shining with a holy light, his words flying before the Throne of Glory.

"The Holy One, Blessed be He uttered the decision: 'Great are the tzaddikim who are ready to relinquish their share in Gan Eden for the sake of others. Because this mitzva is so great, let it be calculated how many people Rabbi Moshe Yehuda Leib redeemed during his lifetime, both they and their children, and their children's children, until the end of time. That number he may redeem here, also.'

"The Book of Records was immediately brought, opened and read. The names of all those who had been redeemed by Rabbi Moshe were counted and their children and their children's children. The final figure was sixty thousand. Rabbi Moshe Yehuda Leib was permitted to take sixty thousand souls from Gehinom to Gan Eden.

"Rabbi Moshe began to walk through Gehinom, looking into countless pits and caves. He found desolate creatures who had suffered for years and who had long ago lost all hope of redemption. One by one he gathered them and when he finished he found their number to be exactly sixty thousand. They all emerged from Gehinom, marching with him at their head, until they arrived at Gan Eden.

"After all sixty thousand souls had entered, the gates were closed."

After recounting this story, Rabbi Levi Yitzchak named his eight-day-old grandson Moshe Yehuda Leib, and blessed him to grow up to emulate the holy tzaddik, Rabbi Moshe Yehuda Leib of Sassov.

Such is the quality of a tzaddik. When it comes to the welfare of others, a tzaddik is utterly selfless. Rabbi Moshe Yehuda Leib was willing to forego his lofty position in Gan Eden, and remain in the tortuous chambers of Gehinom, if, by doing so, he could save another soul. A tzaddik sees beyond the constrictive, narrow perspective of the self. His vision is panoramic, affording him a cosmic view.

Such complete dedication to the Jewish people was demonstrated by our first leader, Moshe.

Shortly after the Jewish people heard the Ten Commandments directly from G-d, Moshe ascended to heaven to receive the entire Torah. A small group of the Jewish nation[305] feared that Moshe would not return. In their panic, they formed an idol.

After this blasphemous betrayal, G-d threatened to destroy the entire nation and create a new one from Moshe's children. Moshe, however, was not interested in fathering a new nation. Out of his deep love for his flock, Moshe declared that if G-d was unwilling to forgive the Jewish people, then "erase me, too, from the book which You have written" (Ex. 32:32).[306]

To be erased from G-d's book did not simply mean that Moshe's name would not be mentioned. It implied, as well, that his entire role and mission in G-d's plan would be forfeited, and his very being would, thereby, be sacrificed. Moshe was boldly stating to the Alm-ghty that if His intention was to annihilate the Jews of that generation then Moshe, too, wanted no part of G-d's plan.

Moshe was prepared to forsake his very being for the sake of his people. He was willing to terminate his special relationship with the Alm-ghty for the sake of his people, the children of G-d.

Today it is difficult to appreciate the magnitude of such self-sacrifice. The concept of looking outward rather than inward, of seeing beyond the confines of how this is going to affect ourselves, is difficult for us to comprehend. Our generation's focus is on "me"—increasing my pleasures, my standards of living, my own personal growth. A successful person is one who has reached the very top, regardless of who and how many he has stepped on along the way. Careers that involve increasing people's pleasure, improving their appearance, and educating them in asserting themselves and obtaining the most out of life for themselves are amongst the most lucrative.

In Judaism, by contrast, the highest and noblest virtue is the ability to negate one's egotistical self. Suppressing selfish aspirations is achieved through the process of bitul,[307] the nullification of one's self for the sake of a greater good. By becoming more selfless, the individual is capable of more fully experiencing his G-dly soul and appreciating his spiritual purpose.

An explanation in Chassidic teachings concerning the characteristics of a kosher animal further develops this concept. Kosher or permitted animals are those that chew their cud and have split hoofs. Non-kosher or forbidden animals are those that do not possess these two characteristics.[308]

The Hebrew terms for forbidden and permitted are assur and mutar respectively. Assur also means "chained" or "bound." Objects forbidden (assur) by the Torah are tied and bound by the power of impurity and negativity. The G-dly light which animates all aspects of creation is "imprisoned" in these objects and cannot be released. That is why a Jew is forbidden to partake of them, for not even the best intentions can elevate such objects.[309]

The term mutar means "released" or "free." Objects permitted (mutar) by the Torah are not tied down and bound by negative, impure forces. When these items are used for good purposes, their spiritual source is absorbed in the realm of holiness.

The kosher food that a Jew eats becomes a part of his flesh and blood and is a source of energy. When man uses this energy for positive purposes, the creative force contained in the food becomes elevated to the realm of holiness. This can only occur, however, when the food is kosher, and its creative energy is mutar, free to ascend to the holy domains of reality. Non-kosher food, on the other hand, is assur, bound to the realm of unholiness.

The concepts of mutar and assur are symbolized by the hoofs of the animals. Those of the non-kosher animals are closed. The holiness in them is, as it were, locked in, and cannot be liberated. The unsplit, closed hoof is bound to pure physicality, to animalistic desires and goals. Animals with such hoofs are, therefore, assur.

The split hoof of an animal indicates that it has a relationship to both good and evil, and, thus, can be sublimated. The split hoof is open, creating a space for holiness to penetrate. The split hoof does not obstruct holiness, but allows it to radiate out even to the earthly matters to which it is connected. A split hoof, therefore, is a sign that an animal is *mutar*.[310]

Man, like the hoof of the kosher animal, must be split and open to G-dliness. When man breaks from his self-centered existence, he allows holiness to penetrate and become a part of him. Contrary to popular thought, by nullifying himself to G-d's will, by observing His commandments, man does not lose his identity or become "imprisoned"; rather he becomes "released" and "free." He opens himself up to his true, essential self which is imbued with G-dliness.

Only by nullifying his egotistic self can man become in tune with his internal spiritual self. He can reach a state of harmony as physical and spiritual work in unison.

Throughout Jewish history, we have had shining examples of exemplary personalities who have demonstrated to us through their actions the way to attain inner harmony. Through the lives that they led and through the teachings that they imparted, they have enabled us to gain wisdom into how to live our lives more meaningfully. Many of these personalities were women.

The tremendous successes and contributions of these women can easily be applied to the difficult decisions facing modern women. Once some of the outside circumstances or superficial details are removed, it is almost uncanny to notice how many of their issues mirrored the challenges of modern times. When viewed properly, their ancient lifestyles can enhance and provide much needed insight to the life of today's modern women.

Throughout the ages, the common denominator experienced by these great Jewish women has been *bitul*, utter selflessness. Although *bitul* was a dominant force in the lives of all great Jewish leaders, both male and female, women have characteristically been endowed with a greater capacity for self-effacement.

Self-effacement expresses itself in several ways. A few of the characteristics which may surface include: *emuna* (faith), *mesirat nefesh* (self-sacrifice) and *bina* (deeper perception and intuition). Indeed Jewish women have been renowned throughout the ages for their exemplary expression of these specific characteristics.

Let's examine these characteristics through a parent-child analogy to discover their relationship to *bitul*.

A child trusts his parents, believes in what they tell him, and follows their directives. He does so because, in his eyes, his parents are perfect. They seem to be all-knowing and all-powerful.

Compared to how he views their all-encompassing stature, his own sense of self is insignificant. All his needs are filled by them, and, without their help, there is little that he is capable of accomplishing.

As the child matures and becomes increasingly aware of his own capabilities, he becomes more independent. He wants less parental involvement in certain areas of his life. Having discovered his independence, he begins to resist more and more of his parents' instructions. He has his own will and doesn't want to subordinate himself to his parents. At times, he will disobey his parents' directives without realizing their benefits, just in order to act on his own. Unaware of his own limited insight, he may actually harm himself.

We could say that the older the child becomes, the more he sees himself as a separate and unique individual. As an infant, he relied on his parents for everything. He had complete trust in them and in their abilities. As an adult he perceives their flaws and shortcomings and is more aware of his own capabilities and talents.

In a parent-child situation, it would be abnormal for the child not to mature in this manner and reach these conclusions. His parents, no matter how intelligent or refined, are, nevertheless, still people. As the child grows and becomes more intellectually and emotionally mature, he becomes capable of judging for himself how to behave.

In contrast, the distance between man and G-d is not even comparable to that of an infant to an adult. A human being is so far removed from G-d, that he would more accurately be compared to a stone than to the Infinite, Omnipotent G-d. Nevertheless, the child-parent analogy is similar in the sense that just as an infant is completely dependent on his parent for all his needs, so are we dependent on G-d. We become concerned with our self only when we lose the awareness that we are merely extensions of G-d.

When an individual constantly recognizes that G-d animates and vitalizes him at every moment, he realizes how insignificant he truly is. This awareness enables man to achieve *bitul*, negation of his sense of self to his Creator.

We can now appreciate the connection between *bitul* and *emuna*. *Emuna* is generally translated as "belief"; in truth, its meaning is much deeper.

To the individual who has achieved *bitul*, the reality of G-d is unshakable, as is his trust in Him. The source of this clarity is his soul, which knows G-d, just as his body relates to physical reality. A person's knowledge of the physical world cannot be termed faith or belief, since it is an absolute knowledge based on the five senses. To the soul, G-d is the true reality.

An individual whose consciousness is connected to his soul clearly perceives the reality of G-d. This awareness is unshakable and will not be affected by any circumstances. Such a level of awareness can only be attained through *bitul*. Man becomes attuned to his soul and perceptive to the reality of G-d to the point that it becomes as clear and as concrete as the physical world—and even more so—only by removing the barrier of self-consciousness.

The individual who has attained *bitul* will also possess *bina*, a deeper, intuitive perception of the inner workings of the world. Since he is not bound by the confines of his own desires, his perception is not slanted by his own self-awareness. He can look at matters with a fuller and clearer vision; he isn't constrained by his own view, as his own personal outlook is non-existent.

Such an individual can more readily achieve the level of *mesirat nefesh*, self-sacrifice. Since the individual has a clear perception of true reality, he will be willing to sacrifice his very self for the sake of what he knows is a higher purpose. Though the life of an individual is his most precious possession, in the face of the Omnipotent, he willingly sacrifices himself for G-d.

Thus Moshe led the way for Reb Moshe Yehuda Leib Sassov, in the above illustration, as well as for numerous other great Jewish men and women throughout our history who willingly sacrificed even their spiritual selves for the Jewish people. This is the highest expression of *mesirat nefesh*, when an individual's spiritual goals and pleasures are sacrificed for the sake of G-d's will or His People.

Emuna, *bina* and *mesirat nefesh* are of the loftiest traits that an individual can aspire to attain in this world. The key to elevating oneself to such levels is *bitul*. The negation of one's self for the sake of the Creator's will is also the only method for attaining true inner harmony.

The lives of our great female role models from our past demonstrated an incredible power of *bitul*. This was the characteristic quality that imbued their lives.

As women, and as Jewish women, and in particular as Jewish women living in today's spectacular times, we must celebrate the power and strength of this quality. And we, too, can tap into our own feminine power and strength to bring more fulfillment and completion into our own lives, and into the world at large.

THROUGH
THE EYE OF A NEEDLE
The Role of Harmony

A woman of valor who can find? She is more precious than pearls... She puts her hand to the spindle and her palms support the distaff..." (Prov. 31: 10, 19).

The needle pierces the pieces of cloth, joining its divisions. To and fro the needle sews, creating a new unity in the disjointed material. As the needle completes its final stitch, the cloth becomes whole.

Man is like the needle. Throughout his life he toils to and fro, connecting the disjointed elements of our material world. Weaving his way through the fabric of life, he sews spirituality into his surroundings. His thread is Torah and mitzvot, through which he imbues the whole of creation with life and purpose, to achieve its G-dly intent.

The needle's tip is sharp and pointy. The stiff cloth bends under the steely tip. Aggressive and forceful, no stubborn cloth will interfere with the needle's path. Pushing ahead, it will unite the many tears of the fabric.

A person can learn from the needle's tip to persevere in accomplishing his G-dly mission. Relentlessly pursuing his goals, one should not be sidetracked by difficulties. With confidence and resolve, one must meet the challenge of infusing every piece of physical matter with spiritual vitality. With perseverance and a head-on approach, one must continue weaving the light of Torah and mitzvot into all aspects of creation.

The other end of the needle seems dull and hollow. It merely tags along, following the lead of its other more assertive half. It neither imposes its rule, nor breaks through any new frontiers.

Yet, as subordinate as it may seem, the eye of the needle provides the power for this tool. The secret of the needle's success lies precisely in the connecting threads housed within this cavity.

The needle's hollow end reminds man of the humility which must accompany his aggressive march ahead. Only with the realization that he is but a vessel—an empty, hollow vessel—can he achieve his mission.

While externally his approach must be confident and assertive, overcoming all outside challenges, he must maintain a deeper, inner understanding that he, too, is merely a created vessel for carrying out a higher Will. Only by his appreciation of his true worth can man achieve his lofty goal of uniting all of creation, permeating it with its spiritual intent.

Man is the pointed, assertive tip of the needle. Woman is its hollow end.

Man fights and harasses the evil of the world; woman imbues it with the thread of harmony, bringing out its latent good.

Man pushes through new frontiers and challenges; woman cultivates these terrains.

Man leads; woman develops.

Man is outer; woman is inner.

Man projects the aggressiveness; woman, the humility.

Man opens new challenges; woman houses life.

Man appears on the forefront; woman carries the meaning and purpose.

Man has the strength of character; woman, the secret of life's mission.

Man takes the lead during the period of exile, woman is the shining force during the era of redemption.

Within creation lies its essential unity—namely, its G-dly core. Though this is the uniting factor of all of creation, this G-dly essence is not always apparent. Woman's role is to unveil this underlying secret— a role that is therefore often a secretive one, directed inward.

By uncovering the inner secret of the hollow eye of the needle, we discover the true strength of woman in her ability to reveal good and integrate it into all aspects of creation.

WORKING
FROM WITHIN
The Role of Cultivator

L ife—it is full of opportunities and choices, a monumental gift
replete with potential. It is a mass of raw matter to be
developed, cared for and transformed into meaning and
purpose. It requires ongoing care and devotion, a constant
infusion of direction and focus.

"Man was born to toil" (Job 5:7).

Creating a higher purpose out of this raw mass of potential is
a lifelong journey of strenuous labor. Nevertheless, we are
cautioned, "It is not up to you to complete the work, but neither
are your absolved from the effort" (*Avot* 2:16).

Inherent in human life itself is the desire to make an impact
upon our surroundings, to employ our abilities to make a
difference. Along with the twinkle of the eye, marking the desire
for life itself, comes the human need to imprint upon humanity,
and on the world around us, our unique contribution.

Rabbi Yitzchok of Homil (1780-1857), one of the foremost
students of Rabbi Shneur Zalman of Liadi, the author of the
Tanya, said:

*"We all look at the same world; but what we see depends on
who we are.*

*"To a child, a coin is a shiny toy; to a laborer, a loaf of bread
after a weary day; to a merchant, a chance to make two coins."*

There are many ways of leaving our imprint upon the world—
indeed, as numerous as the paths life itself holds. But humanity's
true gift is not an accomplishment of temporal, materialistic or
fleeting existence, but the transformation of negativity and the

creation of an everlasting positive edifice. Collectively and individually, we strive for the ultimate bequest: a higher moral, a larger truth, an act of spirituality and G-dliness brought into everyday existence.

Some achieve this through intellectual endeavors—a well thought-out system of living, a theory of equality or altruism. Others fulfill it through emotional or practical endeavors—a smile to a neighbor, or a good word to a downtrodden passer-by.

Whatever the means, if in the right spirit, if infused with the correct intent, both can achieve their goal and endow goodness to the world. Each can bring a higher level of spirituality, a glimmer of G-dliness into our midst.

The purpose of man's creation and the creation of all worlds, higher and lower, is to make for G-d a dwelling place in the material world.[311]

Originally G-d had a desire—a desire to have a relationship with the most physical of beings, within our materialistic, temporal world of action. In order to develop this relationship, we need to attach ourselves with the One who seeks this relationship. Yet how does a finite, physical mortal forge an attachment to the Omniscient, Omnipotent, Infinite Creator?

Rabbi Shneur Zalman of Liadi once overheard his wife referring to him in a conversation with her neighbors, "Mine [i.e., my husband] says..."

Rabbi Shneur Zalman remarked: "Through a single mitzva [the mitzva of marriage], I am yours. With the performance of the mitzvot, how many times over are we G-d's?!"

"For you are my light, O G-d" (2 Sam. 22:29).
"The soul of man is the flame of G-d" (Prov. 20:27).
"A mitzva is a flame, Torah is the light" (Prov. 6:23).

G-d, the Infinite Light, is attached to the flaming soul of man through the commandments of His Torah, called mitzvot,[312] which are themselves shining candles of light.

Torah is the revelation of G-d's wisdom. Studying the Torah imbues our consciousness with this G-dly wisdom.

The direction of Torah study is downwards,[313] from the highest spiritual worlds down into our world of mundanity.

Mitzvot, and particularly prayer, on the other hand, are supplications from our innermost selves, from our very depths. Their direction is upwards, reaching from our lowly world to higher plateaus of the spirit. From below, they rise above.

In our quest to affect creation, there are two divergent approaches: one typifies the feminine essence while the other, the masculine.

Though man and woman in their daily lives utilize both the masculine and feminine modes, each has its own distinct characteristics, which play a major, defining role in their respective missions in life.

R. Yossi questioned Eliyahu, "G-d said, 'I will make for Adam [a woman as] a helpmate.'[314] How is a woman a helpmate to her husband?"

Eliyahu answered, "Man brings home the wheat, yet does he chew the wheat? Man brings home flax, yet can he wear flax?" (Yevamot 63a).

The masculine mode of service is to draw G-dliness down into this world,[315] creating a new dimension of spirituality in our physical surroundings. Man forges into this new territory, utilizing his aggressive talents to fight the world's evil, to bring home his raw game.

Woman, on the other hand, takes this raw mass and refines it. She brings out its inherent goodness by cultivating and nurturing it to reach its highest potential.

Man, from without, reaching for the heavens, brings G-dliness into creation. Woman, working from within, uplifts all of creation.[316]

Man brings down the Divine light of G-d's wisdom into our world. Woman elevates and saturates creation by exposing and developing its inherent good.

Therefore, the prototype of man's service is depicted by Torah study,[317] which takes precedence over all of his other duties and obligations.[318] Prayer[319] and certain mitzvot, on the other hand, embody the prototype of woman's service. Ascending the spiritual rungs of the ladder of prayer, she permeates all of reality with G-dliness.

Both directions in this relationship with G-d are necessary. Bringing spirituality down into creation is just as necessary as elevating all aspects of creation to the Divine.

While both man and woman utilize each other's modes of direction in developing and strengthening their potential, on a practical level, each has intrinsic, unique capabilities that enable them to best fulfill their mission of refining their surroundings.

Through her spiritual makeup and through her particular mitzvot, woman permeates the physical with the Divine. She utilizes her spiritual powers to imbue the very essence of physical reality with its G-dly intent.

Through her singular contribution, woman can transform the unformed matter of life itself, endowing the world the ultimate gift: creating a suitable dwelling-place for G-d in the material world.

WOMEN
OF ROYALTY
The Role of Humility

After our Matriarch Leah's fourth son was born, she joyously named him Yehuda, Judah. In explaining her choice of name, Leah exclaimed: "This time, I thank [*odeh*, root of Yehuda] the L-rd" (Gen. 29:35).

Leah was aware that her husband, Yaakov, was to father the twelve Tribes of Israel. Since Yaakov had married four wives (Rachel, Leah, Bilha and Zilpa), Leah assumed that each would give birth to three children. Thus, when her fourth child, Yehuda, was born, she joyously thanked G-d for giving her this extra blessing.

The essence of Yehuda, as expressed by his name, is a state of gratitude to G-d for an undeserved gift. Therefore, all Jews are called Yehudim, regardless of their actual tribe. This demonstrates how a Jew is forever aware of G-d's graciousness, and thanks Him for all His undeserved gifts.[320]

In fact, the very letters of Yehuda's name allude to total subservience to and appreciation of G-d for undeserved good. The word Yehuda consists of the four letters of the Tetragrammaton (the Ineffable name of G-d, spelled with the Hebrew letters *yud*, *hey*, *vav* and *hey*), with the additional letter *daled*. In Hebrew, *dal* (the root of *daled*) means "pauper."

A beggar relies on the generosity of the public. Everything he has depends on the goodwill and kindness of his benefactors, not on his worthiness or productivity. He is always the recipient of their mercy and charitable acts. Simply put, a pauper is humble.

Yehuda, likewise, regarded himself as a mere pauper, considering all he had as undeserved gifts from G-d. Yehuda represents the sensitivity to perceive that all created beings are merely recipients of G-d's mercy and kindness. He realized that he was sustained not on account of his intrinsic worth, but because of the goodness of the Creator.[321]

Yehuda, therefore, embodied the qualities necessary for a Jewish king. On his deathbed, Yaakov blessed each of his sons, promising Yehuda that the royal families of the Jewish people would descend from him.[322] In fact, Melech HaMashiach, the ultimate King of the Jewish people, must be a direct descendant of King David, a member of the tribe of Yehuda.[323]

A Jewish Monarch

A rightful king of the Jewish people must descend from Yehuda because the king must emulate the essential characteristics embodied by Yehuda. The role of a Jewish king is twofold. On one hand, he personifies grandeur and achievement. He is widely respected and honored greatly by his people. On the other hand, he should be the epitome of humility. He needs to constantly be aware of his subservience to G-d, the true King of Israel, displaying an absolute submission to G-d's will as expressed in the Torah.

For this reason he is obliged to carry a Torah scroll at all times.[324] He must realize that he only exemplifies the sovereignty of G-d, and that all the grandeur surrounding him is completely undeserved. He has to view himself as little more than a common pauper whose every possession originates from charity—a gift from his Creator.

This ideal was achieved by King David, the illustrious king of the Jewish people, and forebear of Mashiach. The letters in David's name begin and end with a *daled*, illustrating his quality of absolute humility. Despite all his accomplishments and royal surroundings, David considered himself a pauper, dependent on G-d's bountiful gifts. He understood that, based on his own merit, he possessed and deserved nothing. Royal power and honor were given to him only as an ambassador of G-d.

For this reason, King David declares four times in Psalms, "I am poor and needy."[325] David's declaration of abject poverty is puzzling, as he belonged to one of Yehuda's wealthiest and most distinguished families. What he meant, however, was that just as a poor person feels indebted to his benefactor, so too, David felt thoroughly indebted to G-d for all that he had achieved.

Hence, a true king of the Jewish people has no independent existence. His very self, completely nullified, is but an expression of G-dliness.[326]

Mashiach's Donkey

For this reason, Mashiach is described as "a pauper riding a donkey" (Zech. 9:9). Mashiach is destined to complete the purpose of creation by totally unifying the spiritual and the physical. He will do so by crowning G-d King over mankind. Hence, the word Mashiach has the same numeric value (358) as *"Hashem Melech, Hashem Molach, Hashem Yimloch—*G-d is King, G-d was King, G-d will be King [forever and ever]" (*Siddur, Pesukei d'Zimra*).□

Nevertheless, Mashiach is depicted as a pauper riding the humblest of beasts. In his own estimation, he is merely a channel for bringing Divinity into physical reality. He is an embodiment of G-d's will on earth and has no will of his own. Therefore, Mashiach is referred to as Bar Nafla, meaning, "the fallen one" (*Sanhedrin* 96b). The soul of Mashiach experiences itself continuously falling and dying. If not for the ever-present Hand of G-d "catching" it, it would crash and shatter. The consciousness of the fall is the reflection of the egoless state of Mashiach.[327]

Accordingly, the animal that Mashiach rides is a donkey. The Hebrew word for donkey is *chamor*, which is comprised of the same root letters as *chumriyut*, material matter. Mashiach, who infuses spirituality into physical reality will consequently elevate the entire realm of *chumriyut*.

Above Materiality

There are three instances in the Torah where an individual used a donkey to aid in the elevation of material matter. When Avraham traveled to Mt. Moria to fulfill G-d's mission of sacrificing his son at G-d's behest, he saddled his donkey, which carried his belongings.[328]

Moshe, too, used a donkey. After his encounter with G-d at the burning bush, Moshe was instructed by G-d to return to Egypt to redeem the Jewish people from Egyptian bondage. On this journey, Moshe put his wife and two sons atop a donkey.[329]□

A donkey is mentioned a third time, in describing Mashiach as "a pauper riding a donkey."

Avraham saddled his possessions on a donkey and Moshe sat his wife and two sons atop a donkey. But only Mashiach, himself, actually rides the donkey. According to Chassidic teachings, this signifies that only Mashiach has the ability to completely synthesize the physical dimension, *chumriyut*, with Divinity.[330]

Elevating the Physical

Before *matan Torah*, (the giving of the Torah), the physical and spiritual did not intersect.[331] Avraham made no lasting impression on physicality. His donkey was not capable of carrying a spiritual person of his caliber. His animal was used only for the purpose of transporting physical possessions.

Closer to the time of *matan Torah*, Moshe used his donkey to carry his wife and sons, who were an extension of himself. Although his essential self had no connection with the physical dimension, nevertheless, there was a connection, albeit limited, between the spiritual and the physical.

The goal of Mashiach is to utilize physical reality for G-dliness, thereby elevating the physical to a state of spiritual. He will do so by being an ultimate expression of royalty devoted exclusively to G-d. Since his own ego will be nullified, his whole existence will be that of a vessel for G-dliness. He will act as the unifying force between the physical and spiritual worlds by being the conduit for G-dliness in this physical world.

Making Room for G-d

The nullification of the ego is a prerequisite for prophecy, a transmission of Divine Will. It is for this reason that during the prophetic experience the prophets invariably speak of themselves in the third person. Moshe himself said, "And G-d spoke to Moshe" (Ex. 4:4; 4:19, etc.). Yaakov said, "Gather around and listen, O sons of Yaakov!" (Gen. 49:2). Devora sang, "Awake, awake Devora!" (Judg. 5:12). There are many other similar examples.

The prophets use the third person because their consciousness has been so elevated that their bodies seem as if devoid of their soul. It therefore appeared as if they were another person. They achieved total detachment from themselves. Only an individual at this level of total indifference to any external influences (including his own) can be a vehicle for revealing the Divine Presence.[332]

To illustrate this complete lack of selfhood, the following account is recorded:

A sage once came to a member of a group who spent much time meditating on G-d's greatness and His world, and asked that he be accepted into their society.

The reply was, "My son, blessed are you to G-d. Your intentions are good. But tell me, have you attained self-effacement [complete objectivity where one has no ego]?"

The sage said, "Master, explain your words."

The meditator said, "If one man is praising you and another is insulting you, are the two equal in your eyes or not?"

He replied, "No, my master. I have pleasure from those who praise me and pain from those who degrade me. But I do not take revenge or bear a grudge."

The other said, "Go in peace, my son. You have not attained self-effacement. You have not reached a level where your soul does not feel the praise of one who honors you, nor the degradation of one who insults you. You are not prepared for your thoughts to be bound on high, that you should come and meditate. Go and increase the humbleness of your heart..."

Similarly, a related episode is told of the Kotzker Rebbe. He was five years old when he asked his father, "Where is G-d?"

His father answered, "G-d is everywhere!"

He replied, "I think G-d is found only where you let Him in."

To perceive G-dliness, an individual must "make room" for G-d in his life. Thus the Jewish monarch, who is a physical representation of G-d's will, must have no sense of self so that his whole being can serve as a vessel for the transmission of G-dliness. This level was attained by King David and ultimately will be perfected by Mashiach.

Feminine Royalty

A woman, too, intrinsically represents this quality of Jewish royalty, where no expression of self interferes between her and the Divine Will.

In the teachings of Kabbala, it is explained in detail that the creation of this physical world came about through a progression of channels of Divine light affecting creation, known as *sefirot*. Each *sefira* imbues creation with its own unique characteristic. To illustrate, the *sefira* of Chochma, Wisdom, contains the attribute of intelligence. The *sefira* of Chessed, Kindness, brings mercy and the element of giving into creation. In contrast, the *sefira* of Gevura, Might, introduces restriction, and so forth with all the remaining *sefirot*.

The final *sefira*, Malchut, is unique in that it lacks its own distinctive character. It represents receiving and is characterized as the *sefira* that "has nothing of its own" (*Zohar* 1:238a, *Eitz Chaim* 6:5). On the other hand, Malchut acts as the unifying *sefira*, harmonizing all of the diverse attributes of the *sefirot* within it, and projecting the *sefirot* downwards into creation.333

Accordingly, Malchut cannot have a definition of its own. Something that possesses characteristics of its own will immediately exclude other characteristics. For example, the characteristic of severity excludes the characteristic of mercy. Malchut, therefore, has no unique, individualistic characteristic so that it may encompass all the *sefirot* within it to project a more focused light into the world.

The six *sefirot* from Chessed till Yesod represent the six basic directions of the three-dimensional physical universe: north-south, east-west and up-down. They represent the fundamental modes of reaching out to the six directions of creation. These *sefirot* are referred to as the masculine *sefirot* because they are directed outward. Malchut, in contrast, is the axis or focal point at the center of the six directions; instead of being directed outward, Malchut is directed inward and integrates all spiritual illumination. Malchut is therefore referred to as the feminine *sefira*.

The Harmony of Shabbat

Sefer Yetzira (1:5) explains that the six days of the week are masculine and that they represent the six outward directions. Shabbat, on the other hand, which is feminine, is the center that draws all six points together. All week long, in our struggle to connect to G-d, we operate in a masculine mode. On the Shabbat, we are on a female level, absorbing the fruits of all we have done during the week. The feminine Shabbat is, thus, the unifying and harmonizing force which is capable of absorbing spirituality from the six masculine days of the week.

According to Kabbalistic literature, women are the physical representation of Malchut. Just as Malchut has no identity other than the unification of all the *sefirot*, so, too, women's identity is nothing more nor less than G-dliness. The essential core of a woman has no definition other than a Divine one.

While men are represented by the various conflicting forces of the *sefirot*, women, like Malchut, are more unified and intrinsically more centered on their G-dly goals. While the paradigm of a man is more diversified, the paradigm of a woman is more focused and consistent in fulfilling her purpose and spiritual calling.

Spiritual Powers

For this reason women are exempt from many mitzvot that men are obligated to perform. The feminine essence is intrinsically bound up with and sensitive to G-dliness. A woman, therefore, does not require the spiritual influences of certain mitzvot, as she already possesses this spirituality.

The mitzva of tefillin, phylacteries, is a prime example of the above concept. One set of tefillin is bound on the arm, near the heart; a second set of tefillin is worn on the head. These positions allude to man's source of strength and desire, as well as his source of intellect. The tefillin, thus, are meant to assist in the subordination of man's desires and reasoning to the Divine Will.

The same is true with regard to other mitzvot which men are obligated to fulfill. The tzitzit surrounding his body connect a man's physical body to G-dliness. The *kippa* worn on the head signifies the subjection of the ego to a greater Being above.

The mitzvot, then, serve as conduits of spiritual energy, strengthening a man's ability to nullify the various elements of his being to the will of G-d. A man's strongly defined emotive and intellectual faculties require the special spiritual energy contained in the performance of mitzvot. A woman, however, does not require these additional powers from outside sources, as she already possesses them from within.

Receiving and Completing

The difference between the masculine and feminine spiritual constitution is represented by their respective roles in reproduction. The man is the giver while the female is the receiver. The man gives to the woman, but she, in turn, produces much more than the man initiated. She receives but ultimately ends up creating and developing something complete. If masculinity is giving, femininity is receiving, developing and completing.

Malchut is likened to a woman's womb. Malchut, too, has the ability to receive and hold the light of the *sefirot*, eventually channeling them into the world in a more complete state.

Since the woman's essence is by nature more harmonized with Divine Will than the man's, an interesting question may be asked. If Mashiach is a physical representation of G-d's will in this world, and women have a stronger inclination to G-dliness, why is Mashiach not a woman? The *halacha* (Jewish law) clearly stipulates that Mashiach will be a male descendant from the House of David.334 Why, we may ask, are women excluded from this position, particularly since they possess a natural bond with G-d's will not found in their male counterparts?

Moshe and Eliyahu

To help us gain a deeper appreciation of the essential difference between the nature of men and women, we will contrast two of the greatest Jewish personalities, Moshe Rabbeinu, and Eliyahu Hanavi, Elijah the Prophet.

Moshe reached the highest level of prophecy attainable by a human being. G-d spoke directly with Moshe, "face to face" (Num. 12:8), as it were. During a prophetic experience, his entire speech center became attached and one with the Divine. No other human being ever had or ever will have a closer relationship with G-d.335 Still, at the age of one hundred and twenty, Moshe ultimately died.

Eliyahu, on the other hand, did not attain a level of such intimacy with G-d. His prophetic experience did not come close to the clarity and directness of Moshe's prophecy. Yet, Eliyahu never died. His body became so completely spiritual that it did not require the experience of death, but rather lived on in the spiritual worlds.

This paradox can be explained by analyzing the unique Divine service of each of these Jewish leaders.

Moshe had attained such a high level of spirituality that his connection to his physical dimension was practically severed. His physical self was so nullified, that it was as if he had no physical self. His soul was so sublime and holy that it was almost detached from his body. Consequently, his soul's effect on his body was limited because of this weak relationship.

Craving Meat

The complete nullification of Moshe's physical dimension was demonstrated when the Jewish people requested meat in the desert. Although the Jewish people were miraculously provided with sustenance in the form of "manna," they longed for real meat. When they complained to Moshe, he responded, "From where can I get meat to give to these people?" (Num. 11:13)

Chassidic teachings explain that Moshe was implying that he could not supply them with physical meat because he could not relate to it. He was so removed from mundane needs that he could not identify with a physical desire to eat meat. Thus, he knew that he would be powerless to provide it.[336]

Immediately following this episode, G-d instructed Moshe to gather seventy Elders and share his responsibilities with them (Num. 11:16). Moshe would not teach the Jewish people directly, rather he would teach Aharon and the Elders, who in turn would instruct the Jewish people.

Moshe's sublime soul was on such a lofty spiritual level that he could not relate to the physical needs or desires of the people. He needed Aharon and the Elders, who could relate better to physicality, to help him lead the Jewish people. In addition, Aharon and the Elders were in a better position to assist the nation in conquering their non-essential desires.

The Ultimate Integration

Mashiach will be the epitome of holiness, but, unlike Moshe, will not be detached from the material. He will be a most righteous individual who will have the power and capability of synthesizing spirituality with physicality. Mashiach will achieve this ultimate perfection not through a detachment from the physical dimension, but by elevating it to the level of Divinity.

To accomplish this synthesis, Mashiach must be a male. Due to her intrinsic selfless nature, a woman could not epitomize this integration. Focusing on Divinity comes more naturally to a woman, since it is part of her essential spiritual makeup. Mashiach's mission is to teach and set an example for all mankind in how to elevate one's physical self. Consequently, Mashiach cannot be a woman, who has a less dominant physical inclination.

On the other hand, as women do have a closer union with the Divine Will, they will prepare the world for Mashiach. Women, with their steadfast faith and spiritual determination, will encourage others to usher in this new spiritual era. Indeed, as our Sages have remarked, "In the merit of righteous women our forefathers left Egypt" (*Sota* 11b; *Shemot Rabba* 1:12). Similarly, the future redemption will occur in the merit of righteous women.[337]

Perhaps this may be hinted at, as well, by the Hebrew words for male and female. Male is *zachar*, which also means "remember." Female is *nekeiva*, which contains the same letters as the word *nekeiv*, or "pierce." This signifies that the appreciation for the male's character is in the past, remembered. A woman will truly be appreciated, however, in the future after the exile has been "pierced" and we have reached the redemption.

Women of the Future

In the eras prior to the redemption, when the quality of self-sacrifice for a higher goal is less understood, men dominate. Women, however, who represent the state of utter nullification to G-d's will, can be truly appreciated only in the future, in the era of Mashiach. When G-dliness finally pervades the world openly, the uniqueness of her Divine essence will shine with remarkable radiance.

By utilizing their spiritual qualities, women pierce through the bitter *galut*, bringing forth the perfect era of the redemption when creation will be imbued with utter Divinity, "as the waters cover the sea bed" (Isa. 11:9).

THE
CREATION STORY
The Role of Redeemer

Against the backdrop of rolling valleys and mountains, and a sun bathing the world with its warmth, creation awaits its finale. Adding infinite texture and destiny to the flow of life force of the fish of the sea, the livestock of the land and the birds of the sky, creation climaxes with the birth of humanity.

The dramatic course of the past six days culminates in the conception of Adam. Against the perpetual rhythm of creation itself, mankind represents it critical zenith.

As G-d breathes into Adam his first breath of life, the challenge and responsibility as well as privilege and destiny of all creation is born. On his shoulders rests the burden and the merit of making his world a home compatible for his Creator.

As such, we would have expected Adam's creation to be recorded in Genesis as the peak event within a flowing story line. Interestingly, though, the birth of mankind is recorded as two almost separate and independent events, in two separate chapters of Genesis.

Creation of Man

And G-d said, "Let us make man in Our image and Our Likeness. They shall rule over the fish of the sea, the birds of the sky and over the cattle, the whole earth and every creeping thing that creeps on the earth."

So G-d created man in His image, in the image of G-d, He created him, male and female, He created them.

G-d blessed them and said to them, "Be fruitful and multiply, fill the earth and conquer it; and rule over the fish of the sea, the bird of the sky and every living thing that moves on the earth..."

And G-d saw all that He had made, and behold it was very good. And there was evening and there was morning, the sixth day.

The first Adam—created as male and female—is created in G-d's image. He is commanded to "conquer," "fill" and "rule over creation."

(Gen. 1: 26-28, 31)

Creation of Woman

These are the products of the heaven and earth....

Now no tree of the field was yet on the earth and no herb of the field had yet sprouted for G-d had not sent rain upon the earth and there was no man to work the soil.

A mist ascended from the earth and watered the whole surface of the soil.

And G-d formed the man of dust from the earth and He blew into his nostrils the soul of life and man became a living being...

G-d took the man and placed him in the Garden of Eden, to keep and to guard it...

G-d said, "It is not good that man be alone, I will make him a helper corresponding to him..."

And man assigned names to all the cattle and to the birds of the sky and to every beast of the field, but as for man, he did not find a helper corresponding to him.

So G-d cast a deep sleep upon the man and he slept, and He took one of his sides and He filled in its place.

Then G-d fashioned the side that He had taken from the man into a woman, and He brought her to the man...

(Gen. 2: 4-7, 15, 18, 20-22)

Keeping and Guarding

In the second account of humanity's creation, we learn of a human being formed "from the dust of the earth" who is charged to "keep and guard" creation.

In this version, we find the necessity of an independent "helper corresponding to him," since at this stage, "it was not good that man be alone."

Much commentary has been written on the unusual and two-fold structure of mankind's coming into being. Clearly, there are two versions to mankind's creation, each accompanied by an independent destiny.

The first Adam is a figure of will and contest. He is dignified in his mastery over creation, existing in the realm of victorious acts. He is the ultimate conqueror.

He rules with his strength and through his conquest. He is functional.

Formed in the "image of G-d," he is commanded to "subdue," "rule" and "conquer" the world.

His role in creation is to banish the earthly darkness, impose rule and order. He acts through a hierarchy of domination and control in an active and aggressive effort to overcome the nature of reality.

He works the earth, beating it until its fruit emerges. He reshapes physical matter, winnowing, plowing and harvesting until he extracts its bounty.

Never satisfied to just be, he breaks through new frontiers, searching for more. He develops, challenges and pushes creation to its limits—and beyond.

First Adam, the conqueror, draws down new potential and abilities—and G-dliness—from the outside.

In the second version, on the other hand, we are introduced to a non-functional, receptive, loyal and submitting being.

He is separated from nature not by his dominion over it, but rather by his covenant to "keep" and "guard" it. He is entrusted to redeem the world, to protect it. He does not rule by authority or dominance, but rather nurture and dialogue.

Formed "from the dust of the earth," he relates to what is, rather than what is to become.

He lives with a vision to make the world a home for his Creator, by uncovering the light already implicit within. He finds G-dliness within the world, rather than importing it from without and imposing it onto creation.

While the first man lives with the assertion of the will, the second lives with its extinction.

The first masters the world, imposing a G-dly rule on creation. The second offers creation in humble dedication to G-d.

If first man is a conqueror, second is a protector and redeemer.

Interestingly, while woman is present at both accounts—"male and female He created them"—in the second version she comes into being as her own independent personage, with her own destiny.

Up until this point, creation, including Adam, was "very good." For in the realm of victorious acts, woman did not play an independent, nor primary, role.

However, in the redemptive, protective role, it becomes very evident that "it is not good that man be alone." The keen necessity of an independent "helper corresponding to him" is born. Man as ruler and master needs an equally powerful and influential creation, "corresponding to him" to be charged with the sometimes contradicting, opposing or parallel redemptive role.

She emerges in the form of Chava, Eve, or Isha, "woman."

Respective Roles

While both male and female are urged to "conquer" and subdue the negative aspects of creation by imposing a G-dly order, the male takes the primary role in this act of conquest.

Similarly, while both women and men are entrusted with redeeming creation, nurturing and uncovering the G-dliness, the female exemplifies this ability.

In resolving the apparent contradiction of emphasis between man as "dust of the earth"—humble dedication to G-d— and man as the "image of G-d"—assertion of the will— woman and man utilize their respective advantages.

Though each role is integral to the Creator's plan, and both man and woman are necessarily partners to both accomplishments, each role respectively assumes a stronger degree of emphasis. The internal rift between "serving and guarding" and "subduing" becomes less of an inner tension as the man and woman each assumes his/her arena of spiritual expertise.

The male affects the creation, by changing it, acting upon it and vanquishing its negativity. And the woman prepares the world to be a home for G-d by redeeming, protecting and discovering the light implicit within it.

Or in other words, the masculine forces represent the cosmic exhale of creation by doing, affecting and impacting upon the outside environment. Man's mission is to "rule and subdue" as a conqueror.

The feminine forces represent the cosmic inhale by being and internalizing. Woman carries the ability of exposing the inner, Divine essence—who you are. Therefore her role epitomizes "guarding and keeping," self-preservation and protection.

Therein lies the intrinsic blueprint of creation and the poignant inner rift for all future generations between manliness and womanhood. Though each necessarily encompasses both the qualities of each other, the inner essence of man and woman is reflected on the very first pages and chapters of Genesis.

And man's and woman's roles, missions or inner dynamics cannot be reduced to the other, and thus neutralized.

Protection and nurturance requires the extraction of evil. Similarly, conquest requires a redemptive vision, and is ultimately validated by it.

But as the pages of our own lives turn, we too become active participants in this march of life. We need to discover a model for synthesizing these two modalities in peaceful harmony.

Man's and woman's contrasting origins, modes and goals are represented in the practical differences of their respective approaches to their day-to-day interaction. These disparities are reflected on a cognitive, emotional and functional level, or in the way that the masculine and feminine respectively thinks, feels and acts.

Against the perpetual rhythm of life itself, we perforce must join together to achieve a melodious duet with a rich and deep resonance, as we discover a joint destiny, celebrating and understanding our differences. Then will come the day when the home that G-d has yearned for will be prepared, and we can all rest from our battles to rejoice in its unity and redemption.

ACTING LIKE A SOLE
The Role of Faith & Acceptance

The mind...the source of inspiration, intelligence and analysis. It is man's crowning glory—his ability to think and discern right from wrong. Though small in mass, it carries the weighty responsibility for the decisions we make. It holds the depth of our understanding, the breadth of our knowledge and the illumination of our inspiration.

The heart...the source of passion and vitality. Vibrating, pulsating, the heart pumps warmth and life to even the furthermost veins and sinews. Infused with emotion, the heart is the seat of feelings and aspirations.

Our eyes...a window to the soul, hold the power of perception, discerning the road even in the darkest of night.

Speech...the power of communication, expression and interaction.

Hands...holding the pen of the poet, the brush of the artist, hands represent the power of giving and taking, of affecting change and of creating.

Legs...a confident stride, the march of an obedient soldier, legs represent the power of movement.

And then at the very bottom of this mass of potential, called the human body, lies the sole of the foot.

The sole does not possess the power of penetrating thought like the brain. Nor does it feel with the force of passion like the heart. It cannot see with the perception of the eyes. Nor can it communicate through speech like the mouth. It cannot give nor create like the arms. Nor can it move or propel the body forward like the legs.

The sole of the foot merely trudges along. Furthermost from the crowning thought of the brain or the vitality of the heart, it seems almost devoid of life and purpose, warmth and feelings.

Yet despite its roughness and externality, herein also lies its greatness. Precisely because it lacks a more integral role, closer to the heart of emotion or the thought of the rational, can it achieve its own purpose. Precisely because of its insensitivity, it can plunge ahead, obediently and fearlessly following the orders of the brain, the yearnings of the heart, the panoramic vision of the eyes and the movements of the legs.

Precisely because it feels so little pain can its naked skin be charged with climbing over the rocky terrain of life's journey. Precisely due to its roughness and callousness, can it feel less pain when its skin is ripped by the jutting sharp edges of the ground it trudges.

Generations...Each historical time period has its own special features and characteristics.

Since the beginning of recorded history, the Jewish people have seen many generations, each unique in accomplishing the specific goals of that period in history. Though each generation is comprised of individuals, the level of the generation can, in comparison to other times, be described as an organic whole.

In some generations, we had the minds of our nation—people who were gifted with a special wisdom to understand the Will of G-d. These were individuals who, due to the depth of their understanding, were able to lead lives in complete accordance with His principles, permeated with a depth of purpose and inspiration.

Other times, we were a nation of hearts. Our belief was infused with vitality and passion. Our lives steadfastly pulsated with warmth and feelings.

In other eras, we were penetrating eyes, seeing beyond ourselves, beyond the here and now. We had a perceptive vision that saw far ahead.

In yet other generations, we may have lacked the knowledge, the inspiration, the depth of commitment or foresight, yet at least we had the instinctive sense to distinguish right from wrong. Judaism was vibrant enough that we could smell it with our noses, hear it with our ears and feel it with our touch.

Yet other times, we lacked even this capacity, but at least we acted with our hands and our legs. Perhaps the emotion or understanding didn't accompany the deed, but the deed was there nonetheless. Our days were filled with actions and mitzvot. We gave with our hands and marched forward with our legs, performing our duties.

And today...after the Jewish people's long trek through history, our generation represents the sole of the foot.

Chosen not because of our merits, perhaps in spite of them, we must continue to learn even though we lack a keen awareness and depth of understanding of G-dliness.

We must continue to stubbornly believe, even though we are missing the passion and warmth.

We must train our instincts to continue to feel, despite their numbness.

And we must propel our hands and legs into action despite their inertia.

Yet, though we must make these attempts wholeheartedly, our uniqueness as a generation lies in none of these avenues. As the generation at the threshold of the redemption, our special merit lies precisely in our deficiencies.

For it is our spiritual insensitivity, which allows us so easily and uncaringly to step on others, that gives us the strength to trample on exile norms and mentalities, and triumph.

It is our poor intellectual perception and reason that allow us to unquestioningly have the faith and *kabbalat ol*, acceptance of the Will of G-d, to continue believing despite the length, the hardships and the apparent injustices of exile.

It is our paucity of passion and principles that allows us to obediently follow the commands of the brain, our leaders, past and present, unreservedly and with total self-sacrifice and devotion.

In such a generation, the unique qualities of women shine particularly brightly.

A woman can utilize her abilities in each time period of our history with its respective dominant qualities. Nevertheless, since the essence of her being is self-sacrifice and *kabbalat ol*, her inner strength is particularly evident in our times, at the threshold of the promised redemption, when the faith, determination and bravery of the sole will bring it to its goal.

For in the end, the sole of the foot is what supports the entire body, carrying its weight as it reaches its final destination by its audacious, simple resolve to plunge forward. We, a generation of soles, stand prepared to support the souls of our nation, thrusting them into this epoch.

Without passion or perception, without thought or personality, but with tenacity and a hardened, stubborn resolve, we will succeed.

For Further Reflection

- What value does Judaism allocate to the woman's role? Is this a positive role for modern times?
- How does the "giver" gain as much or even more than the "recipient"?
- How can we broaden ourselves to be in tune with the needs of another?
- What are women's strengths in the area of "*kabbalat ol*," acceptance of the Divine Will? Give examples from your own life.
- What is true selflessness? What role does it play in your life? Cite an example.
- What effort do you expend in bringing harmony into your life and world? How have you succeeded?
- What is true humility? What role does it play in your life?
- What are examples of working from within to empower or nurture versus working from without to conquer or eradicate? When is each of these qualities necessary? Cite examples from your life of when you used each mode.

Section Six

DIALOGUE
The Feminine Perspective
More Thoughts on
Jewish Womanhood

- Why Husbands Should Buy Their Wives Flowers:
  Reflections on Women and Time-Bound Mitzvot
- Morning Blessings—His Version and Mine:
  A Blessing of Faith
- Thoughts from an Unfocused Mind:
  Pregnancy as a Metaphor for Exile
- Coffee Break: Male and Female Differences Reflected in
  Their Modes of Communication
- It's All in the Packaging:
  A Dialogue on Equality
- A Different Kind of Spirituality:
  The Focus on Another

WHY HUSBANDS SHOULD BUY THEIR WIVES FLOWERS

Reflections on Women and Time-Bound Mitzvot

Have you ever gone into a gift shop and noticed the rows and rows of cards devoted specifically to women—especially mothers, wives and sisters? We don't generally hear of wives buying flowers or chocolates for their husbands.

Ever wonder why these affectionate gifts are so gender-specific? Does a man not appreciate the flowers or chocolates? Is it perhaps a woman's stronger connection with nature that allows her to admire the vibrant colors of the flowers more than her male counterpart? Or is it her poetic, more emotional nature that is so tenderly touched by the few graceful lines of poetry on the attractive card?

No, of course not. While these tendencies may be true, her love for these gifts has really nothing to do with her appreciation of poetry or nature, or whatever other small presents women traditionally receive.

The secret behind these gender-specific gifts is that women thrive on feedback. The cards, the flowers or the small tender presents show that he cares. They represent the time he took out of his day to think about me. It means that he values our relationship.

He took the moments to drive to the store and he deliberated on what I would most appreciate. He remembered to choose my best color or my favorite chocolates. It means the world to me that he showed that he cares.

Women need that feedback.

Every self-help book on improving married life invariably provides practical suggestions to the husband on communicating his care better, listening better and understanding more what his wife is going through. Of course, buying flowers or cards is just one way of expressing that. She may not need the flowers, cards or chocolates, but these tender gestures demonstrate to her that he cares.

A husband neglecting to give his wife the attention that she needs or expects, notices her becoming withdrawn, irritable, upset, or in husband parlance, "nagging." Venture to ask her what's wrong and she's sure to rejoin, "nothing."

Never buy that.

What is a woman implying by her response? She is saying that if you care enough, if I am sufficiently important in your life, you'll keep asking. You'll find a means to try to understand me. You'll keep working on figuring out what's really wrong. If our relationship is as important to you as it is to me, you won't accept my retort at face value, but you'll probe. As most husbands figure out soon enough, woe is to the man who assumes that nothing means nothing!

A man, on the other hand, doesn't need as much feedback. He is comfortable in knowing that you are there for him. You don't need to prove it or demonstrate it nearly as much, or nearly as often. He may be content sitting silently on the couch beside you, just knowing that you are his. He might be doing his thing and you might be doing your thing, but he considers that spending time together. He doesn't need the constant reminders that you are there for him.

But a woman, through her need for feedback, reminds her man that over time their relationship can grow static. Gestures are important to reignite that flame of romance, longing and tenderness. Demonstrating outright consideration and thoughtfulness through these gestures reawakens the original dynamism and passion in the marriage. She brings a message to the relationship that says reaching a comfort level with one another is great, but let's not take one another for granted. Show me regularly that you care, not only in your heart, but also through your deeds.

I know of a wife who complained to her husband that he never buys her anything—not jewelry, not flowers, no cards. His staggered response was, "Honey, do I ever tell you not to spend the money? By all means, if you want jewelry or flowers go out and buy them!" He thought he was being generous, but of course he missed the point entirely of what she was lacking. It's not the time or money that you spent on me, it is the fact that you cared to spend the time and money.

A woman intuitively feels this need in any relationship she is in. She demonstrates through deeds, small and big, regularly, over and over, that she cares and that she loves.

Perhaps this natural dynamic is a reason why women are not obligated in the time-bound mitzvot of the Torah. Some of the traditional reasons given for this are the fact that a woman may be occupied with other more important things, namely her family life and children. Far from binding a woman to the chains of domesticity, this underlines the supremacy that Judaism places on the value of home life, and its precious regard for family and children—a goal that more and more of us are recognizing in today's hectic and turbulent times.

Another reason given for woman's exemption from these time-bound mitzvot is that she doesn't require the spiritual powers of these mitzvot for her unique spiritual makeup. She intrinsically is in tune with the point of the mitzva without the need to perform it.

What I think this means is that in our relationship with G-d, mitzvot serve as connections, ways of becoming closer. Torah is full of dos and don'ts. Things that G-d doesn't like us to do and things that He requests us to do for Him. He tells us, whether you understand this or not, this is what I need for our relationship; this is how you can demonstrate your love to Me. Mitzvot teach us not to take our relationship with Him for granted, but to maintain the connection, keep the passion and dynamism alive.

While a woman is equally obligated to abstain from the negative precepts of the Torah, she doesn't require the constant reminders of the time-bound, positive ones. She intrinsically understands the need for the positive gestures and the feedback, because that is her own need. She intuitively knows how to demonstrate her love and care in her relationship, because that is so much of what she is all about.

Men on the other hand, need to be told specific directions. They need to be instructed, this is how you can show you care.

This is how often you must demonstrate your love. This is the prescribed formula for expressing tenderness.

A woman doesn't need to send her husband flowers, because through the many things she does in her day-to-day schedule, she will find ways to express how much she cares. She doesn't need to buy him chocolates or affectionate cards on a regular basis, because the message of these tender gifts is a message that she already is sending him and knows how to send him all the time—because this is a need of hers.

She doesn't need to wear a *kippa* or bind tefillin daily on her arm or pray at three specific times a day to remind her of G-d's presence in her life, because He is a reality. He is always with her. Not because she is more spiritual. Not because she is a better person. Not because she is greater than her male counterpart. But simply because feedback to a woman is as necessary as the air she breathes. She understands its importance and will find a million ways in her day to live it.

MORNING BLESSINGS
HIS VERSION AND MINE
A Blessing of Faith

I've been noticing recently that my husband is taking a few more minutes to recite his morning blessings. Of course, he has good reason for the extra concentration. I am expecting, G d willing, our sixth child. I know that his thoughts are focused on praying for the health and welfare of his growing family.

But there is one blessing, in particular, about which I wonder: Does he now pause over it for an extra moment of contemplation? Have its words have taken on a deeper significance to him, as he recites, "Thank You, G-d, for not making me a woman"?

As he watches me struggle with my bouts of nausea and lassitude, with my raging hormones and assortment of pains and discomforts, surely he cannot help but feel grateful to be exempt of this burden?

These days, my world has changed dramatically. While I am thrilled with the wonder of a life growing inside of me, and while I am filled with anticipation of this new soul about to make its debut and join the ranks of my children, the long wait is achingly difficult.

Not too long ago, I used to wake up filled with eager energy to tackle the novel challenges of a brand new day. I would look forward to confronting new projects at work, implementing new strategies, devising new programs, formulating new ideas. I reveled, too, in taking care of my home, frolicking with my children and inventing new activities of interest for them.

Nowadays, however, my mornings begin with sickness which progresses into burdensome heaviness, lethargy and immobility.

My days revolve around simply trying to survive one hour after another until a night's fitful sleep provides some refuge from the tormenting moments of sickliness.

This is how my days pass, week after week, month after month.

I no longer feel in control of anything. My brain and body seem to be working hand in hand in a grand conspiracy against me. Any thought with the slightest degree of complexity is too straining to tackle. My burgeoning body is growing way out of control, pounds heaping upon pounds, collaborating against any remaining agility. Energy is a word of the past, as the slightest exertion is burdensome, an effort beyond my capability.

Yet in this state, somehow, a new realization has also dawned—as if a new space of awareness has opened up within me.

I've come to realize, quite simply, that my situation and circumstances are not in my hands to control. While I do the small bit that I can and put forth whatever effort I am able to muster to order and run my life, there is the underlying realization that everything—projects at work, my health, the activities or issues in my children's lives and even my own thought process—are no longer mine alone.

The stark recognition has hit me that You, G-d, are orchestrating it all.

As I'm forced to relinquish my reigns of control, usually such an integral part of my personality, I am faced with a new reality. I am compelled instead to fall back on You and Your control. And as I fall back, relegating it all to You, I find that the fall is surprisingly not hard, that there is the cushion of a new pillow of faith and comfort.

So my husband futilely empathizes with my pains and discomfort and he tries to offer practical assistance. He prays on behalf of me and our family with extra concentration and devotion. And he thanks G-d with a measure of relief for not making him go through this physiologically debilitating and emotionally draining condition. As a man, he can participate in the birth of a new child without the need to be so transformed and so wrung out in the process.

As for me, as I try to focus my unfocused brain on my prayers, I, too, spend slightly more time on my morning blessings.

And I, too, thank You, G-d.

I thank You for all the good in my life. I thank You for my husband and children. And I thank You for the blessing of new life developing within me.

Perhaps I should be able to thank You for my aches and pains, too—knowing full well that the end result will make it all worthwhile—but quite honestly, I cannot. Perhaps it is because I can't really fathom why such absolute joy must be marred with such sickliness. Or perhaps simply because, in the meanwhile, G-d, it hurts.

But the genuine thanks that I do offer You is for the realization, through all this, that this pain—and with it all the suffering in this world, all the good and bad that You have chosen to intermingle in Your creatures' lives—is happening exactly according to Your plan, exactly according to Your wishes.

I thank You for the awareness that You are fully taking care of me. It eases my mind to know that You are working it all out, exactly as it is meant to be.

And falling back into that space, that comforting pillow of faith, in realizing that You are controlling it all—whether I appreciate it or not, whether I understand it or not—makes me say my blessings with slightly more conviction.

I take a moment to pause in reflection as I read the blessing that women have traditionally recited instead of the one my husband has just read. And I think with absolute and honest conviction, "Thank You, G-d, for making me—and Your world—exactly as You want it to be."

THOUGHTS
FROM
AN UNFOCUSED MIND
Pregnancy
as a Metaphor for Exile

I'm not accustomed to my head and body acting disjointedly. Generally, my mind identifies a goal or direction, and the faculties of my body naturally follow through in carrying it out. That is, until lately.

One day, I was functioning like my normal, energetic self. But the next day, my brain had turned into putty, my willpower had evaporated, my limbs had become utterly useless, and my general being had become suffused with a fog-like, heavy lethargy that just wouldn't go away.

All this is not a new experience for me. It actually is quite familiar, though the vividness of my memory has blurred over time.

If past experiences are correct, these feelings will accompany me for a number of months. Nine, in total, to be precise.

(Let me caution you right here: these thoughts aren't intended for those women who experience pregnancy as the height of joyous blissfulness. If your face glows perpetually as you continue to conduct your normal routine in a state of grace and elegance, you just won't relate. Don't even bother reading on. Rather, it's for those of us who, though excited by the prospect of motherhood, spend these nine months in enormous discomfort. It is for those like me, whose only glow on their complexion is a green pallor of non-stop nausea.)

Of course, I try to focus on the beauty of the end goal—the euphoria of a new life that is growing inside of me. I begin my day by filling my mind with positive images, trying to imbue it with a sense of the wondrous miracle forming inside my expanding body. Each morning I convince myself how wonderfully healthy I will feel today—just as the taste of bile rises in my mouth.

What has been bothering me lately, though, is a nagging feeling that something is wrong. At such a special time, my days should be imbued with spirituality. My prayers ought to be heartfelt and intense, my times of Torah study increased, my gratitude evident through the extra good deeds that I undertake.

I should be thanking You, G-d, effusively, for this precious gift You have bestowed upon me by granting me such a central role in the miracle of life. I should be asking You intently for the strength to cope with my discomforts and with the upcoming delivery. I should be seeking Your help with the challenges of a new infant, as I pray for a healthy baby. And, I should be beseeching You for patience and wisdom in dealing with all my other children.

Instead, just getting through each day is a colossal chore. I need to muster all of my remaining energy just to mouth the most rudimentary prayers. Focusing intently and praying passionately is an activity well beyond my capabilities.

This is a special time for me, when I feel Your presence so intimately and constantly within me. I feel surrounded by You and encompassed by my dependency on You. Yet at a time when I need You the most, I am so utterly incapable of expressing or acting upon this connection.

I notice the same situation mirrored in my relationship with my husband. I want us to share the joy of the drama unfolding before us. I want to experience its wonder and ecstasy together. To dream and to speculate in long shared moments of intimate communication. But all I can usually muster is a forced smile or a squeezed hand as I focus all of my energies on getting through my routine, one hour at a time.

Yet, interestingly, despite this lack of open expression, despite this decrease in our time spent together, we both feel the strength of this bond more acutely these days. Somehow, he intuitively senses just what to say when I am feeling sick and unattractive. Somehow, gazing into his eyes is enough to give me a lift when I near despair.

In some strange way, though the circumstances are causing some artificial distance, their underlying cause is bringing us even closer together.

That was what made me think about how our sages compare our current state of *galut* (exile) to the difficulties experienced in pregnancy.

Galut is that time when outwardly we're feeling so distant from You, G-d. We're spiritually uncommunicative. All of our energy is consumed in the daily challenge of just getting through the tediousness of life and survival.

Not much time or energy is left over for any special closeness with You. Spiritually, we are lethargic. Our minds and limbs are unfocused. We are confounded by fatigue, spiritually immobile and apathetic.

Yet, somehow, despite the distance in our communication, despite the lack of intimate spiritual expression, what is emerging from this ordeal is a deeper connection to You. As our very selves become transformed in the pains of this harsh process, we are also giving birth to a new spiritual self that is intimately and essentially connected to You.

Throughout this incessantly long exile, the circumstances of spiritual disconnection and disillusionment may be causing us to feel apart from You. But inwardly, our bond is more potent than ever.

I just ask You, now—with my unfocused thoughts—to give us the strength to get through the pains, agonies and discomforts of these gestations, so that we can finally exult in the birth of that special time.

COFFEE
BREAK

Male and Female Differences Reflected in Their Modes of Communication

W ould you like to stop for a cold drink or a cup of coffee now?" Sara asked her husband as they approached a service station at the side of the highway. The couple had been driving towards their destination for several hours, and now, in the late afternoon, the trip was becoming tiresome.

"No, thanks," Ben replied, wanting to speed up their arrival time.

"Oh," Sara answered with a slight edge in her tone, just as they drove past the station.

Ben was too busy paying attention to the road to detect any change in Sara's demeanor. It took a full fifteen minutes of deafening silence till he finally realized that something was amiss. Mentally, he reviewed their last lines of dialogue before the communication had broken down, but couldn't figure out, for the life of him, what Sara could possibly be upset about.

When Sara asked Ben if he wanted a coffee, her subliminal message to him was that *she* wanted a coffee. Asking him was her way of allowing him to reciprocate and demonstrate his consideration for her. By not reciprocating, in Sara's mind, Ben was being inconsiderate of her needs.

Ben, on the other hand, couldn't fathom why if Sara wanted a coffee, she couldn't simply say so. He certainly wouldn't have minded stopping for her and even delaying the trip—if she only would have explicitly asked.

In previous chapters, we discussed the differences of mission for man and woman, as reflected in the original blueprint of creation—from the very first pages of *Bereishit* (Genesis). We noted, then, how man's primary role was evident in the first chapter (verse 28), when he is enjoined to "fill the earth and conquer it and rule over the fish of the sea, the bird of the sky and every living thing that moves on the earth." He is the goal-oriented "conqueror" who enforces and draws down G-dliness onto creation.

Woman's role, on the other hand, becomes evident in the second chapter (verse 18) of *Bereishit*, when she comes into being, as an independent person "corresponding to him." At this point, humanity is charged with building a home for G-d, in the Garden of Eden, which they are commanded "to keep and to guard" (Gen. 2:15). Woman was charged with "protection" and "nurturance" or "revealing the G-dliness already inherent and impregnated within creation."

While obviously both men and women are urged to "conquer" and subdue the negative aspects of creation, in this area, the male assumes the primary role. Similarly, while both are entrusted with redeeming creation and uncovering the G-dliness within, the female exemplifies this ability. From the very beginning of their creation, man and woman have two respective roles—both integral to the Creator's plan.

Interestingly, more and more studies, articles and books nowadays are coming to the conclusion that gender differences do not only stem from nurture, but also from nature. In other words, psychologists are finally admitting that it is not only society that shapes men and women, but that biology plays an equally significant role.

Each gender was created with unique differences to further their particular role and goal in creation. Moreover, what Torah has been saying for centuries is surprisingly only lately being read in the pages of modern psychology, that "being equal does not mean being the same."

An example of this is a recent study that I read on the managerial styles and skills of men and women. The study found that women are better than men at empowering teams and staff, while men tend to be more speedy decision makers.

"Women ask questions, men tend to give answers," says author and coach Terri Levine.

"Typically, when comparing managers, the dialogue is framed as men's commanding style versus women's team-building or consensus approach," writes Joanna Krotz, a marketing intelligence professional.

The study concluded that woman's stronger ability to keep staffers enthusiastic is vital, and perhaps the most important tool for success in today's competitive small and midsized businesses.

I was considering these statements as I reflected on the different lecturing styles that my husband and I respectively employ. Both of us lecture regularly to adults of all different backgrounds, to enhance their Jewish awareness and education.

My husband will invariably pose a thought-provoking question. As participants venture to answer, he'll brilliantly disprove or discredit their offerings, in order to build up and bring out his central point and hypothesis. He'll demonstrate flawlessly the fallacy of other ways of life to lead all without a shadow of doubt towards his conclusion.

I, on the other hand, might also pose a thought-provoking question. But every answer from participants will receive a complimentary comment. Somehow, I'll discover or elicit from even the more far-fetched responses some point of similarity, some point of worth that can further the principles that I am attempting to convey.

Masculine and feminine modes of communication reflect their respective arenas of spiritual expertise.

The masculine is often more direct and goal-oriented, since he epitomizes the role of impacting and affecting the outside environment. The feminine persona, on the other hand, is more intuitive, since she finds and exposes the common grain of truth and connection inherent in us all.

For this reason, workforce specialists and interpersonal counselors alike are discovering that it is inborn for a woman to ask questions, to empower teams, to build relationships— "guarding" and nurturing—just as it is natural for a man to provide answers, work according to the bottom line and be quicker with decisions— "conquering" and ruling.

It is not coincidental that each gender was provided with precisely the tools that he/she needs to best execute his/her role in making this world a better G-dly home. Unfortunately, the differences in our makeup often cause differences in our communication styles, resulting in unintended discord.

So, while a fellow woman would have intuitively understood Sara's implicit suggestion as her needing a coffee break, expecting her husband to realize this is akin to expecting him to mind-read. Sara, and women as a whole, have to learn how to word their requests directly in ways that allow their husbands to clearly understand their needs. While Sara may automatically intuit her husband's underlying wishes, she cannot be insulted when he doesn't realize hers.

On the other hand, Ben, and men as a whole, must learn to sensitize themselves (with the help of the women in their lives) to picking up on some of the nuances in their wives' tone and words. Occasionally that might mean that Ben has to forgo his immediate goal and sidetrack or delay its outcome in order to become attuned to and aware of Sara's thought process.

Equally important is for both to realize that the underlying differences in their communication is not due to a lack of focus or an insensitivity towards the other, but merely a difference in approach and outlook.

And these differences in approach—as we are taught on the first pages of the Torah—are what make both man and woman such integral and vital partners in transforming our world into a home for G-d.

IT'S ALL IN THE PACKAGING

A Dialogue on Equality

Chana, I've just started attending your courses, and I'm really enjoying them. You've opened my eyes to a new appreciation of Torah. I feel like I've gotten to know you and I see you are a modern and enlightened woman.

"So tell me honestly, don't you ever feel Orthodoxy is unfair in its treatment of women? Aren't the Rabbis degrading to women? Sure, we study the ancient sources, but how about nowadays? I mean, why can't a woman, for example, be called up to read from the Torah?" Vanessa approached me for the first time after one of my Monday evening classes.

Vanessa is a successful entrepreneur who owns a very large retail company selling computer software products in the Toronto area. She is fifty-two years old, but with her professional, natural makeup and her model's figure—thanks to her strenuous workouts with her personal trainer during her lunch break—easily passes for fifteen years her junior. Vanessa has never been married; she travels often and is a confident and articulate woman.

Recently, Vanessa resolved to delegate more of her company's responsibilities to enable her to enjoy more of what life offers. High on her priority list of things that somehow got neglected during her career ladder climb, is her Jewish education, and in particular her Jewish feminine education.

Vanessa's new resolution and her somewhat lighter workweek allowed her to implement two new things in her life.

First, Vanessa spoke to the Rabbi at her Temple and, together with a group of women, began learning for their "bat-mitzva" celebration, several months away. Weekly, the women meet and are taught the proper chants for the reading of the Torah.

They will be "bat-mitzva'ed" in the presence of many family members and friends, and each woman will have the honor of being called up to the Torah to proudly recite the three or four verses in the practiced cantillation. In addition, each woman was preparing to deliver a five- to ten-minute "*d'var Torah*" or lecture on a prepared topic in Judaism. Vanessa had been practicing for weeks already and was beginning to explore different avenues for her speech.

Vanessa's second resolution was to attend a regular Torah class that related to her as a woman. She had checked out the Temple's adult education programs, but somehow, nothing grabbed her.

That was when she happened on a small ad in the local Jewish newspaper promoting a series on "Feminine Voices" given by a woman dean and offering a "text-based exploration of the lives of great Biblical women." The course promised to deliver a "refreshing and provocative understanding of feminine spirituality" as well as "insights in dealing with the daily challenges facing modern Jewish women." It sounded like just what she was looking for.

Vanessa wasn't acquainted with the group offering these courses, but decided nonetheless to invest her time in attending one class and taking it from there. After the first class, she was intrigued and found herself coming back for more.

She enjoyed the hands-on source material, the intellectual presentation and, to her surprise, the other participants. Women who attended were as diverse as they come—in ideology, all the way from the extreme right-wing until the far left, a few even further than her. Many shared their opinions—some of which she outrightly rejected as too narrow-minded and illogical, but nevertheless she found the communication and sharing beneficial.

A group of women formed around Vanessa that Monday evening, some curious to understand the issue themselves, others, to hear how I would deal with it. It wasn't an unusual sight. In this course, no area of Judaism was off-limits and the non-threatening environment encouraged women to open up and explore the issues.

The hour was already late and I knew that I didn't have the time to go through a whole lecture on the different roles and missions of men and women. Nor could I elaborate right then on the mystical composition or the cosmic ramifications of each gender. Throughout the course these ideas were explored and an appreciation was definitely forming. I always stressed the need to go back to the original sources, to remove our preconceived notions and allow each participant to judge for herself.

But for now, Vanessa was waiting for a quick response.

I began outlining the practical ramifications of a woman being called up before a group of men and how this contradicted the vision of modesty according to Judaism. I explained how the laws were made to safeguard a woman's honor and image, and avoid cheapening or selling her physicality, as is unfortunately so prevalent in society nowadays.

Vanessa understood and partially agreed, but I could see that she wasn't entirely convinced.

"Vanessa, do you ever light Shabbat candles?" I asked.

"As a little girl, I remember my mother lighting every week. We never kept Shabbat in the traditional way, but every Friday night we ate a family meal together by her shining candles. I have fond memories of those lightings. A moment of peace and serenity."

"Let me ask you a silly question, Vanessa." I ventured. "The Shabbat candles are traditionally lit by the women and girls of the house, unless of course there isn't a female available." The women all nodded as I cited the law. "Have you ever heard of a movement of men vocally insisting on their right to be the ones to light the Shabbat candles instead?"

The women smiled. "Of course not. But how does this connect to my question?" Vanessa was beginning to get impatient.

"Just a second, Vanessa. Seriously, think for a moment. Why is it that men are not clamoring for this privilege? You yourself said that it is a beautiful moment, and it is a special mitzva to usher in the holy day of Shabbat. So, why don't the men argue for this privilege, instead of playing second fiddle to women's lighting?"

The women's faces were blank. They didn't understand where I was heading. "I'm not sure," Vanessa finally responded.

"Let me tell you of a male that weekly protests this unfair treatment." The women looked curious. "Every Friday, eighteen minutes before sunset, I and my older three daughters light the Shabbat candles. My youngest, an adorable three-year-old boy, stands at the sidelines, protesting that he isn't able to light his own candles like his sisters do—he can merely pretend to do so." Vanessa and the others smiled at the image.

"What I am getting at," I continued, "is that perhaps men don't clamor for this mitzva—or any of our other special mitzvot, like our precious one of mikve—because we aren't marketing ourselves properly."

At the word marketing, Vanessa's trained entrepreneur ears perked up. "How so?"

"Well, a three-year-old without socially imposed impressions appreciates the beauty of a woman's mitzva. But as we mature, maybe we are buying into society's unfair expectations that what a man is commanded to do must be important, spiritual and exciting. On the other hand, society screams loudly, what a woman does—hey, that's just not so important.

"Maybe what Judaism is saying is, don't buy into that vision.

"Man and woman are different biologically, psychologically and spiritually. That doesn't mean one is superior or inferior, but merely that we have different needs and different missions," I continued.

"Maybe it is time that we remove our biased, adult vision and begin to appreciate who and what we are. Let's teach society, as well, to value a true definition of womanhood, rather than exchanging it for what we are not."

Vanessa looked pensive. "Are you saying that the entire premise of wanting to do a traditionally male mitzva is buying into society's chauvinistic notion that women's issues, or in this case, mitzvot, are worth less than men's?"

"I am saying that the purpose of this course is to explore the issues and realize the spiritual importance of each of our mitzvot. We learn from biblical role models, as well, to discover the Torah view on true womanhood. We learn it, understand its value and then we can teach it to the world—"

"You mean *market* it," Vanessa interrupted, "so that perhaps thirty-year-olds will also appreciate what your three-year-old intuitively understood about womanhood and women's mitzvot." Vanessa smiled.

"Of course, you can be a partner in this marketing scheme," I smiled mischievously in return.

"How?" Vanessa's eyes narrowed and her features became serious, as though she was leading a board meeting at that very moment. "Do you mean by continuing to learn at this course?"

"Yes, of course that's true and part of it. But also by being an active participant—by doing."

We continued speaking a little longer that Monday evening, and slowly the group began to disperse. I went home very late and exhausted that evening, but knowing, too, that even in Vanessa's hectic schedule, four days would be enough time for her to buy her own candles to make the world a brighter place on the upcoming Friday night.

A DIFFERENT KIND OF SPIRITUALITY

The Focus on Another

I stand in shul praying. Today is Rosh Hashana, one of the holiest days of the year, but it could be any other day that I'm in shul, or for that matter any time or place when I find myself in the middle of prayers, or, in fact, any spiritual obligation.

I am surrounded by my children. My girls and youngest son are at my side, and my infant is in her carriage right before me. I begin reciting the prayers, beseeching G-d for a good new year, asking Him for a stronger connection, for Him to be a greater and deeper presence in my life. And I am asking for health, for success in raising my children, to properly utilize the talents that He has endowed me with, for livelihood, and for all the things, little and big, that we request in our daily audience with our King of Kings and Father in Heaven.

As I say the words that flow so readily from my lips, my leg is in an automatic mode of perpetual motion, rocking my newborn's carriage back and forth in the vacant aisle before me. Meanwhile, one forefinger is pointing in my young daughter's *siddur*, motioning to her which part the *chazan* is reciting. The other arm is finding its way through the snack bag we prepared for my youngest son, giving him something to nibble on so he is occupied throughout the long service. And my eyes are alternating between scanning my siddur and keeping a watchful gaze on my infant, ensuring that the pacifier remains embedded in her mouth, lest she decide to practice her newly discovered baby vocabulary with her loudest vocal cords and compete with the *chazan*.

And the carriage continues to creak softly as I continue to push it back and forth, back and forth. All this while trying to meditate on the prayers—trying to establish a deeper connection to and awareness of G-d, trying to escape the material clutches of this world, trying to transcend the bounds of physicality.

At some point, the realization hits me that my prayers don't seem to sound all that spiritual, or all that connected. Nor very real, and certainly not very transcendental.

My mind wanders back to those days and years, decades ago, when prayers meant starting at the very beginning, focused until the very conclusion, without any interruptions. I remember back to a time when my mouth read the words and my mind concentrated.

No leg rocking. No fingers pointing. No eyes scanning.

Prayers, just prayers. Just communicating with my Father in Heaven. Standing erect and in humble concentration, just me and my Maker.

Of course, I uttered the same words then, albeit far less swiftly and with greater concentration. I asked for the same requests then, too—for health, for happiness, for success, for livelihood, for wisdom and understanding, for direction and meaning, for no pain or suffering, only a suffusion of goodness in our world.

Not only were my prayers much lengthier in those days, before the obligations of family and children became such an integral part of my life, but the activities of my daily schedule were also suffused with more acts of spirituality. Preparation for a Shabbat or holiday meant learning greater Torah insights, reciting extra Psalms, reviewing the deeper commentaries of the Torah reading.

While I still try to make these a part of my life, preparations nowadays are more about defrosting sufficient chickens, baking the kugels and ensuring that all the buttons are sewn on my children's Yom Tov clothing.

Have I lost my spiritual focus, direction and connection? Were those long-gone prayers and preparations far more meaningful than anything I can ever muster now, with my myriad family obligations?

I thought about this as I stood in shul, mouth and limbs in auto mode. I continued saying the prayers, still asking for those very same things. But now, clutching my gurgling, smiling infant daughter on my shoulder, suddenly the meaning of the prayers grew so much more significant that their prior value seemed almost superficial.

Cradling her tiny head in my arms, my requests for health and life became infinitely more urgent. I need a healthy life and strength, dear G-d. Yes, of course we all want life and I have always asked for it. But now I *need* it.

A day less, a day more, a year less or more, does it really matter? Yes! For this little one, I *need* strength. I *need* wisdom, direction, happiness, peace in our world, sustenance and prosperity—for *her*, for all of *them*.

For these six precious souls that you entrusted to me.

Sure, I can make do with a little more or a little less, a little more or less meaning, a larger house or a smaller one, one outfit more or less, a little more or less understanding, happiness or spirituality in my life. But dear G-d, for the sake of these little ones (and big ones), I now *need* it all.

How much more urgent and pressing each of the words uttered became. It was no longer a matter of *me* speaking to my Creator any more. On my shoulders, together with my infant daughter, I felt the weight of all my children, all their needs, all their wants. For their sake, dear G-d, make it a good day, a good week and a good year. Open up Your infinite treasury of goodness for them and all of us.

So, though as each new child is born, my life becomes more hectic, and my prayers become more rushed or more condensed, the intensity and significance of each word surfaces and provides an entirely deeper definition of wants and needs. And although my day becomes filled with more mundane acts and perhaps fewer minutes of spiritual pursuits, these acts aren't really mundane at all.

They never were. Because even a mundane act for *them* becomes a pressing spiritual pursuit for me.

You see, the focus is not about my needs anymore—neither material nor spiritual. It is all about them. And another's needs, whether little or big, whether spiritual or material, are anything but mundane.

In fact, what can be more spiritual?

For Further Reflection

🌿 What does the blessing of "*she'asani kirtzono*" (the blessing that women say thanking G-d for making them "according to His will") mean to you?

🌿 How is pregnancy a metaphor for exile? Can you give some other personal metaphors from your life?

🌿 How do our modes of communication reflect our different roles as men and women?

🌿 G-d did not choose the spiritual realm, but our physical reality, as a "home." Why?

🌿 Kabbala explains that "a descent is necessary for an ascent." Can you think of any examples in your own life where you had to experience an apparent "descent" before achieving an "ascent"?

🌿 What have you discovered about the Jewish view of womanhood?

🌿 What can YOU add to this dialogue on being a Jewish woman?

GLOSSARY

Ahava—love

Amida—*lit.* standing, as it is a prayer that is to be recited in a standing position, also referred to as Shemoneh Esreh ("eighteen" benedictions); the main section of all obligatory prayers recited daily, instituted by the Men of the Great Assembly (*circa* 3406–3448 (355–313 BCE).

Ani—me

Aron—the ark in the Holy Temple

Assur—*lit,* chained, bound (by the power of impurity); forbidden

Ayin—nothingness

Az Yashir—a song sung at the bank of the Red Sea by the Jewish people expressing their gratitude and thanksgiving to G-d for being freed from the Egyptians. This song is incorporated as part of the daily prayer service.

Baal Teshuva—*lit.* master of return, repentant

Bat Yisrael—daughter of Israel

Beit Hamikdash—the Holy Temple in Jerusalem. The first was built by King Solomon (completed 2935 [827 BCE]), the second, by Zerubavel and Yehoshua (completed 3412 [349 BCE], seventy years after the destruction of the first Temple).

Bina—*lit.,* understanding; the second of the ten Sefirot; the second stage of the intellectual process

Bitul—nullification or subordination of one's ego or personal considerations for the sake of a greater and higher goal (see endnote #307 for more elaboration).

Brit Mila—the circumcision ceremony performed on males on their eighth day of life

Bracha—a blessing made over an item of food or drink or the performance of a mitzva; a blessing given by one individual to another

Chamor—donkey

Chassid, *pl.* **Chassidim**—a follower of Chassidism

Chassidism—the movement within Orthodox Judaism founded in the 18th century by Rabbi Yisroel, the Baal Shem Tov, and stressing emotional involvement in prayer, service of G-d through the material universe, the primacy of wholehearted earnestness in Divine service, the mystical in addition to the legalistic side of Judaism, the importance of serving G-d with inner joy, and the importance of cultivating a spiritual attachment to the saintly and charismatic leader, the Rebbe.

Cheder Hamitot—*lit.* the bedroom chamber, referring to the inner chamber in the Temple called the Holy of Holies

Cherubim—golden forms in the shape of a male and female adorning the ark in the Holy Temple

Chilul Hashem—desecration of the name of G-d, open sacrilegious behavior on the part of a Jew or Jews, bringing the Jewish religion—and by implication the Creator—into disrepute

Chuppa—the square canopy beneath which the wedding ceremony takes place or the ceremony itself

Echad—one

Eishet Chayil—a woman of valor; also the prayer said Friday night (preceding Shabbat dinner) extolling the Jewish woman. (This prayer was originally composed by Avraham for Sara and is recorded in the Book of Proverbs.)

Eitz Hadaat—the Tree of Knowledge in the Garden of Eden; it was forbidden for Adam and Chava (Eve) to partake of its fruit

Eizer Kinegdo—a help mate, the term used in Gen. 2:18 at the creation of woman

Emuna—faith (in the Creator and in His ways)

Galut—exile, the historic exile of the Jews; in the spiritual sense, the loss of connection with G-dliness and the sanctity of Torah life

Gan Eden—the Garden of Eden

Gehinom—purgatory

Haftara—*lit.* the final passage, the passage from the Prophets read in the synagogue after the conclusion of the Torah reading

Havdala—*lit.* separation, the prayer recited at the conclusion of the Shabbat, separating from the holiness of the Shabbat to the mundanity of the weekday

Ishto Kegufo—*lit.* his wife is like his body; a Talmudic phrase used to express how the husband and wife are considered as one body in regards to certain Torah laws

Kabbala—*lit.* received tradition; the Jewish mystical tradition

Kabbalat Ol—self-subjugation and acceptance of the Divine will

Kaddish—prayer recited for a departed relative

Kadosh—holy, separate, set apart

Kedusha—holiness, sanctity

Knesset Yisrael—the Jewish people

Malchut Beit David—the Davidic dynasty

Malchut Yisrael—the dynasty of the ten Israelite tribes which broke off from the Davidic dynasty and established an independent kingdom

Malchut—royalty or majesty; also the tenth and final Divine Sefira or emanation

Mashiach ben David—the Jewish leader directly descended from the House of David who will usher in the Final Redemption by rebuilding the third Temple in Jerusalem, by gathering all the Jews from the four corners of the earth to the Land of Israel, and by bringing eternal peace to the Jews and all of mankind

Mashiach ben Yosef—a great Jewish leader, descending from the tribe of Yosef, who will prepare the world and lead the way for the coming of Mashiach ben David

Mashiach—the Messiah; see Mashiach ben David.

Mati V'lo Mati—*lit.* reaching forth and retreating; a Kabbalistic expression to describe the flow of vitality from G-d to creation in flashes of reaching forth and retreating, revelation and withdrawal

Mayim—water

Megilla—*lit.* a scroll, five of the holy books of Tanach are called megilla, the most famous being Megillat Esther, the scroll of Esther

Memaleh—immanent, the mode of Divine influence which is (as it were) bounded by the finitude of the recipient (in contrast to "Sovev")

Mesirat Nefesh—*lit.* giving up one's life, self-sacrifice; forgoing one's own wishes or desires; the keeping of Torah in spite of physical danger or the fact that it conflicts with one's own wishes or desires

Middot, plural of **Midda**—*lit.* traits, attributes; the seven "lower" Sefirot or emotive attributes of G-d and the corresponding dispositions or character traits in the human psyche

Midrash—*adj.* **Midrashic**—a passage from or any one of the classical collections of the Sages' homiletical teachings of the Torah

Mikve—a pool of water constructed under strict Halachic guidelines used for ritual immersion

Mishkan—temporary spiritual center preceding the Temple

Mitzva—*pl.* **Mitzvot**—*lit.* commandment, one of the 613 Torah commandments

Mutar—*lit.* released, free; permitted

Nachat—joy, pleasure, especially from one's children

Nidda—a woman has this status during and after menstruation until her immersion in the mikve

Parochet—the elaborate curtain in the Holy Temple to separate the inner chamber

Pidyon Shevuyim—the commandment to redeem Jewish individuals who have been captured

Ratzo V'Shov—*lit.* bring forth and draw back; a Kabbalistic expression to describe the flow of vitality from G-d to creation in flashes of running forth and drawing back, reaching and retreating, revelation and withdrawal

Reshimu—*lit.* residue; a Kabbalistic expression describing the residual light or remnant of G-dliness that remained within creation even after the *tzimtzum*

Rosh Chodesh—the holiday of the New Moon

Sanhedrin—Jewish Supreme Court

Sefer Yetzira—one of the most important and ancient mystical works

Sefira, *pl.* **Sefirot**—the Kabbalistic term denoting the ten Divine attributes or emanations of G-dliness through which G-d manifests Himself in both the creation and the sustenance of all beings

Shabbat Chazon—*lit.* Shabbat of vision; the Shabbat prior to Tisha B'Av, when the words of the prophet Isaiah beginning with the word *chazon*, the vision, are read

Shabbat Hamalka—the Shabbat Queen

Shabbat—the Sabbath, the seventh day of the week that is a Day of Rest

Shechina—*lit.* indwelling, the Divine Presence or Immanence in creation, as distinguished from the Divine Transcendence. This term is in the feminine gender, while the transcendent aspect is in the male gender.

Shemitta—the Sabbatical year in the land of Israel occurring every seven years, during which period the earth is left fallow and complex laws regulate the supply and consumption of agricultural products

Shidduchim—marriage matches

Shifcha Canaanit—a Canaanite maidservant

Shiva—the seven day period of mourning following the death of an immediate relative

Sovev—transcendent, the mode of Divine influence which, being infinite, cannot be bounded by the finitude of the recipient, which it is therefore said to "encompass," or transcend (in contrast to *Memaleh*)

Tahara—*lit.* purity; a state of readiness to receive holiness

Taharat Hamishpacha—the laws of Family Purity, whose central observance is abstinence from marital relations during menstruation and a further period of "seven clean days" followed by the wife's immersion in a mikve, after which husband and wife are again permitted to each other

Tahor—a state of *Tahara*

Talmud—the basic compendium of Jewish law, thought and Biblical commentary brought to completion in 4235 (475 CE)

Tameh—a state of *Tuma*

Teshuva—*lit.* return to G-d; in the narrow sense, the act of repentance from all sins of omission or commission; in the wider sense, returning to G-d in the sense of a continuously progressive advance to G-dliness

Tevilla—ritual immersion in the mikve

Tuma—*lit.* impurity; the absence of holiness

Tzaddik, *pl.* **Tzaddikim,** *fem.* **Tzadeket**—a completely righteous individual

Tzedaka—charity

Tzimtzum—*lit.* contraction; a Kabbalistic expression for the initial act of concealment, contraction and withdrawal of the consuming Divine light through a series of stages that made it possible for finite and material substances to come about

Yehudim, *pl.* of **Yehudi**—Jews

Yibum—levirate marriage in which a childless man's brother has an obligation to marry his dead brother's wife

Yomim Tovim—Jewish holidays and festivals

Zohar—*lit.* radiance; a classical and fundamental work containing the mystical teachings of Kabbala composed by Rabbi Shimon bar Yochai, one of the great sages of the Mishna

ENDNOTES

✣ VOICES

CHAVA

[1] Rashi, Gen. 1:27.

[2] See the Ramban (Nachmanides) and Abarvanel, Gen. 1:26.

[3] Ramban, 2:7.

[4] See Tanya, *Likkutei Amarim*, chap. 2, for a more elaborate discussion on this topic.

[5] Rashi, Gen. 3:22.

[6] Radak, Gen. 2:7.

[7] This phenomenon of reproducing without mating exists in certain insects like the aphid, as well as in the flowerpot blind snake. These species reproduce by a process called parthenogenesis.

[8] *Akeidat Yitzchak*, chap. 8.

[9] Commentary of Shmuel David Luzzatto.

[10] Gen. 2:24. Therefore, man, although physically stronger, was the one commanded to cling to his wife and not the reverse.

[11] The next few paragraphs are based on the commentary of Rabbi Samson Raphael Hirsch to Gen. 2:18 and 2:24.

[12] See *Kiddushin* 2b.

[13] Maharal in *Gur Aryeh*.

[14] *Sota* 17a, Rashi, ad loc.; *Pirkei d'Rabbi Eliezer*, chap. 12.

[15] *Sifsei Tzaddik*.

[16] Ramban, Radak and R. Bachya (Gen. 2:20) note that man perceived the nature of each creature and named it accordingly. On a deeper level, the Kabbalists explain that the actual letters comprising the Hebrew name of any being (or object) reflect the spiritual source of that being. Hence, Adam not only understood the nature of each animal, but actually perceived the supernal spiritual source of its existence. See Shalo, introduction to *Beit Hamikdash* 14a; *Ohr Torah* (from the Maggid of Mezeritch) 4b. *Sha'ar Hayichud VeHa'emuna*, chap. 1.

[17] *Akeidat Yitzchak*, chap. 8; Ramban, Gen. 2:20.

[18] *Nidda* 45b.

[19] *Bereishit Rabba* 8:3; *Bava Batra* 58a.

[20] *Chagiga* 12a.

[21] Adam didn't actually die on that day, but rather 930 years later. According to the Midrash (*Bereishit Rabba* 19:8), "the day" refers to G-d's day, i.e., one thousand years (Ps. 90:4), during which time he died.

[22] *Bereishit Rabba* 2:17 on the double wording in the verse "*Mot tamut*— you will certainly die."

[23] The Gra in *Aderet Eliyahu* (Gen. 2:16).

[24] *Zohar Chadash*. R. Yitzchak said: "The serpent is the Evil Tempter." R. Yehuda said: "It means literally a serpent." They asked R. Shimon who told them: "Both these views are the same. It was Samael [the accuser, Angel of Death] who appeared as a serpent...Because the serpent was in reality the Angel of Death, it brought death to the world."

[25] Rashi, Gen. 3:1.

[26] Rashi, ad loc. and on *Sanhedrin* 29a.

[27] *Ha'amek Davar.*

[28] This interpretation is according to Rabbi Avraham Menachem Rappaport, a famous 16th-century Italian sage, in his commentary entitled *Mincha B'lula*. Rashi cites from Pirkei d'Rabbi Eliezer, chap. 13, that her motive was that Adam should not survive her and marry another woman. Considering the sublime spiritual stature of Chava, this must be understood on a deeper level.

[29] See Ramchal, *Adir B'Morom*, p. 11; *Nefesh HaChaim*, note to Gate 1, chap. 6; *Michtav M'Eliyahu* 2:138.

[30] Rashi, Gen. 3:7.

[31] *Zohar*, in the name of R. Chiya.

[32] *Sforno*, Gen. 3:7.

[33] Hirsch.

[34] Rashi, citing *Bereishit Rabba* 19:6.

[35] Hirsch explains "the direction of the day" as westwards, implying that G-d withdrew His Presence westwards (therefore the Holy of Holies in the Temple was in the west and the eternal light of the Menora is turned towards the west).

[36] *Aderet Eliyahu,* ad loc.

[37] *Sanhedrin* 38b.

[38] See *Derech Hashem* 3:8.

39 This obviously raises some serious philosophical questions about man's free choice. Furthermore, since the eating of forbidden fruit was for man's improvement, why did the episode have to occur through sin? These issues are dealt with extensively in Kabbalistic and Chassidic literature (see, for example, *Torat Chaim* from Rabbi Dov Ber of Lubavitch, the Mittler Rebbe, *Toldot* 13a *ff.)* and are beyond the scope of this work.

40 In contrast, when the Torah was given at Mt. Sinai, G-d instructed Moshe to inform the women prior to the men. The verse states, *"Ko tomar lebeit Yaakov vetagid lebnei Yisrael"* (Ex. 19:3). Rashi explains *"beit Yaakov"* refers to the women who were to be spoken to prior to *"bnei Yisrael,"* the men. Women were to be explained the Torah laws first since they are more determined in their faith. Women were entrusted with the responsibility of ensuring that their husbands and children observe the mitzvot punctiliously. Accordingly, being the pillars of Torah's perpetuation, the women should learn about it first.

SARA

41 *Sanhedrin* 99b; *Bereishit Rabba* 39:14; *Zohar* 1:102b; Rashi, Gen. 12:5.

42 In the Temple, there were twelve *Lechem HaPanim,* loaves of bread which were present at all times on the *Shulchan,* the special golden table. These loaves were replaced with fresh ones every Friday. The loaves had the miraculous quality that they would remain fresh for the entire week and that they were extremely satisfying and filling for whoever ate even just a small piece of them.

43 *Shem MiShmuel.*

44 *Malbim,* Gen. 17:15, notes that *Yisca* (Isca), the name that alluded to Sara's prophetic spirit (see *Megilla* 14a), was her primary name. *Sarai* (the name associated with her Abrahamitic mission and used from the time of her marriage) was given to her by Avraham, meaning *"Sharosi sheli—*my princess."

45 Cf. *Midrash Tanchuma, Chayei Sara* 4.

46 These are the twenty-two concluding verses of the book of Prov. 31:1 *ff.* (acrostically arranged alphabetically from *alef* to *tav*) in praise of the "Woman of Valor."

47 *Shemot Rabba* 1:1, *Tanchuma, Shemot* 1, cited in Rashi, Gen. 21:2. According to some Kabbalists this was a general rule that the female prophets attained higher degrees of prophecy than the men did. See Rabbi A. Kaplan, *The Handbook of Jewish Thought* (New York: Maznaim, 1979), p. 111, ftn. 245. Sara's greatness was apparent in how

she was particularly able to identify the spiritual source of the soul. This is the deeper meaning of the statement in the Talmud, *Bava Batra* 58a, that Avraham is resting in the arms of Sara. See *Or HaTorah, Bereishit,* p. 442*ff.*

[48] According to Kabbala, when Avraham and Yitzchak, respectively, called their wives sister (Gen. 12:13, 20:2, 26:7), they were describing the spiritual truth rather than a physical one. Their relationship with their wives was one of *"achoti kalla—*my sister, my bride," meaning that they were exact spiritual counterparts to their wives. See Rabbi A. Kaplan, *Innerspace* (New York: Moznaim, 1990), chap. 11, p.106.

[49] *Bereishit Rabba* 40:5, cited in Rashi, Gen.12:14.

[50] Malbim, Gen. 12:13.

[51] The classical commentaries (see for example Abarvanel, Alshich and Malbim*)* deal with these questions. Avraham's behavior remains, at best, difficult to comprehend without the aid of Kabbala.

[52] See *Sha'ar Hayichud VeHa'emuna,* chap. 1, that every aspect of creation has a spiritual life force which gives it existence. Before G-d created this world, the original creation was called *"tohu v'vohu,"* completely chaotic and confounded. A confounded person perceives an idea that his mind cannot hold. Similarly, the reason for this chaotic existence was that these original vessels of *tohu* were incapable of containing the G-dly light and, therefore, shattered. The vessels together with their G-dly light shattered into 288 sparks, which fell and became integrated into various parts of our physical world. These sparks became the source and power of evil, and the task of the Jewish people is to reunite them once again with G-d. See Rabbi J. Immanuel Schochet, *Mystical Concepts in Chassidus* (New York: Kehot, 1988), chap. 7, and sources cited in *Innerspace*, part I, chap. 10.

[53] See *Likkutei Halachot, Rosh Hashana* 6:7.

[54] The Lubavitcher Rebbe once suggested that this is one of the reasons why, after many centuries of life in Europe, Judaism was recently transplanted to North America. Europe and the rest of the world had already been purified through all the Torah and mitzvot performed by the righteous Jews living there for so many centuries. North America, however, was desolate in this regard and needed this purification as a preparation for the arrival of Mashiach.

[55] See *Bava Metzia* 59a. R. Chelbo said: "One must always honor his wife because blessings rest on a man's home only on account of his wife, for it is written, 'And he treated Avram well for her sake.' And thus did Rava say to the townspeople of Machuza, 'Honor your wives and you will become rich.'"

56 See also *Zohar* 3:81, that Avraham was not afraid for Sara because he saw that the Divine Presence was with her. He saw that an angel walked in front of her, but since he himself did not have this protection, he feared for his own security.

57 *Bereishit Rabba* 41:2, *Tanchuma* 5, cited in Rashi, 12:17.

58 *Midrash Hagadol* emphasizes the righteousness of Sara, who did not consider her own feelings at all but acted solely for the sake of Heaven. See also Ramban, 16:2, who pays particular attention to Scripture's wording, "Avram heeded the voice of Sarai," rather than using a simple version of "Avram did so." According to the Ramban this indicates that Avram did not marry Hagar because he wanted children, but because this was Sara's will.

59 *Bereishit Rabba* 45:1. For Hagar's boasting, see Rashi, 16:4, citing *Bereishit Rabba* 45:4.

60 See Malbim, *Or HaChaim* and Hirsch.

61 Nevertheless, Hagar still only consented to return to Sara's home after the angel promised her that Yishmael would be a "wild and free man" (Gen. 16:12), who would be free from the servitude of Sara. (See Hirsch.)

62 Malbim 16:1. Accordingly, the Midrash *(Bereishit Rabba* 45:1) notes that the Torah emphasizes "she had borne him no child"—Sara bore no children to Avraham but would have given birth to a child if she had been married to another. This view clearly suggests that it was primarily on the account of Avraham, and not Sara, that the birth of Yitzchak was delayed.

63 Rashi, Gen. 17:5.

64 *Yerushalmi Sanhedrin* 2:6. Rav Huna said quoting Rav Acha: The letter *yud* (possessing the numeric value of 10), which was removed from Sarai's name, was divided into two *hey* letters *(hey* has the value of 5); one *hey* was added to Avram and the other to Sarai. This idea would concur with the view of the midrash quoted above that Sara was prepared for a child, but Avraham still required an added dimension of Sara's spirituality.

65 G-d's rebuking Sara through Avraham is especially difficult to understand when keeping in mind the great care that G-d takes to maintain *shalom bayit*, peace between husband and wife. In fact at that very moment G-d was concerned with *shalom bayit*, as the Talmud *(Bava Metzia* 87a) points out that when rebuking Sara's conduct to Avraham, He changed Sara's words, quoting her as saying: "Is it possible that I will have children, when *I* am so old?" In reality, Sara had said that *Avraham* was so old, but G-d changed her words to promote peace, so that Avraham wouldn't be offended. This makes it all the more difficult to understand that G-d would criticize and speak badly of Sara to her

husband, when He had routinely spoken directly to her.

Furthermore, when Avraham heard the news he also reacted in a prayer to G-d of "*Lu Yishmael yichyeh lefonecha*—O that Ishmael might live before You." The *Zohar* (2:32a) records that Rav Chiya wept at the circumstances that led Avraham to marry Hagar and beget a son to whom he became so attached that, though G-d assured him that he would have a son through Sara, Avraham prayed that Yishmael might live before Him. The *Zohar* continues that this prayer which G-d was "forced" to answer is the source of all the suffering the Jews would endure from the Arabs at the time period just prior to the *geula*. Nevertheless, no rebuke is made to Avraham for his reaction.

66 *Chizkuni* 18:13.

67 Rashi, Gen. 21:7 (from *Bava Metzia* 87a), on the words "*Heinika banim Sara*," Sara has nursed *children* (plural).

68 Rashi, 21:8-10.

69 Ramban suggests that this episode happened on the day of Yitzchak's feast. See also *Sforno*. Rashi, 21:9, quotes various opinions (from *Bereishit Rabba* 53:11) about Yishmael's wrongful behavior. One interpretation explains that he was worshipping idols; another states that he was engaged in prohibited sexual activities, while yet another, that he wanted to murder Yitzchak in order to receive Avraham's inheritance.

70 Hirsch 21:12 stresses that Avraham was told to heed the voice rather than the word of Sara. He was to rely on Sara whether or not he understood the reason for the demand, or agreed with it.

71 *Bereishit Rabba* 58:1, brought down in Rashi, 23:1. The age "twenty" is cited because the Heavenly Court does not hold one responsible for sin until the age of twenty.

72 *Midrash Hane'elam, Zohar* 1:122b; *Zohar* 1:135a explains the words "and Sara died in Kiryat Arba" (Gen. 23:2) as the body, which is mortal and composed of four *(arba)* elements (i.e., water, air, earth and fire); while about Avraham it is written, "And Avraham rose above the face of his dead" (Gen. 23:3), alluding to the soul, which transcends death.

73 See Rabbi Shalom Dov Ber of Lubavitch, *Ma'amar*, from the year 5659, beginning with the words "*Lakol tichleh*."

74 *Bava Batra* 16b.

RIVKA

75 *Vayikra Rabba* 8:1, *Tanchuma, Mishpatim* 18.

[76] See Rabbi Y. Ginsburgh, *The Alef Beit* (Northvale, N.J: Jason Aronson, 1991), p. 277

[77] *Sota* 2a.

[78] See *Bereishit Rabba* 58:2, that G-d did not allow the "sun" of Sara to set until the "sun" of Rivka had begun to rise. Furthermore, commenting on the verse (24:7), "G-d of the Heavens will send His angel before you," the midrash (*Bereishit Rabba* 59:10) comments that at the very hour that Avraham was instructing Eliezer to seek a wife for Yitzchak, G-d was preparing two angels: one to take Rivka out of her home and one to accompany Eliezer.

[79] Gen. 24:42; Rashi quoting *Bereishit Rabba* 59:11; *Sanhedrin* 95a.

[80] *Shir Hashirim Rabba* 2:2 (1).

[81] *Zohar* 2:20b.

[82] *Pirkei d'Rabbi Eliezer* 16 and *Yalkut Shimoni*, Gen. 109. Note in the ensuing episode how unusual it was for Rivka to have gone out to the well with a jar on her shoulder. Since Bethuel was very wealthy, it would have been expected of her to take along one of her maidens to carry the jar.

[83] The Talmud (*Pesachim* 87b) says that the purpose of exile is to acquire converts. *Likkutei Torah* (*Naso* 26c) questions how this is possible when such a minute number of converts have been added to the Jewish people. He explains that "converts" in this context refers to sparks of holiness. The purpose of exile is to collect these sparks of holiness that are spread throughout the world.

[84] This is similar to the first redemption from Egypt when G-d did not delay for even one instant. See *Mechilta, Bo*, 24 on Ex. 12:41.

[85] *Zohar* 1:117a.

[86] *Tzidkat HaTzaddik*, sect. 111.

[87] Gen. 24:16 *ff.*

[88] Malbim 24:12.

[89] Malbim 24:13-14.

[90] See Rashi, ad loc. (from *Targum* and *Bereishit Rabba* 60:6).

[91] As in the command to give "a *beka* for every head, a half shekel" (Ex. 38:26).

[92] See *Bava Batra* 9a. See also *Shabbat* 88a.

[93] The Ten Commandments are ten comprehensive principles that imply and comprise the whole of Torah; see *Zohar* 2:90b and 93b; *Bamidbar Rabba* 13:16 and 18:21.

[94] *Shabbat* 88a. See also *Mechilta, Yitro, Bachodesh*, 5.

[95] As represented by the name of G-d (*Yah*) found in the combination of "*ish*" (man) and "*isha*" (woman), which when removed leaves only "*eish*," fire and destruction. See chapter on Chava in this book.

[96] Rambam, introduction to *Mishneh Torah*.

[97] The following is based on *Likkutei Sichot* 1:36ff.

[98] In fact, Rivka's family even attempted to murder Eliezer by poisoning his food. Eliezer was saved, however, in Avraham's merit when an angel switched the plates, and Bethuel was killed instead. *Targum*, Gen. 24:33 and 24:55, and Rashi, 24:55.

[99] Rashi, 24:67.

[100] Rivka had terrible pains during pregnancy. When she would pass the doorways of Shem and Ever where *Torah* was being studied, Yaakov would struggle to exit, while Esav did the same when she passed places of idol worship. Rashi, Gen. 25:22, quoting *Bereishit Rabba* 63:6.

[101] Rabbi Dov Ber was the successor of his father, Rabbi Shneur Zalman, the Baal HaTanya, and was the second Rebbe in the Chabad dynasty. He is also known as the Mittler Rebbe.

[102] Rashi, Gen. 25:27. Esav questioned his father about tithing salt and straw, though he actually knew that there was no requirement whatsoever to tithe these items. See also *Zohar* 1:139.

[103] This is reflected by the great souls who descended from Esav and converted to Judaism, e.g., Ovadia, Onkelos, Shmaya and R. Meir. See *Torah Ohr* 20c.

[104] This concept is explained in detail in the *Ma'amar Bati Legani*, 5715, printed in the *Sefer Hama'amarim Bati Legani* 1:63ff.

RACHEL AND LEAH

[105] *Likkutei Torah, parshat Emor*, 38d. Rachel's name also has the same numerological value as the Hebrew words "and there was light." See Rav Menachem Azarya of Fano, *Yonat Alem*, chap. 5, explained in *Likkutei Sichot* 30:286.

[106] The concept of Rachel (and her children) as the *tzaddik* personality and Leah (and her descendants) as the *baal teshuva* personality can be found in *Likkutei Sichot* 35:152ff.

[107] Gen. 1:11. The present and future concepts of the worlds of perfection and imperfection are based on an essay by Rav Kook in *Ein Aya* 4:44-46.

See also Rav Shlomo Elyashiv, *Leshem*, who explains that Rachel and Leah actually represent one soul, and, had it not been for the sin of the Tree of Knowledge, these two aspects would have remained merged.

108 Occasionally Yosef is referred to as the individual charged with "changing from *acher* [something that negates holiness], into *ben* [literally a son, figuratively meaning bringing into the sphere of holiness]." This appears to be the work of the *baal teshuva* and not the *tzaddik* personality. See *Likkutei Sichot* 35:53, note 38, for an elaboration.

109 *Mei Hashiloach, parshat Vayeitzei.*

110 *Berachot* 34b.

111 See *Zohar* 1:259a, which explains that the Beit Hamikdash is both in the portion of Binyamin and of Yehuda. However, the Altar was specifically in the part of Binyamin despite the fact that Yehuda was the "highest of all the tribes." The reason for this is because Binyamin and Yosef, as Rachel's sons, were on the level of *tzaddikim*, whereas the children of Leah were on the level of *baalei teshuva*.

112 *Bereishit Rabba* 70:16.

113 *Tanchuma Vayeitzei* 4.

114 *Bereishit Rabba* 70:16.

115 *Zohar,* 1:153a.

116 See *Megilla* 13b and *Bava Batra* 123a.

117 *Bereishit Rabba* 70:19.

118 See essay "Rachel," based on the teachings of Rabbi Yitzchak Ginsburgh, in *Basics in Kabbalah and Chassidut,* at www.inner.org/worlds/rachel.htm

119 The concept of Yaakov's in some way "becoming" Esav is taken from an article by Rabbi Ari Kahn entitled "Rachel and Leah" on www.aish.com.

120 *Eitz Chaim, Sha'ar Haklalim.*

121 Gen. 32:29.

122 See essay "Rachel," based on the teachings of Rabbi Yitzchak Ginsburgh, in *Basics in Kabbalah and Chassidut,* at www.inner.org/worlds/rachel.htm.

123 *Berachot* 60a.

124 *Me'am Lo'ez* on Gen. 30:18. The Torah says "[Yaakov] lay with her that night [*balayla hu*]" (30:16). Actually the Hebrew expression for

"that" is *ha-hu*, rather than *hu*, as it appears. The verse can therefore be read, "he slept with her that night, He did," meaning, G-d was pleased with Leah's actions.

125 *Me'am Lo'ez* on Gen. 30:18.

126 *Me'am Lo'ez* on Gen. 34:1, quoting *Bereishit Rabba*. In *Bava Batra* 15b, this is mentioned, deriving from the verse, "You speak like an outraged woman" (Job 2:10). The woman against whom an outrage had been committed was Dina (abducted by Shechem).

There is another opinion that Shimon married her, or that she remained a spinster.

127 The above understanding of Dina's outgoingness is based on *Likkutei Sichot* 35:150 *ff.* It is noted there that Dina's "outgoingness" did have the effect of elevating the people of Shechem in that they became circumcised before their deaths on her account. Furthermore, the women of Shechem—those to whom Dina "went out" to have a spiritual effect upon—were taken captive by the children of Yaakov and remained with the tribes.

128 *Targum*, Gen. 30:21.

129 This is also demonstrated by the fact that each of the tribes was born with a twin, but both Dina and Yosef were not. See *Pirkei d'Rabbi Eliezer* 34.

130 See *Bereishit Rabba* 73:5. See also *Me'am Lo'ez* on Gen. 30:25, 26 (ftn.334). Rav Yonaton Eibeshitz in his work *Ya'arot Dvash* (vol. 1, essay 12) explains that the power to defeat Esav's wicked offspring, Amalek, must come from a child of Rachel. Timna, the concubine of Elifaz, who gave birth to Amalek, was originally a princess. Timna went to the patriarchs to convert but was not accepted. She then became a concubine to Elifaz, saying it is better to be a concubine in this family (Elifaz, as Esav's son, was Yitzchak's grandson) than a princess elsewhere. If the power of Amalek emanated from the self-sacrifice of Timna, the power to defeat Amalek must come from the same source—namely, from a child of Rachel, who demonstrated enormous self-sacrifice in giving over the prearranged signs so that Leah would not suffer humiliation.

131 See *Zohar* 1:158: "All the deeds of Leah are hidden. Therefore, it doesn't mention her death in the Torah, whereas the death of Rachel is recorded. Leah was hidden in the Cave of Machpela, while Rachel was buried on the way [in the open]."

132 Introduction to *Midrash Eicha*.

133 The above is based on an essay in *Likkutei Sichot* 30:236.

❧ DEEDS

LIGHT OF ETERNITY

134 See *Ohr Chaim* on Ex. 27:20 as well as many other places: "'And you shall take for yourself pure olive oil'—this hints to Torah, which is compared to oil. Just as oil lights up the world, so too, does Torah."

135 *Likkutei Sichot* 12:149, 5:445-446 and *Iggrot Kodesh* 4:228.

136 Only three mitzvot involve actual light. They are lighting Shabbat candles, lighting the Menora of the Beit Hamikdash and lighting the Chanuka menora.

137 *Sefer BeShT, Bereishit* 82; *Maggid Devarav LeYaakov* 135; *Ma'or Veshemesh* on Ex. 31:16.

138 Isa. 40:28.

139 The world was actually created with the letter *"hey,"* the easiest letter of the Hebrew alphabet to pronounce. See *Bereishit Rabba* 12:2, *Eitz Yosef*, ad loc.

140 *Zohar* 2:135b.

141 Dayan I. Grunfeld, *The Sabbath* (New York: Feldheim, 1981), p. 19.

142 This custom is most likely based on the greeting mentioned in the Talmud, *Shabbat* 12b, "Enjoy the Shabbat rest in peace."

143 Rabbi M. Glazerson, *Revelations about Marriage* (Jerusalem: Raz-Ot Institute, 1988).

144 For a broader understanding of the term *Malka*, Queen, or *Malchut*, Royalty, and its connection to the feminine, refer to the chapter Malchut: The Feminine *Sefira* in this book.

145 See *Zohar* 2:63b, where it is stated that Shabbat and Yom Tov are days from which we draw strength and blessing for the weekdays.

146 *Zohar* 3:52a.

147 *Yevamot* 62b; cf. *Bereishit Rabba* 17b, where it is explained that a wife provides a man with forgiveness, peace, life and completion.

148 A prime example of this would be the pig that will become kosher in the era of Mashiach. For this reason a pig is called in Hebrew, *"chazir,"* meaning "return," because of its future potential of returning to the forces of holiness, to the point that it will be permitted for kosher consumption. As our sages have said, "Why is the swine called *chazir*? Because in the future, G-d will give it back (*l'hachaziro*) to Israel." This does not imply that the laws of the Torah will undergo any change, as the

Torah is eternal. However, the *chazir* is forbidden because of its nature, as expressed in its lack of the kosher signs. In the future, its nature will be transformed and it will have the "correct" signs. See *Likkutei Sichot* 12:75 for sources and discussion.

[149] See *Yalkut Shimoni*, Ruth 606. See the Arizal, introduction to *Sha'ar Hagilgulim*, 20, who explains that the generation of the final redemption are the very same souls as those freed from Egypt. Just as these women were primarily responsible for the first redemption from Egypt, so too, these women will herald the final redemption.

KNEADING G-DLINESS

[150] The minimal requirement of flour in order to recite a blessing is 3 lbs. and 11 oz. or 1.666 grams. For over 2 lbs. and 11 oz., *challa* would be separated without reciting a blessing. A small piece (approximately one ounce) of *challa* is separated while the dough is still whole and undivided and it is set aside to be burnt. The following blessing is recited: Blessed are you, L-rd our G-d, King of the Universe, who has sanctified us with His commandments and commanded us to separate *challa*.

[151] *Vayikra Rabba* 15:6.

[152] Rambam, *Hilchot Deot* 3:2.

[153] *Likkutei Sichot* 18:183-186.

[154] See *Tanya, Iggeret Hakodesh* 19.

[155] *Keter Shem Tov* 194, See also *Likkutei Sichot* 1:177.

[156] *Beitza* 17a.

[157] *On the Essence of Chassidus* (New York: Kehot, 1978), chap. 19.

[158] Cf. *Kohelet Rabba* 2:24, "All references to food and drink in Ecclesiastes refer to Torah and mitzvot."

[159] Ibid.

[160] The modern word, "to weld," *lehalchim*, is from the same root.

[161] See Gen. 39:6, where Yosef says that Potifar "entrusted everything he had to Yosef's hands, taking account of nothing except the bread (*lechem*) he ate." See Rashi, ad loc., who explains *lechem* as referring to Potifar's wife.

162 See Imagery section in this book, where it is explained how women are compared to the *sefira* of Malchut, the unifying and harmonizing *sefira*. Malchut serves as the axis or focal point directing and encompassing all the *sefirot* within it to project a focused and unified light into our functioning and completed world.

MYSTERIOUS NIGHTS

163 This term originates in the Talmud (*Makot* 7b) regarding the laws of cities of refuge. It is "borrowed" in Chassidic texts to refer to the metaphysical axiom that every ascent must be preluded by a descent.

164 *Ben Sira*, chap. 25, verse 1.

165 Furthermore, the letter *beit* relates primarily to the wife, who is the mainstay of the home, *bayit*, and the source of its blessing. Therefore, the Sages customarily refer to their wives as "my home."

166 *Zohar* 3:59a.

167 See Gen. 1:27—"In the image of G-d, He created them, male and female He created them." Cf. Hirsch on Gen. 2:18 and 2:24.

168 *Kiddushin* 2b. Therefore the verse states, "He who finds a wife, finds good" (Prov. 18:22). Since the wife is a part of man, until they become united as a couple, she is regarded as the part of him that is lost.

169 *Sefer Habahir*, attributed to Nechunia ben Hakana, trans. by Rabbi A. Kaplan (Weiser, 1979).

170 Cf. *Tanya*, chap. 46.

171 *Shir HaShirim Rabba* 1:2; Rashi, 2 Kings 11:2; Song of Songs 1:16; 2 Chronicles 22:11. King Solomon built the Temple and House of G-d in which G-d, the celestial groom, and Israel, His bride, consummate their union. Interestingly, King Solomon penned the *Song of Songs*, describing the consummate expression of spousal love.

172 The laws of Family Purity are quite detailed, and, as such, beyond the scope of this book. There are several excellent books available in English.

173 Ra'avad, *Sefer Baalei HaNefesh*, introduction.

174 See Hirsch on Lev. 20:18, where he explains that the laws of *nidda* are mentioned immediately following the forbidden sexual relationship with one's sister. He suggests that the Torah is teaching us that during the period when physical contact is forbidden, the couple should form other non-physical bonds, such as those that normally join brother and sister.

320

Further support for this is found in *Song of Songs* with the recurring use of "my sister, my bride" (Song of Songs 4:9-10; 5:1; 8:1).

[175] *Holy Letter of Nachmanides* (Rabbi Moshe ben Nachman, 1194-1270).

[176] Deut. 31:17.

[177] See *Mateh Ephraim* 625. The custom to immerse in the *mikve* on *erev Shabbat* is based on the *Zohar* and the Arizal. See Sh'laah, *Masechta Shabbat, perek Ner Mitzva.*

[178] See *Likkutei Sichot* 2:310-365.

[179] Deut. 31:17. See commentary of Baalei Tosafot. This expression also contains an allusion, since the Hebrew word for face, *panim*, also means inner dimension. When G-d hides His face, His inner dimensions are still being expressed. They are, however, working in a hidden manner.

[180] Perhaps this explains why, after having given birth to a baby boy, a woman must wait a minimum of seven days before beginning her pure days count; while after a baby girl is born, she must wait a minimum of fourteen days. Since the female child inherently carries a higher degree of holiness, due to her own biological, life-creating capability, a greater void, or *tuma*, remains after her birth. Thus, the greater *tuma* after a baby girl's birth reflects her greater capacity for *kedusha* (due to her creative powers) and necessitates the longer wait to remove this *tuma*.

[181] Tzemach Tzedek, *Sefer Halikutim*, vol. 6, s.v. *nidda.*

[182] Tzemach Tzedek, *Sefer Halikutim*, vol. 6, pp. 38-40.

[183] Rambam, *Hilchot Melachim*, 12: 4-5.

[184] For an elaboration of this concept, see Rabbi Yitzchak Ginsburgh, *The Covenant of Marriage* (Jerusalem: Gal Einei, 1990), pp. 49-59. These three levels of Divine service are mentioned in *Keter Shem Tov* 28.

[185] For an elaboration of the self-sacrifice and faith of Esther, refer to the chapter "Esther: A Paradigm of Self-Sacrifice" in the third section of this book.

[186] See *Likkutei Sichot* 3:749.

[187] *Yalkut Shimoni* 1:3; *Likkutei Halachot (Yoreh Deah) Mikve* 1. I am indebted to Rabbi A. Kaplan, *Waters of Eden* (New York: NCSY, 1976) for this source as well as several others in this chapter.

[188] *Yoreh Deah* 121:1.

[189] *Avoda Zara* 75b; Rambam, *Hilchot Ma'achalot Assurot* 17:3. Note that this differs from the laws of kashrut, where the law stipulates that a mixture of sixty times is required to effect nullification.

190 Rabbi S. R. Hirsch on Ex. 30:18.

191 *Targum*, Judges 10:8.

192 *Berachot* 55a.

193 See *Likkutei Torah, parshat Tzav*, p. 14b, for an extensive discussion of this subject.

194 For this reason, the name by which Moshe is called in the Torah is the name given to him by the Egyptian princess, Batya. She named him Moshe because "from the waters I have drawn him (*mishitihu*)" Moshe's name, alluding to his connection to the water, reflects his spiritual essence. Moshe, like a water creature, and like all the *tzaddikim* of each generation, was at all times connected to his Divine source and cognizant of the Divine will.

195 *Nidda* 15b; *Mishneh LaMelech* on Rambam, *Hilchot Tumat Met* 2:1.

196 See Rashi, Gen. 7:4, who explains that the flood lasted for forty days to correct the sin of the people who "perverted the embryo that is formed in forty days," through their sexual immorality. The concept of the flood as purification is found in Rabbi Shneur Zalman of Liadi, *Torah Ohr, parshat Noach*.

197 *Yerushalmi, Berachot* 9:2.

198 Gen. 1:10.

199 *Yoreh Deah* 201:2.

200 See *Sefer Hachinuch, Vayikra*, mitzva 173.

201 For a greater discussion on many of the concepts in this chapter, see Rabbi A. Kaplan, *Waters of Eden* (New York: NCSY, 1976).

202 Zech. 13:2.

❧ TIME

203 *Ta'anit* 2a.

204 Rambam, *Hilchot Tefilla* 1:1-2.

205 *Keter Shem Tov* 194.

206 See Rambam, *Hilchot Megilla* 2:18. See also *Yalkut Mishlei* 9, which states, "All festivals shall be forgotten in times to come, but the days of Purim shall never be forgotten." Chassidic teachings explain that other holidays will not be celebrated in the era of Mashiach since the spiritual light and revelation emanating from them will be completely

overshadowed by the light and revelation of Mashiach. However, the light of Purim can never be eclipsed.

207 See Rashi, Esther 1:1.

208 There is a difference of opinion among the Sages (*Megilla* 13a) as to whether Hadassa was her proper name and Esther was later added, or vice-versa. Both names are descriptive of her virtues. Hadassa is derived from the Hebrew word *hadas*, "myrtle," because of her similarity to the beautiful and fragrant myrtle to whom the righteous are compared (Zech. 1:8); Esther from *Istahar* (the Perisan word for moon), as beautiful as the moon. (Rashi, Esther 1:7). Esther was on such a spiritual level that she actually attained prophecy. (*Megilla* 14a)

209 *Megilla* 13a.

210 *Tosefot, Ketubot* 57b.

211 *Esther Rabba* 2:15.

212 This is learned from the passage in Esther 2:7 describing Esther's background, "*Lokcha Mordechai lo lebat*" (Mordechai took her in as a daughter when she became orphaned). The Talmud explains: "Do not read *lebat* as a 'daughter' but read it similarly as *lebayit*, a 'home,' meaning a wife" (*Megilla* 13a). It is self-evident that this was not written openly, due to the peril to Mordechai's life.

213 The greatness of Mordechai is further revealed in the *Zohar*, which states that Mordechai possessed no less than the soul of Moshe himself.

214 Commentary of R. Elisha Galico (prominent 16th-century Talmudist and Kabbalist).

215 *M'not Halevi*, Esther 2:15.

216 *Megilla* 13a.

217 Rav Yonasson Eybeschetz, *Ya'arot Dvash*.

218 The commentaries offer various explanations for keeping Esther's Jewishness secret. Ibn Ezra (Esther 2:10) explains that had she declared her faith, she would have been forced to transgress. See also Rashi, *Yosef Lekach* and R. Eleazar of Worms for other explanations.

219 *Megilla* 13b. See also *Midrash Shocher Tov* 22:26, who quotes Esther's heartfelt prayer to G-d before she appeared voluntarily before Achashverosh to plead for her brethren: "My G-d, why have you forsaken me...? I have been placed in the bosom of this evil man for so many years and no miracles have helped me. Jewish women have three special commandments and I keep them even here..."

220 *Megilla* 15a.

221 See *Sanhedrin* 74b. Esther was never an active participant in adultery, and her initial revulsion was never eroded. See also *Megilla* 15a; *Tosefot, Ketubot* 57b; and *Shita Mekubetzet, Ketubot* 3b.

222 Rashi, *Yosef Lekach* (Esther 2:11).

223 *Seder Hadorot* traces the time to the Jewish year of 3395.

224 Rashi (Esther 1:2) notes that Achashverosh was a usurper to the throne and his first three years involved political insecurity. *Megilla* 11b elaborates that Achashverosh was not deserving of the throne, but owed his status to his vast wealth and lavish distribution of money with which he purchased his royal position, thus giving him dominion.

225 *Esther Rabba*; Ibn Ezra (Esther 1:1).

226 Achashverosh ordered Vashti to appear unclothed to show her true beauty to all present. When Vashti indignantly refused, she was summarily executed.

227 *Yalkut Shimoni.*

228 *Megilla* 12a.

229 Jer. 29:2. Yermiyahu's prophecy that the Jews would return to Israel after a 70-year period actually began from the destruction of Jerusalem and the exile of King Tzidkiyahu, ending in the second year of the reign of Daryavesh II, son of Achashverosh and Esther, who gave permission to rebuild the Holy Temple. This elusive prophecy caused many miscalculations, and was only properly interpreted by Daniel.

230 See Rav Galico; *Me'am Lo'ez* (Esther 1:5).

231 The first verse of the Bible at the creation of the Universe states, *"Bereishit bara Elokim*—In the beginning G-d created." Rashi interprets the irregular usage of *"Bereishit"* as "for the sake of *reishit"*— those that are called "firsts," i.e., foremost and most important. They are: a) the Torah and b) the Jewish people; and it is for them that the world was formed. *Tanna DeVei Eliyahu Rabba,* chap. 14, states that of these two, the Jewish people are first and foremost. (See also *Bereishit Rabba* 1:4.) Esther, through her behavior, demonstrated just how deeply she perceived this lofty quality of the nation of G-d.

232 Rabbi Akiva was tortured to death by the Romans. As his flesh was being torn with burning iron combs, he confessed to his students how he had waited his whole life to fulfill the words of the Shema, *"Bechal levavcha u'vechol nafshecha*—to love G-d with all one's heart and life." It was only now, as he was being murdered for the sake of G-d, that he was finally able to literally serve G-d with his life. The *Beit Yosef* in his *Maggid Me'isharim* mentions how he prayed to merit to die *"al kiddush Hashem."*

233 Up until now, Esther was halachically permitted to resume relations with her husband, Mordechai, because each meeting with the king had been forced upon her under penalty of death. Now, however, she was taking the initiative. Such an action on her part would be considered infidelity, even if Mordechai himself had ordered it and it was the proper and heroic thing to do. Consequently, she could never again live with Mordechai.

234 Although Esther listened to Mordechai, who was the leader and prophet of the generation, and her behavior was hence permissible, she did not know its effect at the time of her action.

235 There are several instances when we see this phenomenon that a *tzaddik*, a righteous person, can atone for the Jewish people through his sufferings and hardships. This is only possible if the Jewish nation has completely repented. For this reason, Esther insisted that the Jewish people "fast for me and do not eat or drink for three days" (Esther 4:15), to ensure total repentance from their sin of participating in the feast. Once they had done their part (as mentioned above, for an entire year the Jewish people lived in a state of danger rather than renounce their religion), then the extra amount of atonement needed could be accomplished through Esther. Although Judaism stresses the independent responsibility of every individual, nevertheless, the soul of all Jews are united like one body. The *tzaddik* represents the spiritual head of the nation and whatever affects the heart affects the whole body. Thus, the *tzaddik*, through his service, can provide atonement for the Jewish people (if the above prerequisite of *teshuva* is present).

236 *Megilla* 12a.

237 *Sota* 11b; *Shemot Rabba* 1:12; Rashi, Ex. 38:8.

238 These mirrors were later donated by the women to the Tabernacle. At first Moshe was reluctant to use such seemingly vain tools. But G-d attested to the merit of the women in using these mirrors to encourage their husbands, by instructing that the mirrors be melted down and made into the *Kiyor*, the Priests' washing basin.

239 Rashi, Ex. 1:15. See also *Shemot Rabba* 1:13 and *Sota* 11b.

240 *Shemot Rabba* 1:13.

241 Rashi, Ex. 1:17.

242 *Sota* 12a; *Shemot Rabba*.

243 Rashi, Ex. 2:2

244 *Bava Batra* 91b. Ruth lived to see her royal descendant, David Hamelech's son Shlomo, ascend the throne.

245 Moav refused food or passage through its land to the men, women and children of the Jewish nation, who had recently been freed from their servitude in Egypt. See Deut. 23:5.

246 *Seder Hadorot* and *Tzemach David.*

247 See *Targum,* Ruth 1:1. Elimelech was from the leaders of the generation. Rashi refers to Elimelech as the *parnas hador.*

248 Rashi, Ruth 1:2. Ruth and Orpa were the daughters of Eglon, King of Moav.

249 *Ruth Rabba:* "The Merciful One never begins His retribution by taking a human life...first their horses, their donkeys, and then their camels died. Then Elimelech. And lastly his two sons."

250 *Bava Batra* 91b. All the above-mentioned punishments were due to the family's leaving the Land of Israel.

251 Ruth 1:16-17.

252 Malbim (Ruth 1:18) explains that the word *"eemutz"* used in the verse denotes not only inner strength but also perseverance.

253 Ibn Ezra, Ruth 1:17. Ruth swore that she would never forsake the Torah of the Jews or the Oneness of G-d.

254 Malbim, Ruth 1:16, 17. Ruth stated: "I do not expect luxuries and I am prepared to be a mere lodger because there is only one object in my going"—to live as a Jew and to die as a Jew.

255 *Yevamot* 76b.

256 See *Iggeret Shmuel,* Ruth 1:22.

257 *Yalkut* 601: "People exclaimed: 'In the past she used to travel in a covered carriage and now she walks barefoot. In the past she wore a cloak of fine wool and now she is clothed in rags. In the past her appearance was full from food and drink, now it is shrunken from hunger. Could this be Naomi?'"

258 *Targum,* Ruth 1:6. The famine ended on account of the prayers and righteousness of Boaz.

259 *Iggeret Shmuel,* Ruth 1:6. Naomi told Ruth: "It is not that I hold you in low esteem that I permit you to so degrade yourself by gleaning like a common pauper; I permit you only because of the circumstances and our dire needs, which demand it."

260 Rashi, Ruth 2: 1.

261 *Iggeret Shmuel,* Ruth 2:4.

262 *Shabbat* 113b: "Was it, then, Boaz's custom to inquire about young

girls? Rabbi Elazar answered: 'Her halachic knowledge and exemplary conduct caught his attention. She would glean two ears but would not glean three.'" (In accordance with the law in *Mishna Peah* 6:5.)

[263] *Ruth Rabba*: "She would stand while gleaning the standing ears and sit while gleaning the fallen ears. The other women hitched up their skirts, she kept hers down. The other women jested with the harvesters, while she remained reserved. The other women gathered from between the sheaves, while she gathered only from that which was definitely abandoned."

[264] *Iggeret Shmuel*, Ruth 2:8. Boaz said to Ruth: "You heard me discussing you with my servant. Don't think I inquired about you because of any displeasure at your presence. To the contrary, I insist that you stay and glean in my fields exclusively."

[265] Rashi, Ruth 3:2.

[266] Malbim, Ruth 3:4. See Deut. 25:5-10 for the laws of *yibum*.

[267] Explanation here is based on the Alshich, *Introduction to Megillat Ruth* and 3:9. The basis of the Alshich can be found in *Midrash Rabba*, Gen. 50:16, as pointed out by Rabbi A. Rotenberg in his essay printed in the English Alshich, *Harvest of Majesty* (New York: Feldheim, 1991). See also *Seder Hadorot, Boaz*.

[268] See Gen., chap. 18-19.

[269] *Midrash Rabba*, Ruth 3:10.

[270] *Yalkut Shimoni* 608.

[271] *Midrash Rabba*, Ruth 8:1. David Hamelech said to G-d: "How long will they speak angrily and say, 'Is he not of unworthy lineage? Is he not descended from Ruth the Moabite?'"

[272] Translation taken from Rabbi Aryeh Kaplan, *The Living Nach* (New York: Maznaim, 1994).

[273] Adam sinned by disregarding G-d's command and eating from the forbidden Tree of Knowledge. He did this on the instigation of the serpent. The human body became defiled by this act, and as a result is not capable of living forever.

[274] The story and concepts in this chapter are based on *Yalkut HaMachiri* and developed by *Sefer Hatoda'a* (Jerusalem: Yad Eliyahu Kitov, 1976), section on Sivan and Shavuot.

[275] Deut. 23:5.

[276] See Gen., chap. 38 and *midrashim* and commentaries on that chapter.

277 In the verse in the Psalm where David says he was a "stranger" to his brothers, the Hebrew word for stranger (*muzar*) is from the same root as *mamzer*, illegitimate son.

278 Radak and Abarvanel on I Samuel 16:3.

279 This event occurred even after David was crowned king. However, according to commentaries, it is possible that they didn't understand the implications of the anointing. (It has been suggested that they assumed that Shmuel was anointing David as a new student in his school of prophecy.) Though this was an honor, and an act that would validate David's lineage, only once David actually became king to the entire nation did his brothers realize his true greatness.

280 Malbim.

281 *Midrash Tanchuma, parshat Va'eira* 6.

282 The Hebrew word in this verse for builders, *bonim*, has the same root as the word for sons, *banim*.

283 See *Torah Ohr*, end of *parshat Vayigash* and *Siddur im Dach*, p. 276.

284 Text of *Sheva Berachot*, based on Jer. 33:10-11.

IMAGERY

285 The understanding of the "*kav* and *reshimu*" in this chapter is based on an essay by Rabbi Yanki Tauber in *Week in Review*. vol. 8, no. 24, expounding on a letter dated Adar 18, 5704, as printed in *Iggrot Kodesh* 1:267-268.

286 Eitz Chaim, *Heichal Adam Kadmon* 1:2; *Sha'ar HaHakdamot*, 4 and *Otzrot Chaim*, introduction to *Sha'ar Hagilgulim*.

287 For a further discussion and elaboration of these concepts see Rabbi J. I. Schochet, *Mystical Concepts in Chassidut* (New York: Kehot, 1988); Mattis Kantor, *Ten Keys for Understanding Human Nature* (New York: Zichron Press, 1994) and Rabbi Simon Jacobson, *A Spiritual Guide to the Counting of the Omer* (New York: VHT, 1996).

288 See *Iggeret Hakodesh* of the *Tanya*, chap. 4, for a discussion on the descent of the Divine Light through the letters of *Havaye*.

289 This is a reason why the Hebrew letter *hey* has the shape of the letter *yud* contained within it (as the *hey* is composed of a *daled* and a *yud*).

290 As our sages commented, "When they were exiled to Edom, the Shechina went with them." *Mechilta* on Ex. 12:41; *Sifrei* on Num. 10:35 and 35:34; *Megilla* 29a.

²⁹¹ *Sefer Yetzira* 1:5.

²⁹² See, for example, *Iggeret Hakodesh,* chap. 26, where it is explained that on Shabbat it is a duty to eat "all delightful things" and to consume meat and wine (*Shulchan Aruch, Orach Chaim* 250:2) since the *kelipat noga* itself is elevated along with the *chitzoniyut* of all the worlds. For a further elaboration of the feminine aspect of Shabbat, see *A Light of Eternity* in section 2 of this book.

²⁹³ See Gen. 1:27, where man's creation is described as "in the image of G-d."

²⁹⁴ *Tikkunei Zohar* 19:40b and *Zohar Chadash* 11a.

²⁹⁵ For an elaboration on this theme, refer to *Mysterious Nights—the Mitzva of Mikve* in section 2 of this book.

²⁹⁶ See, for example, *Iggeret Hakodesh*, chap 26, quoting introduction to *Tikkunim* 17a, which states: "*Malchut,* that is the Mouth and we call it the Oral Torah."

²⁹⁷ Note that the Talmud (*Kiddushin* 49b) states that ten measures of speech were given to the world; nine were allocated to women.

²⁹⁸ The following concept is based on *Iggeret Hakodesh*, chap. 20, p. 131.

²⁹⁹ See the chapter *Working from Within,* in section 5 of this book.

³⁰⁰ The Written Torah refers to the Five Books of Moses. The Oral Torah or Tradition refers to all other books of Torah including the Mishna, Talmud, and works of *Halacha* and Kabbala. Originally, the Oral Torah was not recorded in written form, only taught and transmitted verbally, from generation to generation. Eventually, historical circumstances necessitated that it be written, for its preservation.

³⁰¹ The following concept is based on *Iggeret Hakodesh,* chap. 30.

³⁰² Ex. 20:10; Deut. 5:14.

³⁰³ Therefore, woman is the source of blessing and well-being, as our Sages have noted, "Life without a wife is devoid of joy, blessing and well-being" (*Yevamot* 62b).

³⁰⁴ Zech. 14:9.

✽ VISION

³⁰⁵ See Ex. 32. The only *Jews* actually involved in the making of the calf were the *erev rav.* They were Egyptians, who, after witnessing the great miracles during the Exodus, decided to convert to Judaism. They did not,

however, completely rid themselves of their idolatrous tendencies. The influence of their past surfaced during the incident of the Golden Calf. The cause for their mistake was as follows:

Moshe had told the Jewish people that he would return after a period of forty days. These Jews made a mistake in their calculation. (Moshe ascended in the middle of the day and the Jews mistakenly counted that day as the first of the forty days. In actuality, the count began from the following day.) When Moshe failed to return after their calculated forty-day period, they panicked and created the Golden Calf.

Furthermore, there was no intention, even on the part of those participating in the sin of the Golden Calf, to create an actual idol. They merely intended to fashion a physical entity to serve as a conduit for spiritual light to be drawn into this world. This function had been previously served by Moshe. (See Kuzari 1:97; Ramban, Ex. ad loc.)

Even though only a small portion of the Jewish people were actually involved (about three thousand out of approximately two million), G-d held the entire nation responsible because they did not attempt to dissuade the conspirators. See R. Chaim Vital, *Eitz Hada'at Tov*, Ex. 32. This is a clear indication of the immense responsibility that one Jew has to another.

306 According to Rashi, the book refers to the Torah. Abarvanel suggests that it refers to the book of life, that is, "kill me."

307 The term *"bitul"* is a halachic term. It is, for example, used to describe the process in which, under certain (very specific) circumstances, a non-kosher food becomes nullified when mixed with a large quantity of kosher food. The non-kosher food is then termed *botul*; it loses its own identity and becomes identified as the majority substance. Chassidic literature borrows the term to express the nullification of the self into the all-encompassing Essence of G-dliness.

308 Lev. 11:1-8.

309 See *Tanya*, chap. 7.

310 Based on Tzemach Tzedek, *Ohr Hatorah, Vayikra*, 1:pp. 45-47.

311 *Midrash Tanchuma* 58, explained and elaborated in *Tanya*, chap. 36.

312 Mitzva can also mean an attachment, from the Aramaic word *"tzavta,"* connection or attachment. Since the soul, which is an actual part of G-d, was separated from its source within G-d and sent to this lowly world, it requires mitzvot to reconnect it to G-dliness. See *Likkutei Torah, Bechukotai* 45:3, 47:2 and elsewhere.

[313] The following is based on *Reshimot,* an entry in the Lubavitcher Rebbe's personal journal, compilation #149, published for *parshat Beha'alotcha.*

[314] Gen. 2:18.

[315] In Chassidic terminology, this *avoda,* spiritual service, is called *milema'ala lemata,* bringing the spiritual influence from on High to below.

[316] In Chassidic terminology, this *avoda* is called *milemata lema'ala,* uncovering the G-dliness within creation.

[317] Women, on the other hand, are exempt from the actual obligation of theoretical Torah study other than those parts that assist them in fulfilling the laws. See *Kiddushin* 29b. Parenthetically, this is in no way meant to remove women from the domain of Torah study, *per se.* Those areas where a woman is required to study, by obligation, are certainly all-encompassing, and include the entire body of practical laws in which she is obligated, plus all works of philosophy and mysticism which would increase her depth of appreciation for the mitzvot or love, fear and knowledge of G-d. As many have noted, it would be a most respectable accomplishment for any male scholar to master all these disciplines and be proficient in all these areas. Furthermore, a woman receives reward (under the category of a voluntary mitzva) for studying even theoretical areas in which she has no formal obligation. Nevertheless, prayer versus Torah study, as explained further, depicts the prototype for a woman's service.

[318] See *Berachot* 20b. See the following note, explaining man's exemption from prayer and mitzvot. A woman, by contrast, is not exempted from the general mitzva of prayer (although she is not obligated to pray at specific times), since she has no similar obligation to study Torah.

[319] *Shabbat* 11a, where the Talmud explains that a man whose "profession is Torah study is exempt from prayer" (i.e., a man who is constantly studying Torah is exempt from prayer and other mitzvot).

[320] *Chiddushei HaRim al HaTorah,* p. 45; *Sfat Emet* (5648), beginning of *Vayigash.*

[321] See *Sfat Emet,* ibid.

[322] Gen. 49:8-10, where Yaakov's blessing to Yehuda is quoted as: "Yehuda, you, your brothers shall acknowledge...Your father's children will bow down to you...The scepter shall not depart from Yehuda, nor a scholar from among his descendants until Shilo arrives." "Shilo" refers to the Messianic age (*Sforno*) or to Mashiach himself (*cf. Sanhedrin* 98b).

[323] Rambam, *Hilchot Melachim* 11:4; *Perush HaMishna, Sanhedrin,* 13 *Ikkarim,* #2.

324 *Hilchot Melachim* 3:1.

325 Ps. 40:18; 70:6; 86:1; 109:22.

326 In reality, self-abnegation is the method by which a Jew's true self is expressed. By nullifying his artificial, external desires and selfhood, a Jew is capable of hearing and acting upon the dictates of his G-dly soul. Thus, an individual who has succeeded in attaining this level of self-abnegation still maintains individualistic self-expression, *viz.* the unique qualities and capabilities with which G-d has endowed his G-dly soul.

327 Rabbi Y. Ginsburgh, *The Aleph Beit* (Northvale, N.J: Jason Aronson, 1991), p. 208.

328 Gen. 22:3.

329 Ex. 4:20.

330 *Likkutei Sichot* 1:70ff.

331 "The heavens are [the domain of] G-d, while the land He gave to human beings" (Ps. 115:16) signifies that before *matan Torah* the spiritual worlds were separate and completely unrelated to the physical worlds.

332 See Rabbi A. Kaplan, *Inner Space* (Jerusalem: Moznaim, 1990), p. 138 and sources quoted there.

333 See *Tanya, Iggeret Hakodesh*, chap. 20.

334 Rambam, *Hilchot Melachim* 11:4.

335 Num. 12:6: "When I [G-d] speak through one of you...I will speak in a dream. Not so my servant Moshe..." See also Rashi, Num. 30:2. The uniqueness of Moshe's prophetic powers is one of the 13 *Ikkarim*. See also *Zohar* 3:232a; *Likkutei Torah, Bechukotai* 50a. The Talmud (*Yevamot* 49b) states that all prophets experienced prophecy through a non-illuminating *ispaklaria*, whereas Moshe saw it through an illuminating *ispaklaria*. Moshe saw through a "clear glass" while the other prophets saw a reflection in a "mirror." This means the prophecy of every prophet was being reflected through his mind; he was not actually seeing the spiritual impact itself, but how his mind interpreted it. In Moshe's prophecy, on the other hand, the spiritual feeling was not translated into imagery but was actually articulated as words. See R. Bachya, Lev. 1:1.

336 See *Likkutei Torah, Beha'alotcha* 31, 4.

337 See *Yalkut Shimoni*, Ruth 606. The Arizal (*Sha'ar Hagilgulim*, intro. 20) explains that the generation of the redemption is the very same souls as those freed from Egypt. Therefore, just as the merit of women caused

the redemption from Egypt, so too, these same women will herald the final redemption.

ABOUT THE AUTHOR

Chana Weisberg is the editor of **thejewishwoman.org**, the most popular Jewish educational site on the web for women. Many of her articles, blogs and videos appear there as well as on its parent's site **chabad.org**.

Chana Weisberg is the author of five books including *Listening to the Whispers* (Menucha, 2012), *Divine Whispers* (Feldheim, 2005), *The Crown of Creation* (Mosaic Press, 1996) and *The Feminine Soul* (Jacobson and Davidson, 2001). Her books have received rave reviews and become popular texts in study groups and educational institutions the world over.

Weisberg lectures worldwide on a wide array of issues relating to women, relationships, the Jewish soul, faith, parenting, self-esteem and Jewish mysticism. She brings personal warmth, humor, inspiration and down-to-earth relevance to her talks. The hallmark of her lectures is her extraordinary ability to skillfully articulate profound subjects in a down to earth style, appreciated by beginners and knowledgeable listeners alike, and adding practical meaning to participants' lives.